FIFTY YEARS OF *MEDIEVAL TECHNOLOGY AND SOCIAL CHANGE*

This volume brings together a series of papers at Kalamazoo as well as some contributed papers inspired by the fiftieth anniversary of the publication of Lynn White Jr.'s, *Medieval Technology and Social Change* (1962), a slim study which catalyzed the study of technology in the Middle Ages in the English-speaking world. While the initial reviews and decades-long fortune of the volume have been varied, it is still in print and remains a touchstone of an idea and a time. The contributors to the volume, therefore, both investigate the book itself and its fate, and look at new research furthering and inspired by White's work. The book opens with an introduction surveying White's career, with a bibliography of his work, as well as some opening thoughts on the study of medieval technology in the last fifty years. Three papers then deal explicitly with the reception and longevity of his work and its impact on medieval studies more generally. Then five papers look at new cast studies areas where White's work and approach has had a particular impact, namely, medieval technology studies and medieval rural/ecological studies.

Steven A. Walton is an associate professor of history at Michigan Technological University, having previously taught at the Program in Science, Technology, and Society and the Center for Medieval Studies at Penn State University. He is a former president of AVISTA.

AVISTA Studies in the History of Medieval Technology, Science and Art is a peer-reviewed series published by Routledge that promotes the cross-disciplinary objectives of AVISTA (The Association Villard de Honnecourt for Interdisciplinary Study of Medieval Technology, Science and Art). Volumes in the series focus on research in the areas of the history of medieval technology, science, architecture and art. The society takes its name from Villard (Wilars) de Honnecourt, an elusive persona of the thirteenth century whose autograph portfolio contains a variety of fascinating drawings and descriptions of both the fine and mechanical arts.

www.avista.org

AVISTA President
George Brooks

AVISTA Publications Director
Jennifer M. Feltman

Series Editorial Board
George Brooks
Robert Bork
Ellen Shortell
Sarah Thompson

Titles in the series include:

Fifty Years of Medieval Technology
and Social Change
Edited by Steven A. Walton

The Long Lives of Medieval Art and Architecture
Edited by Jennifer M. Feltman and Sarah Thompson

*The North Transept of Reims Cathedral:
Design, Construction and Visual Programs*
Edited by Jennifer M. Feltman

*AVISTA Studies in the History of Medieval Technology, Science and Art
Volume 13*

Fifty Years of *Medieval Technology and Social Change*

Edited by

STEVEN A. WALTON

LONDON AND NEW YORK

First published 2020
by Routledge
2 Park Square, Milton Park, Abingdon, Oxon OX14 4RN

and by Routledge
52 Vanderbilt Avenue, New York, NY 10017

Routledge is an imprint of the Taylor & Francis Group, an informa business

© 2020 selection and editorial matter, Steven A. Walton; individual chapters, the contributors

The right of Steven A. Walton to be identified as the author of the editorial material, and of the authors for their individual chapters, has been asserted in accordance with sections 77 and 78 of the Copyright, Designs and Patents Act 1988.

All rights reserved. No part of this book may be reprinted or reproduced or utilised in any form or by any electronic, mechanical, or other means, now known or hereafter invented, including photocopying and recording, or in any information storage or retrieval system, without permission in writing from the publishers.

Trademark notice: Product or corporate names may be trademarks or registered trademarks, and are used only for identification and explanation without intent to infringe.

British Library Cataloguing-in-Publication Data
A catalogue record for this book is available from the British Library

Library of Congress Cataloging-in-Publication Data
Names: Walton, Steven A., editor. | White, Lynn, Jr., 1907–1987. Medieval technology and social change.
Title: Fifty years of medieval technology and social change / [edited by] Steven A. Walton.
Other titles: Medieval technology and social change
Description: Abingdon, Oxon ; New York, NY : Routledge, 2019. | Series: AVISTA studies in the history of medieval technology, science and art | Includes bibliographical references and index.
Identifiers: LCCN 2019009920 (print) | LCCN 2019017693 (ebook) | ISBN 9781317135401 (adobe) | ISBN 9781317135395 (mobi) | ISBN 9781317135388 (epub) | ISBN 9781472475497 (hbk) | ISBN 9781315582313 (ebk)
Subjects: LCSH: Technology and civilization. | Civilization, Medieval. | Social history—Medieval, 500-1500.
Classification: LCC CB478 (ebook) | LCC CB478 .F49 2019 (print) | DDC 303.48/30902—dc23
LC record available at https://lccn.loc.gov/2019009920

ISBN: 978-1-4724-7549-7 (hbk)
ISBN: 978-1-315-58231-3 (ebk)

Typeset in Times New Roman
by Apex CoVantage, LLC

Printed and bound in Great Britain by
TJ International Ltd, Padstow, Cornwall

Contents

List of contributors		*vii*
List of figures		*x*
Acknowledgments		*xii*

1 Introduction and bibliography of works by Lynn White, Jr.   1
  Steven A. Walton

2 Does the history of technology stand on the shoulders of giants?   30
  B.B. Price

3 Lynn White's "Roots" and *Medieval Technology and Social Change*: the view from outside medieval studies   70
  Elspeth Whitney

4 Determined disjunction: Lynn White's *Medieval Technology and Social Change* then and now   90
  Steven A. Walton

5 Of cranks and crankshafts: Lynn White, Jr. and the curious question of mechanical power transmission   107
  George Brooks

6 A Romanesque box hoist in Liège: a possible precursor of medieval tower-clock frames?   134
  C.R.J. Currie

7 Industrial milling and the prolific growth of the Cistercian order in the twelfth and thirteenth centuries   150
  Christie Peters

8	Cistercian nuns and forest management in northern France *Constance H. Berman*	165
9	Cold, rain, and famine: three subsistence crises in the Burgundian Low Countries during the fifteenth century *Chantal Camenisch*	187
	Index	198

Contributors

Constance H. Berman is a specialist on medieval social and religious history, concentrating on the history of women. She received her PhD from the University of Wisconsin, Madison, and is now Professor of History and Collegiate Fellow in Liberal Arts and Sciences at the University of Iowa, Iowa City. Her many publications include *Medieval Agriculture, the Southern-French Countryside, and the Early Cistercians* (Philadelphia, 1986); *The Cistercian Evolution* (Philadelphia, 2000/2010); *Women and Monasticism in Medieval Europe* (Kalamazoo, 2002); *Medieval Religion: New Approaches* (London: 2005); *The White Nuns: Cistercian Abbeys for Women in Medieval France* (Philadelphia, 2018), research for which included material for the current article. She was coeditor with Alison Beach and Lisa Bitel of the late June L. Mecham's study, *Sacred Communities, Shared Devotions. Gender, Material Culture, and Monasticism in Late Medieval Germany* (Brepols, 2014).

George Brooks is Professor of Humanities at Valencia College in Orlando, Florida. He specializes in medieval culture and history of science and technology and is currently president of AVISTA (The Association Villard de Honnecourt for the Interdisciplinary Study of Medieval Technology, Science and Art). Keenly interested in the carpenter engineers (the ingeniators) of the medieval era, he also builds reconstructions of their work, including several catapults. He lives in Orlando with his wife and two daughters.

Chantal Camenisch completed her PhD in Economic, Social, and Environmental History in 2011 at the University of Berne. Her thesis "Endlose Kälte. Getreidepreise und Witterungsverlauf in den burgundischen Niederlande im 15. Jahrhundert" ("Endless Cold. Grain prices and weather conditions in the Burgundian Netherlands in the 15th Century") was published by Schwabe Verlag Basel press in 2015. She is currently a senior research fellow in the Department of Economic, Social and Environmental History at the University of Bern and focuses on economic and environmental history of the late Middle Ages and early modern period.

C.R.J. Currie is Senior Research Fellow, Institute of Historical Research, School of Advanced Studies, London University. He holds a DPhil from Oxford University (1976). From 1972 to 2002 he worked for the Victoria County History (VCH) of England and became the general editor of the VCH series from 1994 to 2000. He still occasionally contributes to the VCH, as for example, the accounts of buildings in Janet Cooper, *The Victoria History of Herefordshire, Eastnor* (London 2013), and "Bosbury" (in progress). He was Vice-President and President of the Vernacular Architecture Group (2011–14 and 2007–11, respectively), a contributor to the Toits d'Europe project in 2008–09, and a co-translator of *Roof Frames from the 11th to the 19th Century*, edited by Patrick Hoffsummer (Turhout, Brepols, 2009).

Christie Peters is Head of Science and Engineering Library and eScience initiatives at the University of Kentucky in Louisville. Christie has a Master of Library and Information Studies from the University of North Carolina at Greensboro and an MA in history from the University of Houston under the direction of Sally Vaughn. Her thesis focused on the early utilization and development of industrial milling technology by the Cistercian order in France.

B.B. Price is Professor of History and Multidisciplinary Studies at Glendon College, York University in Toronto, having taught previously at the Massachusetts Institute of Technology. Her writings span topics within the ancient, medieval, and early modern eras, with a focus on the intersection of the histories of technology and science, and elements of intellectual and philosophical history, such as the transmission of artisan practices, rituals reflecting mastery of technical skills, and institutional structures to protect acquired knowledge. She has published numerous articles and several books, including Medieval Intellectual Thought. She is also the editor of the History of Medieval Science Series of the Pontifical Institute of Medieval Studies Publications Programme, editorial manager for the *Journal of Income Distribution*, and publisher's liaison for Ad Libros Publications Inc., a small academic publishing house in Cambridge, Massachusetts.

Steven A. Walton is Associate Professor of history at Michigan Technological University, having previously taught at the Program in Science, Technology, and Society and the Center for Medieval Studies at Penn State University. He held numerous positions with AVISTA since graduate school: President (2009–2013), Vice-President (2004–9), layout editor for the *AVISTA Forum Journal* (2006–2010), and webmaster (1992–2013). His works spans medieval to modern and tends to focus on the intersection of the history of technology and military production, as in sword manufacture, fortification, cannon foundries, or torpedo research and development, which has resulted in over a dozen articles and two previously edited books. He is also simultaneously editor of two journals: *Vuclan: The Journal for the History of Military Technology* (Brill) and *IA: The Journal of the Society for Industrial Archeology* (SIA).

Elspeth Whitney received her PhD from the Graduate Center of the City University of New York. She is Professor of History at the University of Nevada, Las Vegas, where she teaches medieval history, early modern history, and women's history. She is the author of *Paradise Restored: The Mechanical Arts from Antiquity through the Thirteenth Century* (1990) and a series of articles on the Lynn

White Thesis in Environmental Ethics, History Compass, and elsewhere. She has also written on gender and the medieval theory of the humors and complexions, as well as on the historiography of the European witch hunts.

Figures

4.1	Frequency of use of terms linked to the study of Lynn White and *Medieval Technology and Social Change*, 1900–2008	98
4.2	Frequency of use of terms linked to the study of medieval technology and science, 1900–2008	100
4.3	Count of entries related to 'Technology' in print version of the *International Medieval Bibliography*, 1968–2003	102
5.1	The first unambiguous depiction of a hand-cranked mechanism from the Utrecht Psalter (ninth century)	116
5.2	"Fortuna" cranking her wheel from Herrad von Landsberg, *Hortus Deliciarum*, folio 215 (twelfth century)	117
5.3	Hand-cranked rotary grindstone from the Luttrell Psalter, B.L. Add MS 42,130 (fourteenth century)	118
5.4	Hurdy-gurdy operated by hand crank from the Luttrell Psalter, B.L. Add MS 42,130 (fourteenth century)	119
5.5	Hoisting device operated by hand crank from the Bedford Hours, B.L. Add. 18,850, folio 17*v* detail (fourteenth century)	120
5.6	The Hierapolis gravestone showing marble sawmill, after *Journal of Roman Archaeology* 20 (2007): fig. 3	122
5.7	Reconstruction of the Hierapolis sawmill mechanisms	124
5.8	Hellenistic vase painting with a possible crank in the British Museum, room 73 (fourth century BCE)	130
5.9	Greek temple key, MFA acc. 01.7515 (bronze, date and provenance uncertain)	130
6.1	Turret clock of *circa* 1600 to 1620 from Cassiobury (Hertfordshire, England), now in the British Museum	136
6.2	Left half of the frame of East Hendred church clock, after E.R. Manley	137
6.3	Windlass at Norwich cathedral	139
6.4	Clasped-arm hoist above the crossing of nave and transepts at Auxerre cathedral	140
6.5	St. Barthélemy, Liège, nave roof	143
6.6	Pegging of the rail, strut, and rafter	144
6.7	Isometric view showing the pulley rebate and the windlass axle in relation to the box	145

6.8	The windlass axle from the north	146
7.1	Annotated plan of Clairvaux abbey from Nicolas Milley, *Archicoenobii Claraevallensis ichnographia* (1708)	155

Acknowledgments

First and foremost, I'd like to thank Bert Hall, my own graduate advisor and one of Lynn White's graduate students – making White my academic grandfather, as it were – for his training and inspiration in studying pre-modern technology. Although I never met White himself, I have always imagined that Bert was much like him: interested in a myriad of subjects, able to relate disparate strands of evidence into a penetrating cultural analysis, and, above all, a fount of knowledge that to the untrained observer seemed like so much random trivia but, when asked, knowledge that could be woven into a compelling hypothesis about why, unlike the Cistercians, Franciscans never developed much industry or why the Boeing 747 beat out the McDonald-Douglas L-1011 in the jumbo jet market (that was a rather long story told in a hot L-1011 stuck on the far side of the tarmac in Halifax, Nova Scotia – though blessedly the crew had opened the doors to let a crosswind blow though – on the way back from SHOT 1996 in London).

To reach a bit further back, I went to college the year that Lynn White, Jr., died. In my junior year, Paul Hyams at Cornell was kind enough to recognize that White's work was the bridge between my major of mechanical engineering and my captivation by the Middle Ages, and he handed me White's second set of collected essays, *Medieval Religion and Technology* (1978). It hit me like an electric shock: "Yes: This." The year before, I think, I had taken the late Robert T. Farrell's course on Old English as an elective and had done a term paper on weapons in Old English battle poems (Maldon, Brunanburh, and Finnsburg) and, in the process, had noted an interesting use of the Anglo-Saxon adjective "mill-sharpened" for the swords used by King Aethelstan and the Saxons against the invading Danes. The link was forged when I read White's dissection of the image of the sword-sharpening grindstone in the Utrecht Psalter as a symbol of the chosen where he related that "[t]he iniquitous are content to employ an old-fashioned whetstone. The virtuous, in spectacular contrast, are using the first known example of the rotary grindstone." In that context, the word *mylenscearpum* from the Battle of Brunanburh poem immediately leapt to mind, and I had my first publication (at Bert Hall's insistence in week one of graduate school). When I eventually read White's *Medieval Technology and Social Change* (1962) – I honestly can't remember when or where – the proverbial penny dropped: this was the field I wanted to pursue that could hybridize my knowledge and interest in engineering, science, and technology and my general passion for the Middle Ages and Renaissance.

At just about the same time, I discovered the AVISTA group at the International Congress on Medieval Studies at Kalamazoo (I should probably thank Bob Farrell again in that it was he that allowed a silly engineer to tag along in the van in 1991, which gave me that first hit of the ICMS) the very year that Tarver was demonstrating his traction trebuchet. Whether youthful optimism, folly, or providence, at that moment I could then see where I could fit my knowledge of technical subjects into medieval studies. And despite a number of faculty who told me to remain an engineer, build a career, and do medieval technology as a hobby (I won't name them, though I do respect they were probably offering more sober advice than my young ears wanted to hear at that time, and I have, in the years since, offered similarly sobering advice to undergraduates, some of whom disregarded me, went on to grad school, and are, I think, the better for it), after one year in grad school for engineering, I went to Toronto to study with Bert Hall, and my fate was sealed. I'm exceptionally pleased to be able to bring this book together to honor the legacy of Lynn White, Jr.

John Smedley at Ashgate got the publication process going, but then due to his well-deserved retirement, Michael Greenwood at Routledge then shepherded the project through the production process. To my colleagues at friends at AVISTA and the authors in this volume, who just seemed to trust that I would get this done, thank you for your astounding patience. Our society has given me an intellectual home at the ICMS at Kalamazoo for well over two decades. As White was an encouraging founder of AVISTA (not quite a founding member, as I understand it, as he was no longer attending the ICMS by the time AVISTA was forming in the 1980s), it is also fitting that this collection of essays should appear under their banner. Although our acronym is not a Latin word, even though it sounds like it ought to be, I have always thought that it was a sort of pseudo-diminutive of avis "bird", but which also means something rare or special, as well as an omen. Thus, it may be that the formation of AVISTA has been a portent of special things at ICMS and of rare and valuable scholarship on medieval technology, science, and art. We hope that this volume continues to fill that role.

Chapter 1

Introduction

Steven A. Walton

Half-century anniversaries are special, whether they be the golden wedding anniversary or a retrospective on a world event, a work, or a life. This volume began with a desire to have a series of sessions at the Kalamazoo International Congress on Medieval Studies and at the Leeds International Medieval Congress in 2012 to celebrate the semicentennial of Lynn White Jr.'s *Medieval Technology and Social Change* (Oxford University Press, 1962; hereafter *MTSC*). It was hard to find people to speak. Some thought that the idea had merit but had nothing to contribute; some asked whether there was anything more to say on the topic; no one, at least, said that it was a bad idea. Ultimately, many expressed some concern that it was so difficult to find people to speak on what it seemed should be a notable anniversary. The essays in this volume may go some way to explain that difficulty.

In retrospect, during the editing of these papers, it seemed like the explanation was twofold. On one hand, it is like the golden wedding anniversary couple who have outlived many of their friends. The generation of scholars who came of age under White's direct tutelage or during the time when his works were in the ascendant are now retiring, and the academic bloodline of White's studies has not left a strong lineage. The present editor is a sort of academic grandchild of White, but while I am certainly one of the fortunate ones who has found a permanent berth in academe, I find myself in a position where there is no opportunity whatsoever to engage with medieval technology in my teaching or research expectations. Even stranger, I find it slightly frustrating when I am introduced as the colleague who "does medieval technology" because it is neither my main focus and because I have, for expediency and by my own proclivity (having learned it from White's publications and my graduate experience), a much greater chronological and geographical range. Somehow to be pigeonholed as "the medieval technology guy" does not quite sit right; perhaps it is in line with an anonymous blogger who wondered (in the context of White) "why . . . a medievalist would have anything to say about the future."[1]

---

1 "Lynn White – Historian of Medieval Technology & Futurist," *Consortium for History of Science, Technology and Medicine* [blog], June 25, 2012, online at www.chstm.org/content/lynn-white—historian-medieval-technology-futurist.

Second, however, is that White is both widely cited and paraphrased and yet thoroughly disproved . . . and somehow those two cognitively dissonant stances live in a state of truce. From the beginning, reviews damned his work as "obscure and dubious deductions from scanty evidence about the progress of technology."[2] Yet such criticism has not done in the work. As Candace Barrington nicely summed it up, White had a "stormy reception [with] sometimes grudging acceptance of his basic premises," yet the "broad outline of his thesis remains in place[, even] if not the tighter chronology and specific players."[3] Or as one anonymous MIT student wrote, "White's book remains well-written, thought provoking, methodologically interesting, and wrong."[4] And despite Alex Roland's claim that White "sparked useful lines of research" – though it may be that that spark was sometimes more of a squib than a wildfire – he admits that *MTSC*, "for all its weaknesses, appears to have some life left in it."[5] In other words, White may have often been wrong, yet he seems to have remained right.

This is a far cry from when White received the Dexter Prize in 1970 for "an outstanding book on the history of technology" (in fact, only the third such prize ever awarded) for his *Machina ex Deo: Essays in the Dynamism of Western Culture* (1968) from the Society for the History of Technology (SHOT). At that time, SHOT extolled the importance of the field in the prize citation:

> Throughout a long and brilliant scholarly career, Lynn White, Jr., has studied the medieval roots of the western European technological enterprise, and his many published articles and books bear witness to the depth of his scholarship and to the originality of his findings. In *Machina ex Deo*, however, Dr. White clearly articulates the convictions underlying his years of research and reveals himself not only as an outstanding historian but eminent philosopher of history. His central theme is that to understand our present complex technological culture, we must scrutinize the past with the full recognition that technology has been a constant and, indeed, a central force in the social matrix. Dr. White has gracefully and skillfully demonstrated the importance and the value of the study of the history of technology and has simultaneously exhibited how it should be written. The Dexter Prize has been awarded to *Machina ex Deo* because it is a work of lasting

---

2 P.H. Sawyer and R.H. Hilton, "Technical Determinism: The Stirrup and the Plough," *Past & Present* 24 (1963): 90–100 at 90.

3 Candace Barrington, "White, Lynn Townsend, Jr.," in *Handbook of Medieval Studies: Terms – Methods – Trends*, ed. Albrecht Classen (Berlin: De Gruyter, 2010), 2711–15 at 2714–15.

4 "Student Book Review: Medieval Technology and Social Change," *MIT Open Courseware* (2016) online at https://ocw.mit.edu/courses/history/21h-383-technology-and-the-global-economy-1000-2000-fall-2016/assignments/medieval-technology/.

5 Alex Roland, "Once More into the Stirrups: Lynn White Jr., Medieval Technology and Social Change," *Technology and Culture* 44, no. 3 (2003): 574–85 at 584.

value not only for historians of technology but for all men [*sic*] who seek to comprehend the present by searching into the past.[6]

At that time, such an exploration of the centrality of Western-ness was just about being overwhelmed by the beginning of what are now collectively known as "identity studies" and history itself began to take a turn at that very moment toward the "postmodern condition."[7] These replaced the focus on the elite foundations of Western civilization that had been built by historians and philosophers like Leopold von Ranke, who defined history as the political machinations of the powerful (and, of course, in his wonderfully passive and simplistic construction, *wie es eigentlich gewesen*, or "what actually happened"),[8] and Jacob Burckhardt, who alternatively and simultaneously drew our attention to cultural history, although still in support of the grand Western Civ narrative. What is curious, however, is that these cumulative narratives about the Western world that, in 1970, saw SHOT praising White for rooting out the origins of Western technological civilization have, over time, relatively withered as alternate concerns have come to the fore in the historical profession. There was even for a short time a "Lynn White Society" special interest group in the early 1990s at SHOT, but it did not last.[9]

Neither does what now looks like a wishful Eurocentric outlook in finding the roots of modernity in medieval Europe – an outlook willingly and explicitly tied to Western Christianity in White's work, it must be noted – entirely explain the eclipse of White's scholarship (or perhaps it is merely the dimming of his nova, to use a stellar

---

6 Anonymous, "The Dexter Prize," *Technology and Culture* 12, no. 2 (1971): 233–34.

7 The phrase is from Jean-François Lyotard, *The Postmodern Condition: A Report on Knowledge* (Minneapolis: University of Minnesota Press, 1984), a translation of his *La Condition postmoderne: rapport sur le savoir* (Paris: Minuit, 1979), but we might point to the more pragmatic relativism of Hayden White, *Metahistory: The Historical Imagination in Nineteenth-Century Europe* (Baltimore: The Johns Hopkins University Press, 1973) and his earlier work in the 1960s that began to question the centrality of the Western identity in history.

8 The literature on this historiography is vast, but I have found Andreas Boldt, "Ranke: Objectivity and History," *Rethinking History: The Journal of Theory and Practice* 18, no. 4 (2014): 457–74, most stimulating.

9 Kelly DeVries, pers. comm., October 9, 1996. Paula Findlen and Kenneth Gouwens noted in the late 1990s that at that time, while other eras and areas of the "core" of Western civilization have faded somewhat, the European Renaissance seems to have held its own; "The Persistence of the Renaissance," *The American Historical Review* 103, no. 1 (1998): 51–54. In that special *AHR* Forum there is an article by Findlen on "Possessing the Past: The Material World of the Italian Renaissance" (83–114) and myriad sidelong glances at *the* Renaissance superstar, Leonardo, yet no discussion whatsoever about the broader mechanical genius of the period (we think of Leonardo on paper, of course, but should not forget Taccola, Brunnelsechi, etc.) towards which White's research pointed.

metaphor that White would have appreciated). White quite happily acknowledged the West's debt to the East when he knew of it, although he made the still valid point that the West seems to have done more with these technologies, or at least done it more impactfully on a global scale, than did the Asian cultures.[10] Today trying to make that argument may itself be suspect, even if the hemispheric differential was still there.[11] Indeed, it was White's belief that the study of technology was central to the study of history that led to the founding of SHOT, and White was president of the young society from 1960 to 1962. Notably, however, when White was asked to define technology (this was in 1957 when the society was being planned), he replied in writing that he "did not wish to categorize, but wanted to plunge in and let 'substance splash' wherever it will." Still, he was quite willing to speak at a conference sponsored by *Encyclopedia Britannica* on the topic of "The Idea of Technology," giving a paper on "The Act of Invention: Causes, Contexts, Continuities and Consequences."[12]

Previous responses and retrospectives

At the philosophical level, the implied technological determinism of White's whole approach immediately riled historians and philosophers.[13] Technological determinism is itself both a problematic and a durable position, one that is routinely

---

10   Lynn White, Jr., "Tibet, India, and Malaya as Sources of Western Medieval Technology," *The American Historical Review* 65, no. 3 (1960): 515–26, and see E. H. Gombrich, "Eastern Inventions and Western Response," *Daedalus* 127, no. 1 (1998): 193–205, and Leonid E. Grinin and Andrey V. Korotayev, "The Technological Competition after the Twelfth Century: A Quantitative Analysis," in *Globalistics and Globalization Studies: Global Evolution, Historical Globalistics and Globalization Studies*, ed. Leonid E. Grinin, Ilya V. Ilyin, Peter Herrmann, and Andrey V. Korotayev (Volgograd: Uchitel Publishing House, 2017), 143–63.

11   For a fundamentally perceptive analysis of one specific technology and its East–West history, see Tonio Andrade, *The Gunpowder Age: China, Military Innovation, and the Rise of the West in World History* (Princeton, NJ: Princeton University Press, 2016).

12   Thomas P. Hughes, "Shot Founders' Themes and Problems," *Technology and Culture* 50, no. 3 (2009): 594–99 at 595. White's paper was published in *Technology and Culture* 3, no. 4 (1962): 486–500 (and rpt. in his *Machina ex Deo* [1970], 107–32), which was a publication of the proceedings of the conference, with contributions from Jacques Ellul, Melvin Krantzberg, A.R. Hall, and Aldous Huxley and commentaries by dozens of other notables of the day.

13   Sawyer and Hilton, "Technical Determinism," and Donald A. Bullough, "*Europae Pater*: Charlemagne and His Achievement in the Light of Recent Scholarship," *English Historical Review* 85 (1970): 59–105, esp. 85–88. And more generally, see Merritt Roe Smith and Leo Marx, *Does Technology Drive History? The Dilemma of Technological Determinism* (Cambridge, MA: MIT Press, 1994) and Thomas Kaiserfeld, "Technological Determinism," in *Beyond Innovation: Technology, Institution and Change as Categories for Social Analysis* (London: Palgrave Macmillan, 2015), 93–101.

disavowed if enunciated yet tacitly subscribed to when unexamined. Take, for example, a critique of White's position on the matter:

> Not all scholars accept this version of technological omnipotence. Lynn White, Jr., has said that a technical device "merely opens a door, it does not compel one to enter." In this view, technology might be regarded as simply a means that humans are free to employ or not, as they see fit – and White recognizes that many nontechnical factors might affect that decision. Nevertheless, several questions do arise. True, one is not compelled to enter White's open door, but an open door is an invitation. Besides, who decides which doors to open – and, once one has entered the door, are not one's future directions guided by the contours of the corridor or chamber into which one has stepped? Equally important, once one has crossed the threshold, can one turn back?[14]

Alex Roland added a slightly different perspective to the debate, which still functions even if one takes what White was arguing was about "cultural artifact[s] with the enormous power to shape society," or even "grand scale" Marxian causation:

> White's argument functions on the level that Carlo Cipolla and William H. McNeill have used to explain the rise of the West. As in their studies, technology seems most deterministic when viewed from afar. When viewed in detail, it seems more responsive to human control, but only up to a point. People often entrain a technology that then goes on to dictate the course of history, as railroad timetables did on the eve of World War I.[15]

Some problems with White's main theses – which, for convenience, I shall refer to as the 'military thesis' on the stirrup and mounted shock combat, the 'agricultural technology thesis' on the plow and three-field rotation, and the more general 'mechanical revolution thesis,' which are to be found as the three sections of *MTSC* – became evident quite quickly. The military thesis lasted less than a decade until more detailed research, notably by Bernard S. Bachrach, put that one to rest. That said, the fact that it was a misconception needed reiteration three decades after that (and that it continues to be trotted out) shows its seductiveness.[16] From about the

---

14   Melvin Kranzberg, "Technology and History: 'Kranzberg's Laws'," *Bulletin of Science, Technology and Society* 15, no. 1 (1995): 5–13 at 5. The quote from White is from Lynn White, Jr., *Medieval Technology and Social Change* [hereafter *MTSC*] (Oxford: Oxford University Press, 1962), 28.

15   Alex Roland, "Theories and Models of Technological Change: Semantics and Substance," *Science, Technology, and Human Values* 17, no. 1 (1992): 79–100 at 92. White did, in fact, famously cite Marx's dictum that "The hand-mill gives you society with the feudal lord; the steam-mill society with the industrial capitalist" from *The Poverty of Philosophy*, ch. 2.

16   Bernard S. Bachrach, "Charles Martel, Mounted Shock Combat, the Stirrup, and Feudalism," *Studies in Medieval and Renaissance History* 7 (1970): 49–75; Roland,

turn of the millennium, the core agricultural thesis – the one that we all may well still teach – began to be slowly pushed aside though rarely explicitly repudiated. And when such sidelining or de-emphasis occurred, it seems to be done without explicitly calling out White by name, as in this example from 2001: "The supposedly key role of tools, field rotation and technology in renewed agricultural productivity and demographic expansion is now downplayed."[17] Finally, even while many, especially in the engineering world, still see the Middle Ages as "dark" (e.g., "Design methodology returned to the level of a craft [after the Roman period], and no noticeable advancements were recorded until the time of Leonardo da Vinci"),[18] the mechanical revolution thesis still reigns, even while the argument that the medieval centuries as ages of innovation gets weaker and weaker by the day.[19]

Indeed, White's overall arguments still retain currency even when partially disproved or undermined. One example of this sort of academic cognitive dissonance comes from a recent survey article on the tenth century:

> Agricultural productivity may have benefitted from widespread adoption of technological improvements, a theory popularized by Lynn White Jr., who saw

---

"Once More into the Stirrups" (note 5); and Peter Burkholder, "Popular [Mis]Conceptions of Medieval Warfare," *History Compass* 5, no. 2 (2007): 507–24. For the nature of such seductive theses, see George Raudzens, "War-Winning Weapons: The Measurement of Technological Determinism in Military History," *The Journal of Military History* 54, no. 4 (1990): 403–34. Recently it has shown up, again, to explain "The Rise of the West," in *The Ascent of GIM, the Global Intelligent Machine: A History of Production and Information Machines*, ed. Teun Koetsier (Cham, Switzerland: Springer, 2019), 128–29. White is not indexed in Robert S. Ehlers, Sarah K. Douglas, and Daniel P. M. Curzon, eds., *Technology, Violence, and War: Essays in Honor of Dr. John F. Guilmartin, Jr.*, History of Warfare 125 (Leiden: Brill, 2019), which does have a section on "The Pre-Industrial World, 1300–1800," although the three articles are on gunpowder, ship rigging, and Mughal military technology, areas White was not directly concerned with.

17 Paul Freedman, "Georges Duby and the Medieval Peasantry," *The Medieval History Journal* 4, no. 2 (2001): 259–71 at 271 although the citations there do not refer to White at all. See also Adriaan Verhulst, "The 'Agricultural Revolution' of the Middle Ages Reconsidered," in *Law, Custom, and the Social Fabric in Medieval Europe: Essays in Honor of Bryce Lyon*, ed. Bernard S. Bachrach and David Nicholas, Studies in Medieval Culture 28 (Kalamazoo, MI: Medieval Institute Publications, 1990), 17–28.

18 T. G. Chondros, "The Development of Machine Design," in *International Symposium on History of Machines and Mechanisms. Proceedings of HMM 2008*, ed. Hong-Sen Yan and Marco Ceccarelli (Cham, Switzerland: Springer, 2009), 64.

19 Richard Holt, "Medieval Technology and the Historians: The Evidence for the Mill," in *Technological Change: Methods and Themes in the History of Technology*, ed. Robert Fox, Studies in the History of Science, Technology and Medicine 1 (Amsterdam: Harwood Academic Publishers, 1996), 103–21; Steven A. Walton, "Review Essay: The Greeneian Reappraisal of the Context of Medieval Technology," *AVISTA Forum Journal* 14, no. 1 (2004): 25–28.

horseshoes, a new horse collar, and a post-invasion shift to heavy plows and the three-field system all leading to 'an agricultural revolution of the early Middle Ages' that 'provided surplus food which, from the tenth century on, permitted rapid urbanization'. White was severely criticized by scholars who claimed that the technological developments he heralded had been adopted much earlier. Nonetheless, on some things he may have been right: tenth-century England, for example, saw the 'decisive' reintroduction and triumph of the heavy plow, a new expansion of arable, more exploitation of water-power, and new Benedictine communities intent on improving their holdings; or again, although the debate on horse equipment has shifted from questions about padded collars and horseshoes to a cluster of technological devices related to carts and plows, evidence does suggest, if not 'revolution', at least tenth-century progress.[20]

And later, the same author again rescues White's thesis in a discussion of the agricultural and demographic "turnaround":

Even Lynn White Jr. had been careful to note the Carolingian roots of the agricultural and technological innovations to which he attributed Europe's resurgence – what he had claimed as distinctive was their more widespread diffusion at the start of the High Middle Ages.[21]

Whether this sort of argumentation is an example of how there is no crucial element that can prove *or* disprove White's overall thesis[22] or an element of willful disbelief on the part of authors that the Middle Ages could *not* have been the "revolutionary" time they wish it to be (or an element of both), this is the sort of continued engagement that White and *MTSC* have engendered. As Barrington put it neutrally, "[t]hough many details of his various theses have been either modified or reversed, [at least] his early work encouraged the study of medieval technology."[23]

In other areas, the claims of White and other medieval technological historians have fallen apart – or become more complex – by further archaeological discoveries, a source of information White was keenly attuned to. The crank had been claimed to be a uniquely medieval invention from the last quarter of the fourteenth century. The problem is that since at least 1980s, a third-century CE Greek

---

20 John Howe, "Re-Forging the 'Age of Iron' Part II: The Tenth Century in a New Age?" *History Compass* 8, no. 9 (2010): 1000–22 at 1001.

21 Ibid., 1005.

22 A meta argument that would be good to remember in general, for theories in history are not always like a detective story where there is and must always be a "smoking gun" that Sherlock Holms or Hercule Poirot can dramatically reveal, only for the perpetrators to mutter, "And I would have gotten away with it, too, if it hadn't been for you meddling kids."

23 Barrington, "White, Lynn Townsend, Jr." (note 3), 2711.

sarcophagus from Hierapolis (Phrygia, Greece) and excavated sixth-century sites in Ephesos and Gerassa, both in Asia Minor, make it clear that waterwheels were used at that time to drive cranks used for industrial-scale marble-sawing.[24] And so here we have cranks (a medieval "invention"), a mill wheel used for industrial production (another medieval "invention"), and the multiplications of action by a water wheel (what White claimed as a medieval intensification, at the very least) all clearly attested in the late antique eastern Mediterranean. It is clear that cranked machine technology was in complicated use a millennium before it is "supposed" to exist. Similarly, White's dismissal of a late Roman engraved gemstone depicting Eros turning a cranked grindstone[25] because cranks were not known at that time starts to fall apart, as does the dismissal of the only ancient textual source that is taken to *possibly* allude to a crank, Plutarch's Life of *Marcellus* (14.8). As the modern editors of that text note, "since the crank does not otherwise appear in ancient machinery, this interpretation is probably incorrect,"[26] but with the knowledge of clearly cranked marble saws across the late antique world, the link in the now obviously circular argument is broken. Kevin Kelly nailed it by saying, "Technology could be seen everywhere in the ancient world except in the mind."[27]

White's name remains current at a superficial level, although other proponents of the mechanical revolution idea – or, more generally, that there was something fundamentally important about the European Middle Ages, as Eurocentric as that may be – like Lewis Mumford and Jean Gimpel seem to have faded or tarnished to a certain degree.[28] The reasons for this are no doubt partly due to fad and fashion, but one durable difference between the sort of story that White told about the Middle Ages and what at least Mumford offered (and, to a certain extent, Gimpel) was that White was generally an optimist about the value of technology and of Western inventiveness. After his initial optimistic *City in History* (1962),

---

24 Tullia Ritti, Klaus Grew, and Paul Kessener, "A Relief of a Water-Powered Stone Saw Mill on a Sarcophagus at Hierapolis and Its Implications," *Journal of Roman Archaeology* 20 (2007): 138–63 at 139, and see George Brooks, "Of Cranks and Crankshafts: Lynn White, Jr. and the Curious Question of Mechanical Power Transmission," this volume.

25 Michael Angelo Causeo dela Chausse, *Le Gemme Antiche Figurate* (Rome: Gio. Giacomo Komarek Boemo, 1700), 37 and fig. 99: "amore rotatore."

26 John William Humphrey, John Peter Oleson, and Andrew N. Sherwood, *Greek and Roman Technology: A Sourcebook* (London: Routledge, 1998), 50, no. 2.34.

27 Kevin Kelly, "The Name of What We Do," The Technium [blog] November 24, 2004, online at www.kk.org/thetechnium/the-name-of-wha/.

28 One recent specialist article argued for the continuing relevance of Mumford's thesis concerning the clock, though it seems that his name and the use of *Technics and Civilization* largely waned after the 1970s. But see Teun Koetsier, "Lewis Mumford Revisited," in *History of Machines and Mechanisms: Proceedings of the Fifth IFToMM Symposium on the History of Machines and Mechanisms*, ed. Carlos López-Cajún and Marco Ceccarelli, History of Mechanism and Machine Science 32 (Dordrecht: Springer, 2016), 171–81.

Mumford was clearly a deep pessimist about the role of technology in human affairs.[29] Gimpel, too, with his quasi-imperialist attitudes of the simultaneous greatness of the medieval machine and its fitness for raising up third-world conditions, seemed to feed off the technological nihilism of modernism in the late 1970s.

There have been a number of retrospectives of White's works and influence, suggesting that his work has clearly had an impact, even if half a century on little of it underpins specific studies of "medieval technology and social change."[30] There have been three focused reviews of White's work and specifically of *MTSC*: In 1998, Bert Hall, one of White's students (and, full disclosure, the present editor's graduate advisor) considered *MTSC* at thirty; then the noted scholar in the history of technology, Alex Roland, revisited *MTSC* as part of the Society for the History of Technology's "Classics Revisited" series at about its fortieth anniversary; and finally, in 2009, Shana Worthen, another of Hall's students, wrote a review article in *History Compass*.[31]

---

29 See Everett Mendelsohn, "The Politics of Pessimism: Science and Technology Circa 1968," in *Technology, Pessimism, and Postmodernism*, ed. Yaron Ezrahi, Everett Mendelsohn, and Howard Segal, Sociology of the Sciences 17 (Dordrecht: Springer, 1994), 151–73. At the very least, it is difficult to imagine today such a self-assured essay as A.F. Titley, "The Importance of Medieval Studies in the Teaching of History," *History* 23, no. 90 (1938): 97–199.

30 Here I omit the considerable literature on reviewing the impact of this key article "The Historical Roots of Our Ecological Crisis," *Science* 155 (1967): 1203–7. On that I defer to Elspeth Whitney, "Lynn White's 'Roots' and *Medieval Technology and Social Change*: The View from Outside Medieval Studies," this volume, and her "Lynn White Jr.'s 'The Historical Roots of Our Ecologic Crisis' after 50 Years," *History Compass* 13, no. 8 (2015): 396–410. Also see the following: Robin Attfield, "Social History, Religion, and Technology: An Interdisciplinary Investigation into Lynn White, Jr.'s 'Roots'," *Environmental Ethics* 31, no. 1 (2009): 31–50; Martin Meganck, "Lynn White Revisited: Religious and Cultural Backgrounds for Technological Development," in *Engineering, Development and Philosophy: American, Chinese and European Perspectives*, ed. Steen Hyldgaard Christensen, et al. (Dordrecht: Springer, 2012), 379–95; and Todd LeVasseur, *Religion and Ecological Crisis: The "Lynn White Thesis" at Fifty* (New York: Routledge/Taylor & Francis Group, 2017), the last of which I have not seen. To these, we might also add a broader reflection, Bert S. Hall and Ranald M. Macleod, "Technology, Ecology and Religion: Thoughts on the Views of Lynn White," in *Design and Production in Medieval and Early Modern Europe*, ed. Nancy Van Deusen (Ottawa: Institute of Mediaeval Music, 1998), 149–62.

31 Bert S. Hall, "Lynn White's *Medieval Technology and Social Change* After Thirty Years," in Fox (ed.), *Technological Change*, 85–101. Roland, "Once More into the Stirrups" (note 5). Shana Worthen, "The Influence of Lynn White, Jr.'s *Medieval Technology and Social Change*," *History Compass* 7, no. 4 (2009): 1201–1217. Hall and Worthen also had access to Judith Machen, "Cultural Values and the Vitality of the West: The Mind of Lynn White, Jr." MA thesis, University of Oklahoma, 1993, which I have not seen.

Hall made a number of points, being, of these authors, the most personally acquainted with White. Perhaps the most important was that White was truly a pathfinder, developing a hybrid field of history of technology (when such barely existed in America for the premodern era at all when he was in graduate school in the 1930s), cultural anthropology, and the history of religion. His orientation derived from his training in political, institutional, and cultural history, rather than the economic or science and engineering backgrounds from which most other historians of technology arrived at the field. But this background was leavened by his exposure to the ethnography of the American Alfred Kroeber and the French Marc Bloch (and the *Annales* School's focus on *mentalité*), although White never met either man. Hall provides a biographical and somewhat psychological survey of White's career and influences and does the best job of the three main retrospectives in taking up each of White's three theses in *MTSC* and laying out his argument and the critics' attacks. His conclusion is that White became an "outrider" (not an out*lier*, which is an aberrant data point, but an out*rider*, which is not a false positive but which does not "fit" the data set) in his home field of medieval studies. By extension, then, it is not hard to recognize that he never became an "in-rider" in the history of technology as he worked across both worlds but not fully within what was or became the usual province of either. Hall ends without saying that White was right or wrong. Rather, he encourages us to "recontextualize medieval technology [and] decide what it means" to us: "build from the base that [White] left" and "move forward in directions we choose" (101).

Roland, on the other hand, was asked to write his piece for the SHOT "Classics Revisited" series, but expressed misgivings in the very first paragraph: "the strenuous criticism it attracted almost from the start, and the accumulation of four decades of subsequent scholarship, call into question its continuing viability" (574). Nonetheless, he cautiously argues that one can, and should, still assign him to students, despite White's arguments being "relegate[ed] . . . to the category 'destroyed'" (579). After again rehearsing White's arguments in the three sections of *MTSC*, and then recapitulating the strongest critics of each section (in most cases not arguing against them or, at best, agreeing to disagree), Roland still wonders "how a scholar whose major work was so thoroughly disparaged by his peers could within a decade be elected to the presidency of the Medieval Academy of America, the History of Science Society, and the American Historical Association" (579) (White was also president of SHOT when *MTSC* came out). His "resolution" to this seemingly contradictory evidence is to ask us to recognize White as a soft determinist, making "modest, cultural claim[s] for inevitability" (580). The arguments in *MTSC*, as well as its harsh criticism, were of their time of the 1960s, where "many scholars worried that confirmation of the phenomenon in history would only add to its impetus in contemporary life, when the nuclear arms race and other perils of modernity seemed rife" (581). Roland readily admits to White's breezy overstatement or oversimplification in the text and his padding footnotes with favorable evidence to bolster his rhetorical case, and also notes that "he wrote with impish mischievousness, a teasing provocation" (583). Yet his answer is that while *MTSC* may be battered and down, "keep using it until something better comes along": "broad outlines of his paradigms still stand" (583). All three of White's "revolutions" may not have occurred in quite the order that White described (or posited), but they did roughly happen: there was a change in medieval mounted warfare, there was a revolution in agriculture in the Middle Ages, and, by the time of the Renaissance, the machine "design space" as it would now be called was considerably more elaborate than it was at the end of the Roman Empire.

As a side note, John Lienhard reacted to the publication of Roland's article in his audio podcast, "Engines of our Ingenuity," and described *MTSC* as a "delicious flawed beginning."[32] He noted that *MTSC* came out the same year as Kuhn's *The Structures of Scientific Revolution*, and called the books "the two most significant works of history since WW-II," noting that they "redirected historical thinking" while at the same time becoming "lightning rods for criticism." Furthermore, "[b]oth books were audacious. Both made fearless generalizations. Both clearly were flawed in many ways. Both have been dented by their critics. And both remain standing." Perhaps overstating both their impact by comparing them to *Origin of Species* – overstated because Darwin *did* create a whole new, ever-expanding field, which neither White nor Kuhn can claim to have done, although the latter at least left us with the "paradigm shift" meme – Lienhard suggests that Kuhn remains much stronger by having been "stripped . . . of his original hyperbole" by his critics, though this is not quite what White's critics have done. Lienhard here is paraphrasing Roland's 2003 article suggesting that White's critics have "filled in blanks and corrected errors," subjecting "a grand generalization to a vigorous shaking" and have thus "reasserted [*MTSC*'s] importance."

Worthen, like this introduction, reviews the previous historiography on *MTSC* and quite rightly characterized it as "controversial, inspiring, and accessible," which helps us understand both its simultaneously eclipse and its longevity. Her retrospective of *MTSC* praised it as a "model of multi-disciplinary methodology," and noted its wide, if sometimes superficial, resonances within popular discourse. In her summarizing of the three essays within the work, Worthen notes that White's engagement with the material artifacts of the past was for its time quite novel for medievalists, at that time much more – and yet still – textually driven.[33] Her more important observation, however, is that nearly one-third of *MTSC* is endnotes which

---

32 John H. Lienhard, "No. 1835: Revisiting Stirrups," Engines of our Ingenuity [podcast] [2004], online at www.uh.edu/engines/epi1835.htm.

33 White at times has more in common with historical archaeologists such as James Deetz's canonical *In Small Things Forgotten: An Archaeology of Early American Life* (Garden City, NY: Anchor Press/Doubleday, 1977). He also resonates well in the modern field of material culture studies, as for example, Steven Lubar, "Machine Politics: The Political Construction of Technological Artifacts," in *History from Things: Essays on Material Culture*, ed. Steven Lubar and W. David Kingery (Washington, DC: Smithsonian Institution Press, 1993), 197–214 and the other essays in that volume.

are packed full of potential future leads on research projects.[34] It is unclear and probably unknowable how many scholars have started swimming in a specific pool where White had only dipped his toe. But ultimately, Worthen reiterates a crucial point that White is the one who made technology an element of medieval history: indeed, he was "the apostle of Western technological development."[35] Whether one chooses to see technology as causal, or transformative, or merely set dressing, it existed and influenced things in the Middle Ages as much as if not more than the romances and charters, and is a topic that needs to be grappled with.

White's *MTSC* is still a considerable presence on college syllabi. Judging from the *Open Syllabus Project*, it finds a home in a number of different fields. It is apparently most often assigned in conjunction with survey texts on the Middle Ages, such as Southern's *The Making of the Middle Ages*, Block's *Feudal Society* or Pierrenne's *Mohammed and Charlemagne*. Its main use is in classes is with standard works on the history of science and technology and in science studies, such as Kuhn's *The Structure of Scientific Revolutions*, Mumford's *Technics and Civilization*, Cowan's *A Social History of American Technology*, or Winner's *Do Artifacts Have Politics?*[36] Most notable in this analysis is that *MTSC* is paired relatively infrequently with very recent scholarship, though that may be a function of how collegiate syllabi are built. *MTSC* is also taught far more often than White's collected essay volume, *Medieval Religion and Technology* (noted as "indispensable to the historian of technology" by Gombrich),[37] which suggests that the argument that flowing through *MTSC*, so flawed as it has been shown to be, makes the work an excellent teaching resource in a way that the individual studies of *Medieval Religion and Technology* do not seem to be.[38]

Ultimately, bringing the articles in the present volume together has helped highlight where White's views have been influential as well as where they no longer seem to resonate. White had a prolific career, as can be seen by the bibliography of his works that follows this introduction (all the more notable in that he was in college administration for fifteen years). And although White received both of the highest honors that SHOT bestowed, it is doubtful that his corpus would receive as much attention today. Approaches to history of technology, and to history itself, have changed. Still, White was one of the scholars who brought cultural and anthropological perspectives to bear on history and consciously relied on material

---

34 One such research project just happens to be Shana Worthen, "The Memory of Medieval Inventions, 1200–1600: Windmills, Spectacles, Mechanical Clocks, and Sandglasses," PhD dissertation, University of Toronto, 2006.

35 Worthen, "The Influence of Lynn White," 1211.

36 Open Syllabus Explorer, online at http://explorer.opensyllabusproject.org/text/483566, accessed February 18, 2016.

37 Gombrich, "Eastern Inventions and Western Response" (note 10), 198–99.

38 It is also curious to that *MRT* is paired with texts on management and law, suggesting that its value is in its investigation of the ideas of intellectual property and invention that suffuse the essays.

and iconographical sources to inform his historical interpretations. We can do well to heed Alex Roland's assessment of White's legacy:

> *Caveat lector*. All students should be taught early in their reading careers that the better the writer, the more the reader must be on guard. All good writers will exercise the maximum rhetorical suasion of which they are capable to bend readers to their views. . . . [White] was a provocateur, and he did provoke. This is what good books do. *Medieval Technology and Social Change* is still a good book. We should keep reading and recommending it until another grand synthesis provides a more compelling view of its topic.[39]

The present volume

Of the nine contributions in this volume, three (Chapters 2–4) are historiographical reflections on White and his work, while five (Chapters 5–9) are studies directly or indirectly inspired by White's work and/or approach. The former group presents interesting observations that supplement those made by Hall, Worthen, and Roland, noted earlier, while the latter group offers new ways to extend the kinds of questions White liked asking in depth, breadth, or reach.

B.B. Price opens her essay – itself now a historical artifact, having been written in 1995 – with the invocation of Bernard of Chartres and his modest idea that those with the greatest perception are not to be themselves elevated but that we recognize that they "stood on shoulders of giants." Her in-depth survey of the works of Lewis Mumford, Lynn White, and Jean Gimpel with respect to medieval technology orients readers who might not be familiar with their influences (in both directions) as well as their interconnections. The essay does, however, beg the question of how we can 'stand' on their works and what this could mean for the future of medieval technology studies. The answer is not so patently obvious, as Price recognized then, and which has perhaps become more poignant today. In a Lynn White Memorial Lecture at the University of California, Los Angeles in 2003, Kelly DeVries rather audaciously pointed out to the assembled audience they had never hired anyone to replace White in terms of topic or theme, so the study of medieval technology was, for all intents and purposes, no longer in evidence in its *cathedra*.[40] More recently, a number of articles have bemoaned the perceived dwindling of medieval and early modern studies at the doctoral level, at least in North America.[41] It is most interesting to realize that even back in 1995, Price

---

39 Roland, "Once More into the Stirrups" (note 5), 584–85.

40 Kelly DeVries, "Lynn White and the Invention of Medieval and Renaissance Technology," The Annual Lynn White Lecture, UCLA Center for Medieval and Renaissance Studies, May 22, 2003.

41 For an area of some relevance to medieval technological studies, see John D. Hosler, "Pre-Modern Military History in American Doctoral Programs: Figures and Implications," *The Journal of Military History* 82, no. 2 (2018): 565–82.

wrote in this essay that while Mumford, White, and Gimpel certainly believed that "there is a place for the history of medieval technology within the greater study of the history of technology," they made their arguments for that, even then, with a "sigh . . . both a sigh of relief and of resignation."

By comparison, Whitney and Walton's articles look at, respectively, how one single part of White's work has continued to inspire, while the topic of his oeuvre, "medieval technology" has experienced a rise and fall in the last half century. Elspeth Whitney's specific contemporary assessment of the legacy of White's article on "The Historical Roots of Our Ecologic Crisis," demonstrates how this piece of his work has catalyzed an entire industry of ecotheological criticism and continues to inspire both deep and broad criticism. The problem, it would seem, is that the Middle Ages has generally been ignored in the development of the field of environmental history, so White's thought-provoking article has taken on a shibbolethic stature. Ultimately, she concludes that while medieval historians have "gotten beyond Lynn White" – even while other authors in this volume recognize his simple, sweeping narratives continue to resonate with teachers – those who study ecotheology need to "catch up" to unpack the role of religion, and Christianity, in particular, in the attitude of humans toward nature. Steven A. Walton's essay takes a bibliometric approach to note how *MTSC* has had a discernable rise *and* fall in popularity, peaking in the 1980s and 1990s. On one hand, this can be seen as a life course of a scholarly work as new work supplants it, yet *MTSC* is the sort of work that has at once been thoroughly criticized yet never replaced. The essay also is sanguine about the future of a field – if one can even call medieval technology a field – when the cornerstone of its foundation is so seriously eroded. Continuing worries about the state of the field by its few practitioners seem confirmed by this study, though there are enough who continue to be inspired by White's work as they (re)discover it that it will carry on in some fashion. The strength of allied fields like ecotheology or medieval architectural studies (which White never talked about) is an encouraging sign.

The volume then moves on to five case studies that are very much in the vein of White's work. The two essays by Currie and Brooks take on Lynn White's third section of *MTSC*, considering the mechanical revolution of the Middle Ages and reflect nicely on each other. C.R.J. Currie's piece engages in the type of analogical thinking that White was fond of, speculating that the arrangement of the frames for hoists in church and cathedral ceilings used to raise building materials to vertiginous heights would have been simple and direct analogies for clockmakers when the latter appeared in the later thirteenth century all across Europe. Both machines involve ropes and pullies, and to support a hoist axle is not conceptually different from supporting a clock's going and striking trains. These hoists and clocks were also occurring within the same ecclesiastical cultural context, making the idea a natural one for transference. But in the absence of explicit proof, such a transference must remain speculative . . . in the same way as George Brooks's essay on the idea of the humble yet transformative crank. Brooks reviews the evidence White and others have made for the crank, noting that evidence that has come to light since their time has pushed back the use of that fundamental mechanical linkage to the late antique period at least. He then posits that such a machine part could be seen even further back in relation to what are interpreted to be Greek locks and keys. Both these essays open new possibilities for investigation and our understanding, and Brooks asks us to consider why it is that we believe overarching theories in the first place and reminds us all that making a positive argument to dismiss contrary evidence may be a bad move.

The next two contributions approach a cornerstone of two of the theses that White championed – the agricultural and the industrial – namely, that the Cistercians were, as Anna Gotlind phrased it, "the messengers of medieval technology."[42] Christie Peters looks at the 'Cistercian thesis,' a theme of which White was a proponent, although he did not do nearly as much as later authors to develop. She asks whether their noted milling activity was as forward-looking or revolutionary as it has been proposed. What she finds, with a more in-depth look at the records of existing mills around Citeaux and its daughter houses, is that the Cistercians in this formative period were far more likely to take over *existing* mills than they were to build anew. This partly deflates the revolutionary side of the thesis, but her further argument explains that it was an internal mandate of the order to be self-sufficient, which led to their industrial intensification, which led to surplus and profit, which, in turn, led to them being able to expand even more. So rather than seeing Cistercians as having spread medieval technology *de novo*, she sees them as having benefited from it being already widespread in twelfth-century France. Constance H. Berman takes a different tack on Cistercian nun's holdings, with a deep dive into the charters, gifts, and rent agreements with respect land ownership and exploitation of the woodland in the Paris region in the thirteenth century. In figuring out who held the land, who granted the land, how rents and profits from the land were used, and especially in looking at the products of the forest in as much detail as her sources allow, she paints a much more complex picture of Cistercian nuns and forests land development. She characterizes it as "a picture of Cistercian prudence and rationality," and at least for these houses, she shows that they were not pioneers (as in breaking new ground and clearing old-growth forests) but, rather, managers of existing woodlands. Thus, both essays expand our understanding, even while slightly undermining the traditional, simple narrative.

The final contribution to this volume demonstrates the new directions that the broad sorts of questions White pioneered have taken in the last few decades. That is, in *MTSC*, White looked at the causes and effects around technologies of agriculture and industry, as well as the social relations around them in the Middle Ages, but he spent far less time – indeed, in places, no time – examining the natural environment in which these great developments took place. Chantal Camenisch exemplifies the way in which White's insights have been extended with the expansion of medieval studies into environmental history. While not taking on White's agricultural revolution

---

42   Anna Gotlind, *The Messengers of Medieval Technology? Cistercians and Technology in Medieval Scandinavia* (Alingsas: Viktoria Bokforlag, 1990).

thesis explicitly, Camenisch demonstrates quite clearly that we must remember we are always at the mercy of the climate. No amount of three-field rotation or horse collars can make up for killing frost after the blossoms have set or a summer and fall so wet that the grain does not ripen and even the little that managed to make it into the barn rotted before it could be milled. Ending with this detailed reading of chronicles for weather information which are then correlated with political and economic developments in the Burgundian Low Countries, also known from the textual history, rather amusingly brings us back again – yet *contra* – the second sentence of the preface to *MTSC*: "the most remarkable [illusion] is the belief that the surviving written records provide us with a reasonably accurate facsimile of past human activity."[43] Camenisch's chronicles, however, are exactly the kind of alternative sources of information, even if they are textual, that White begged historians to utilize.

Bringing the sorts of studies full circle truly does help us understand medieval technology (and environment) *and* social change.

Bibliography of works on medieval technology by Lynn White, Jr.

With more than 200 items listed in the following, White's output is quite staggering, to say nothing of the breadth of scholarship with which he was able to engage. The following is only the subset of his oeuvre as listed in his SHOT obituary,[44] reorganized, elaborated, and updated using the WorldCat bibliography. Included are all his works on medieval topics as well as those on the history of technology, engineering, and science (including some of the former that are not on technology, and some of the latter group that are not medieval). Omitted here are a number of popular articles, particularly on women's education, from the time he was president of Mills College, as well as a number on public religion from throughout his career.

	\multicolumn{7}{c}{Lynn White, Jr.'s Scholarly Output*}
	1930s	1940s	1950s	1960s	1970s	1980s	Total
Articles	6	5	6	29	28	7	81
Book Reviews	1	7	12	21	12	2	55
Shorter Contributions	1	0	2	4	10	2	19

*Excluding books, edited books, and works outside the fields of medieval studies and history of technology and engineering.

---

43 White, *MTSC*, vii.
44 Bert S. Hall, "Lynn Townsend White, Jr. (1907–1987)," *Technology and Culture* 30, no. 1 (1989): 199–213. The bibliography there was compiled by Hall and Bradford Blaine, both White's former students.

Books

Latin Monasticism in Norman Sicily (Cambridge, MA: Mediaeval Academy of America, 1938; rpt. 1968).

Translation
Il monachesimo latino nella Sicilia normanna (Catania: Dafni, 1984).

What Accelerated Technological Progress in the Western Middle Ages? (London: Heinemann, 1961).

Medieval Technology and Social Change (Oxford: Clarendon Press, 1962).

Translations
Tecnica e Società nel Medioevo, trans. Alessandro Barghini (Milano: Il saggiatore, 1967; 2nd ed. 1970; 3rd ed. 1976).
Die Mittelalterliche Technik und Der Wandel Der Gesellschaft (München: H. Moos, 1968).
Technologie médiévale et transformations sociales, trans. Martine Lejeune (Paris: Mouton, 1969).
Tecnología medieval y cambio social, trans. Ernesto Córdoba Palacios (Buenos Aires: Paidós, 1973).
中世の技術と社会変動 (Chūsei no gijutsu to shakai hendō), trans. Hoshimi Uchida (Tōkyō: Shisakusha, 1985).

Reviews of MTSC

1962

Anon. in *Times Literary Supplement* (September 7, 1962), 676.
L. Badash in *American Notes and Queries* 1 (1962): 30–31.
A.R. Bridbury in *Economic History Review* 15 (1962): 371–72.
J. Habakkuk in *The Economist* 202 (1962): 1230.
J.R. Hale in *The Spectator* 208 (1962): 340.
G.C. Homans in *American Journal of Sociology* 68 (1962): 396.
S. Lindroth in *Lychnos: Annual of the Swedish History of Science Society* (1962): 527–29.
R. Reynolds in *Manuscripta* 6 (1962): 172–73.
G. Ruthmann in *Revue d'histoire economique et sociale* 40 (1962): 569–70.

1963

H.A. Cronne in *History* 48 (1963): 199–200.
W. Endrei in *Technikatorteneti Szemle* 1 (1963): 253–54.
M.F. Farmer in *American Anthropologist* 65 (1963): 982–83.
G.E. Fussell in *Journal of the Royal Society of Arts* 111, no. 5078 (1963): 148–49.

A.R. Hall in *Nature* 198 (April 6, 1963): 61.

D. Herlihy in *Agricultural History* 37 (1963): 43–45.

R. Hilton and P.H. Sawyer, "Technical Determinism: The Stirrup and the Plough," *Past & Present* 24, no. 1 (1963): 90–100.

M. Keen in *Oxford Magazine* (May 24, 1963): 328.

L. Mumford in *Endeavour* 22 (1963): 52.

J. Needham in *Isis* 45 (1963): 418–20.

T. Raworth in *The Month* 30, no. 7 (July 1963): 52–55.

R.W. Southern in *History of Science* 2 (1963): 130–35.

J. Strayer in *Technology and Culture* 4 (1963): 62–65.

L. Thorndike in *American Historical Review* 68 (1963): 93–94.

A. Timm in *Jahrbucher fur Nationaliikonomie und Statistik* 175 (1963): 294–95.

1964

M. Clagett in *Speculum* 39 (1964): 359–65.

M.A. Hoskin in *English Historical Review* 79 (1964): 139.

H.M. Robertson in *South African Journal of Economics* 32 (1964): 306–8.

M.W. Thompson in *Medieval Archaeology* 8 (1964): 314–15.

1965 and Later

J. Boussard in *Le Mayen Age* 71 (1965): 583–85.

E. Cuozzo in *Revista storica italiana* 81 (1969): 600–3.

K. Schulz in *Deutsches Archiv fur Erforschung des Mittelalters* 25 (1969): 278–79.

The Legacy of the Middle Ages in the American Wild West (Cambridge: The Mediaeval Academy of America, 1965).

Medieval Technology: Transfers and Spinoffs, The First Annual Rolf Buchdahl Lecture on Science, Technology and Values, November 3, 1981 (Raleigh, NC: Division of University Studies, North Carolina State University, 1984).

Collected Works

Articles in these works are noted below in square brackets
with either *MxD* and *MRT* and the page ranges.

Machina Ex Deo: Essays in the Dynamism of Western Culture (Cambridge, MA: MIT Press, 1968) [*MxD*].

Reissued as
Dynamo and Virgin Reconsidered: Essays in the Dynamism of Western Culture (Cambridge, MA: MIT Press, 1976); not to be confused with White's 1958 article by that name.

Translations
機械と神：生態学的危機の歴史的根源 (Kikai to kami: Seitaigakuteki kiki no rekishiteki kongen), trans. Seizō Aoki (Tokyo: Misuzu Publishing, 1972).
Machina ex deo: la tecnologia y la cultura (Mexico, FD: Asociados, 1973).

Medieval Religion and Technology: Collected Essays (Berkeley: University of California Press, 1978) [*MRT*].

Editorial Works

Frontiers of Knowledge in the Study of Man (New York: Harper & Row, 1956).

Translations
Marzhā-yi dānish (Tihrān: Markazī: Intishārāt-i Ābān, [25]36 [1978] / Tehran: Marlazi, 1961)
Fronteros del conocimiento en el estudio del hombre (Buenos Aires: Eudeba, 1963)
As fronteiras do conhecimento: um estudo do homem (Rio de Janeiro: Fundo de Cultura, 1963).

The Transformation of the Roman World; Gibbon's Problem after Two Centuries, UCLA Center for Medieval and Renaissance Studies Contributions, vol. 3 (Berkeley: University of California Press, 1966).

Viator: Medieval and Renaissance Studies, vols. 1–5 (Berkeley and Los Angeles: University of California Press, 1970–1974) (with R. Rouse and A.H. Kelly, co-editors).

Memorials

"Obituary," in *G.E. von Grunebaum 1909–1972: In Memoriam* (Los Angeles: Near Eastern Studies Center, UCLA, 1972).
"Robert James Forbes (1900–1973)" [Obituary], *Technology and Culture* 15, no. 3 (1974): 438–39.
"Charles Donald O'Malley: *Vita*," in A.G. Debus (ed.), *Medicine in Seventeenth Century England* (Berkeley: University of California Press, 1974), 1–5.
"Memorial: Gray C. Boyce," *Speculum* 57 (1982): 703–5 (with P. Kibre and Joseph R. Strayer).

Personal Papers

"Papers," University of California, Los Angeles, collection no. 1541. 18 boxes (9 linear ft.) 9 oversize boxes, 1937–1985. Finding aid available at http://oac.cdlib.org/findaid/

ark:/13030/tf1489n73x. Teaching and research material related to the career of history professor Lynn White. Includes exams, lecture notes, publications, correspondence, manuscripts, bibliographic files, and photographs for publications.

Festschriften

Bert S. Hall and Delno C. West (eds.), *On Pre-Modern Technology and Science: A Volume of Studies in Honor of Lynn White, Jr* (Malibu, CA: Undena Publications, 1976).

Nancy van Deusen (ed.), *The Medieval West Meets the Rest of the World*, Musicological Studies 62/2 (Ottawa: Institute of Mediaeval Music, 1995).
In the preface van Deusen writes, that "This project surely would have interested the distinguished, provocative, and influential scholar in whose memory the conference which formed the occasion for the interaction documented by this volume was held, Professor Lynn White, Jr. . . ., conceptual leader in an emerging field of the study of medieval technology" who was "'at home' . . . creating a capacious intellectual environment where he was . . . an intellectual explorer to the end of his life[,] observing the 'resonances' of medieval concepts with other world cultures" (v).

The following volume is not strictly speaking festschrift *for White himself, but is a* festschrift *genealogically "once removed", and very much followed in the same vein:*

Nancy van Deusen (ed.), *Design and Production in Medieval and Early Modern Europe: Essays in Honor of Bradford Blaine*, Claremont Cultural Studies/Wissenschaftliche Abhandlungen 62/4 (Ottawa: Institute of Mediaeval Music, 1998).
Blaine was a student of White's with a dissertation on "The Application of Water-Power to Industry During the Middle Ages" (1966) and van Deusen both invokes White as mentor and inspiration and makes that association explicit: "a feature Lynn White and Brad Blaine share[d]" was "a conviction that mental constructs hold undeniable consequences for social action – and bear responsibility for an outcome within the real world" (xi).

Articles
(including chapters in edited volumes and conference proceedings)

1930s

"The Charters of St. Michael's in Mazzara," *Revue Benedictine* 45 (1933): 234–41.
"A Forged Letter Concerning the Existence of Latin Monks at St. Mary's Jehosaphat before the First Crusade," *Speculum* 9, no. 4 (1934): 404–7.
"For the Biography of William of Blois," *The English Historical Review* 50, no. 199 (1935): 487–90.
"The Byzantinization of Sicily," *The American Historical Review* 42, no. 1 (1936): 1–21.
"La date de la mort de S. Garland d'Agrigente," *Annalecta Bollandiana* 57 (1939): 105–8.

1940s

"Changes in the Popular Concept of 'California'," *California Historical Society Quarterly* 19, no. 3 (1940): 219–24.

"Technology and Invention in the Middle Ages," *Speculum* 15, no. 2 (1940): 141–59 [*MRT*, 1–22].[45]

"Christian Myth and Christian History," *Journal of the History of Ideas* 3, no. 2 (1942): 145–58 [*MxD*, 33–56].[46]

"The Significance of Medieval Christianity," in G.F. Thomas (ed.), *The Vitality of the Christian Tradition* (New York: Harper & Row, 1944), 87–115.

"Natural Science and Naturalistic Art in the Middle Ages," *The American Historical Review* 52, no. 3 (1947): 421–35 [*MRT*, 23–41].

1950s

"The Changing Past," *Harper's* 209 (November 1954): 29–34.[47]

"The Spared Wolves," *The Saturday Review* 37, no. 40 (November 13, 1954) [*MxD*, 169–80].

"The Vitality of the Tenth Century," *Medievalia et Humanistica* 9 (1955): 3/26–29.

"The Changing Canons of Our Culture," in Lynn White, Jr. (ed.), *Frontiers of Knowledge in the Study of Man* (New York: Harper & Row, 1956), 301–16 [*MxD*, 11–32].[48]

"Dynamo and Virgin Reconsidered," *The American Scholar* 27 (Spring 1958): 183–91 [*MxD*, 57–74].

"Of Renaissance Engineering," *Books and Libraries at the University of Kansas* 20 (February 1959): 1–2.

1960s

"Technology in the Middle Ages," *Technology and Culture* 1, no. 4 (1960): 339–44.

"Tibet, India, and Malaya as Sources of Western Medieval Technology," *The American Historical Review* 65, no. 3 (1960): 515–26 [*MRT*, 43–57].

---

45 Reprinted in Herman Ausubel, ed., *The Making of Modern Europe* (New York: Holt-Dryden, 1951), 47–58 and in A.F. Havighhurst, ed., *The Pirenne Thesis* (Boston: Heath, 1958), 79–83.

46 Reprinted in P.P. Wiener and A. Noland, eds., *Ideas in Cultural Perspective* (New Brunswick, NJ: Rutgers University Press, 1962), 544–57.

47 Reprinted in R.M. Ludwig, ed., *Essays Today* (New York: Harcourt Brace, 1956) and in Lynn White, Jr., ed., *Frontiers of Knowledge in the Study of Man* (New York: Harper & Row, 1956), 68–79.

48 Also rpt. in, *The Voice of the Carleton Alumni* 22 (March 1957): 5–15.

"Eilmer of Malmesbury, an Eleventh Century Aviator: A Case Study of Technological Innovation, Its Context and Tradition," *Technology and Culture* 2, no. 2 (1961): 97–111 [*MRT*, 59–73].[49]

"The Social Responsibility of Scholarship: Is Clio a Tutelary Muse?" *The Journal of Higher Education* 32, no. 7 (1961): 357–61 [*MxD*, 1–10].

"The Act of Invention: Causes, Contexts, Continuities and Consequences," *Technology and Culture* 3, no. 4 (1962): 486–500 [*MxD*, 107–32].[50]

"The Context of Science," in C.F. Stover and L. Hatch (eds.), *Science and Democratic Government* (Santa Barbara, CA: Center for the Study of Democratic Institutions, 1963), 148–59 [*MxD*, 95–106].[51]

"The Medieval Roots of Modern Technology and Science," in K.F. Drew and F.S. Lear (eds.), *Perspectives in Medieval History* (Chicago: University of Chicago Press, 1963), 19–34 [*MRT*, 75–91].[52]

"What Accelerated Technological Progress in the Middle Ages?" in A.C. Crombie (ed.), *Scientific Change: Symposium on the History of Science, University of Oxford, July 1961* (London and New York: Heinemann, 1963), 272–91.[53]

"The Discipline of the History of Technology," *Journal of Engineering Education* 54 (1964): 349–51.

"Theophilus Redivivus," *Technology and Culture* 5, no. 2 (1964): 224–33 [*MRT*, 93–103].[54]

"The Legacy of the Middle Ages in the American Wild West," *Speculum* 40, no. 2 (1965): 191–202 [*MRT*, 105–20].[55]

"Conclusion: The Temple of Jupiter Revisited," in Lynn White, Jr. (ed.), *The Transformation of the Roman World* (1966) [see Edited Books], 291–311.

"On Intellectual Gloom," *The American Scholar* 35 (Spring 1966): 223–26 [*MxD*, 133–42].

"Pumps and Pendula: Galileo and Technology," in C. Golino (ed.), *Galileo Reappraised* (Berkeley and Los Angeles: University of California Press, 1966), 96–110 [*MRT*, 121–32].

"The Changing Middle Ages," in F. Sweeney (ed.), *The Knowledge Explosion* (New York: Farrar, Straus and Giroux, 1966), 161–80.

---

49 Reprinted in M. Kranzberg and W.H. Davenport, eds., *Technology and Culture: An Anthology* (New York: Schocken, 1972).

50 Ibid.

51 Reprinted as "Science, Scientists and Politics," in *Science, Scientists and Politics*, ed. R. Hutchins, et al. (Santa Barbara, CA: Center for the Study of Democratic Institutions, 1963), 13–16 and in A. Vavoulis and A.W. Colver, eds., *Science and Society: Selected Essays* (San Francisco: Holden-Day, 1966), 69–74.

52 Reprinted in W.C. Scoville and J.C. La Force, eds., *The Economic Development of Western Europe: The Middle Ages and Renaissance* (Lexington, MA: Heath, 1969), 60–75.

53 Reprinted in D. O'Conner and F. Oakley, eds., *Creation: The Impact of an Idea* (New York: Scribner's, 1969), 84–104 and translated as, "Was beschleunigte den technischen Fortschritt im westlichen Mittelalter?" *Technikgeschichte* 32 (1965): 201–20.

54 A review of C.R. Dodwell, ed. and trans., *Theophilus, Presbyter: The Various Arts* (London: Thomas Nelson, 1961) and C.S. Smith and J. Hawthorne, eds. and trans., *Theophilus, Presbyter: On Divers Arts* (Chicago: University of Chicago Press, 1963).

55 Reprinted in *The American West* 3, no. 2 (Spring 1966): 72–79, 90.

"'Civilizing' the Engineer by 'Civilizing' the Humanist," in W.H. Davenport and D. Rosenthal (eds.), *Engineering: Its Role and Function in Human Society* (New York: Pergamon Press, 1967), 141–52.

"Engineers and the Making of a New Humanism," *Journal of Engineering Education* 57, no. 5 (1967): 375–76 [*MxD*, 143–50].

"Jacopo Aconcio as an Engineer," *The American Historical Review* 72, no. 2 (1967): 425–44 [*MRT*, 149–73].

"More Pieces to the Chinese Puzzle," *Isis* 58, no. 2 (1967): 248–51.

"Technology in the Middle Ages," in M. Kranzberg and C.W. Pursell (eds.), *Technology in Western Civilization* (Oxford: Oxford University Press, 1967), vol. 1, 66–79.

"The Historical Roots of Our Ecologic Crisis," *Science* 155 (1967): 1203–7 [*MxD*, 75–94].[56]

"The Life of the Silent Majority," in R.S. Hoyt (ed.), *Life and Thought in the Early Middle Ages* (Minneapolis: University of Minnesota Press, 1967), 85–100 [*MRT*, 133–47].

"Methods of Organizing Medieval Studies Programs," *Chronica* 2 (1968): 3–8.

"The Contemplation of Technology," *Engineering Education* 59 (October 1968): 101–5 [*MxD*, 151–68].[57]

"The Invention of the Parachute," *Technology and Culture* 9, no. 3 (1968): 462–67 [*MRT*, 175–80].

"The Necessity of Witches," (1968) in *MxD*, 169–79.

"Kyeser's 'Bellifortis': The First Technological Treatise of the Fifteenth Century," *Technology and Culture* 10, no. 3 (1969): 436–41.[58]

"The Expansion of Technology, 500–1500," in C. Cipolla (ed.), *The Fontana Economic History of Europe, Vol. 1: The Middle Ages* (London: HarperCollins, 1969), 143–74.

"The Iconography of *Temperanita* and the Virtuousness of Technology," in Theodore K. Rabb and Jerrold E. Seigel (eds.), *Action and Conviction in Early Modern Europe: Essays in Memory of E.H. Harbison* (Princeton, NJ: Princeton University Press, 1969) [*MRT*, 181–204].

---

56 This famous essay has also reappeared in or as "St. Francis and the Ecological Backlash," *Horizon* 9 (1967): 42–47. *Sunrise* 16 (September 1967): 364–75. "What Hath Man Wrought?" *Americas* 19 (May 1967): 11–19. *The Bulletin of the Conservation Council of Ontario* 14, no. 4 (1967): 10–11 and 15, no. 1 (1968): 2–5. *Sierra Club Bulletin* 52 (1968): 123–27. P. Shepherd and D. McKinley, eds., *The Subversive Science* (Boston: Houghton Mifflin, 1969), 341–51. I.G. Barbour, ed., *Western Man and Environmental Ethics: Attitudes toward Nature and Technology* (Reading, MA: Addison-Wesley, 1973), 18–30. Rajaram Krishnan, Jonathan M. Harris, and Neva R. Goodwin, eds., *A Survey of Ecological Economics* (Washington, DC: Island Press, 1995). The essay was also translated as "A crise ecologica de nosso tempo," *Americas* 19 (June 1967): 11–19. "Die historische Ursachen unserer okologischen Krise," in *Welt im Wandel*, ed. Thilo Koch (Munich: Bruckmann, 1973). "Le radici storicoculturale della nostra crisi ecologica," *Il Mulino* 22 (1973): 257–63. "Las raices históricas de nuestra crisis ecológica," *Revista de Occidente* 143–144 (February–March 1975): 150–64. It has also appeared in numerous ecological readers; see Elspeth Whitney's essay in this volume.

57 Reprinted in *American Institute of Aeronautics and Astronautics Journal* 8 (February 1970): 22–27.

58 A review of Gotz Quarg, ed. and trans., *Conrad Kyeser aus Eichstätt*, Bellifortis (Düsseldorf: VDI-Verlag, 1967).

1970s

"History and Horseshoe Nails," in L.P. Curtis (ed.), *The Historian's Workshop: Original Essays by Sixteen Historians* (New York: Alfred A. Knopf, 1970), 47–64.

"Medieval Uses of Air," *Scientific American* 223, no. 1 (August 1970): 92–100.

"The Origins of the Coach," *Proceedings of the American Philosophical Society* 114, no. 6 (1970): 423–31 [*MRT*, 205–16].

"Cultural Climates and Technological Advance in the Middle Ages," *Viator* 2 (1971): 171–201 [*MRT*, 217–54].

"Medieval Borrowings from Further Asia," *Medieval and Renaissance Studies*, no. 5 (1971): 3–26.

"Harness and Saddlery," *Encyclopedia Britannica* (Chicago: Encyclopedia Britannica, 1972), 118a–120b.

"The Flavor of Early Renaissance Technology," in B.A. Levy (ed.), *Developments in the Early Renaissance* (Albany: State University of New York Press, 1972), 36–57.

"The Medieval Meeting of East and West," *Journal of the Blaisdell Institute* 7, no. 2 (1972): 13–25.

"Continuing the Conversation," in I.G. Barbour (ed.), *Western Man and Environmental Ethics: Attitudes toward Nature and Technology* (Reading, MA: Addison-Wesley, 1973), 55–64.

"Death and the Devil," in Robert S. Kinsman (ed.), *The Darker Vision of the Renaissance: Beyond the Fields of Reason* (Berkeley and Los Angeles: University of California Press, 1974), 25–46.

"Indic Elements in the Iconography of Petrarch's *Trionfo Della Morte*," *Speculum* 49, no. 2 (1974): 201–21.

"Technology Assessment from the Stance of a Medieval Historian," *American Historical Review* 79, no. 1 (1974): 1–13 [*MRT*, 261–76].

"The Diffusion of the Lateen Sail," *Proceedings of the 13th International Congress of the History of Science, Moscow, August 18–24, 1971* (Moscow: Institute for the History of Science and Technology, 1974), section 4, 212–20 [*MRT*, 255–60].

"Christians and Nature," *Pacific Theological Revue* 7 (Summer 1975): 6–11.

"Medical Astrologers and Late Medieval Technology," *Viator* 6 (1975): 295–308 [*MRT*, 297–316].

"Medieval Engineering and the Sociology of Knowledge," *Pacific Historical Review* 44, no. 1 (1975): 1–21 [*MRT*, 317–38].

"The Crusades and the Technological Thrust of the West," in V.J. Parry and M.E. Yapp (eds.), *War, Technology and Society in the Middle East* (Oxford: Oxford University Press, 1975), 97–112 [*MRT*, 277–96].

"The Study of Medieval Technology, 1924–1974: Personal Reflections," *Technology and Culture* 16, no. 4 (1975): 519–30 [*MRT*, xi–xxiv].

"Tools and Civilization," *Perspectives in Defense Management* 24 (Winter 1975–1976): 33–42.

"Food and History," in Dwain N. Walcher, N. Kretchmer, and Henry L. Barnett (eds.), *Food, Man, and Society* (New York: Plenum/Boston: Springer, 1976), 12–30.

"The Embryology of Columbus' Discovery," *Bulletin of the American Academy of Arts and Sciences* 29, no. 6 (1976): 33–48.

"La Vita Della Maggioranza Silenziosa, trans. by Erica Vinay Angelini," in Robert S. Hoyt (ed.), *Vita e Pensiero Nell'alto Medioevo* (Napoli: Liguori, 1977).

"Medieval Europe Foresaw Planes, Cars, Submarines," *Smithsonian* 8 (October 1978): 114–23.

"Science and the Sense of Self: The Medieval Background of a Modern Confrontation," *Daedalus: Journal of the American Academy of Arts and Sciences* 107, no. 2 (Spring 1978): 47–59.

"The Flowering of Medieval Invention," in *The Smithsonian Book of Invention* (Washington, DC: Smithsonian Books, 1978), 64–71.

"An Appeal from the Consumer," in R. Berger and H. Suess (eds.), *Radiocarbon Dating* (Berkeley and Los Angeles: University of California Press, 1979), 37–40.

"The Ecology of Our Science," *Science 80* (1979): 72–76.

"The Mystery of Inventiveness," in John G. Burke and Marshall C. Eakin (eds.), *Technology and Change* (San Francisco: Boyd & Fraser, 1979), 39–41.

1980s

"Substitutes for Human Muscle: Past Crises," in Melvin Kranzberg (ed.), *Energy and the Way We Live* (San Francisco: Boyd & Fraser, 1980), 7–9.

"Technological Development in the Transition from Antiquity to the Middle Ages," in *Tecnologia, economia e societa nel mondo romano: Atti del convegno di Como, 27–29 settembre 1979* (Como: Banca Popolare Commercio e Industria, 1980), 235–51.

"Agriculture and Nutrition: Northern Europe," in Joseph Strayer (ed.), *Dictionary of the Middle Ages*, vol. 1 (New York: Scribner's, 1982), 89–96.

"The Eurasian Context of Medieval Europe," in Daniel Heartz and Bonnie Wade (eds.), *International Musicological Society, Report of the Twelfth Congress, Berkeley, 1977* (Kassel: Barenreiter, 1982), 1–10.

"St. Francis of Assisi," *Bohemian Club Literary Notes* 43 (Winter 1983): 17–19.

"Science in China," *Isis* 75, no. 1 (1984): 171–89 (with Jonathan D. Spence).[59]

"Technology, Western," in Joseph Strayer (ed.), *Dictionary of the Middle Ages*, vol. 11 (New York: Scribner's, 1988), 650–64.

Shorter contributions

1930s

"An Undergraduate Curriculum in Medieval Studies at Stanford University," *School and Society* 50, no. 1280 (July 1939): 55–57.

1950s

"Meetings," *California Historical Society Quarterly* 31, no. 1 (1952): 83–88 (with J.N. Bowman).

"Symposium on the Tenth Century: Introduction," *Medievalia et Humanistica* 9 (1955): 3.

---

59   A review of Joseph Needham, *Science and Civilisation in China*, 11 vols. to that date (27 vols. to 2015) (Cambridge: Cambridge University Press, 1954) and other works.

1960s

"Preface," in P. Boissonnade (ed.), *Life and Work in Medieval Europe* (New York: Harper & Row Torchbooks, 1964), xiii–xiv.

"Beyond the Ordinary Dimension," *UCLA Alumni Magazine* 42 (Fall 1967): 15–17.

"Christian Impact on Ecology," *Science* 156, no. 3776 (1967): 737–38 (with Ernest S. Feenstra, Renato Baserga, Cesare Emiliani, and Shale Niskin).

"Memoirs of Fellows and Corresponding Fellows of the Mediaeval Academy of America," *Speculum* 42, no. 3 (1967): 587–94 (with Curt Bühler, Taylor Starck, Archer Taylor, Gray C. Boyce, Frederic C. Lane, Gaines Post, Kemp Malone, et al.)

1970s

"Intercultural History," *Science* 168, no. 3932 (1970): 728.

"Introduction: The Reticences of the Middle Ages," in R. Berger (ed.), *Scientific Methods in Medieval Archaeology*, UCLA Center for Medieval and Renaissance Studies Contributions, vol. 4 (Berkeley and Los Angeles: University of California Press, 1970), 3–14.

"Tools" (in "History of Inventions" series), *The Sunday Times* (June 21, 1970), 20.

"Introduction," in W.S. Hudson and L.J. Trinterud (eds.), *Theology in Sixteenth and Seventeenth-Century England* (Los Angeles: William Andrews Clark Memorial Library, 1971), i–ii.

"Foreword," in D.R. Hill (ed. and trans.), *Jbn al-Razziiz al-Jazari, The Book of Knowledge of Ingenious Mechanical Devices* (Dordrecht and Boston: Reidel, 1974), xiii.

"Foreword," in Ernest A. Moody (ed.), *Studies in Medieval Philosophy, Science, and Logic* (Berkeley and Los Angeles: University of California Press, 1975), vii–viii.

"Introduction," in R. Westman and J.E. McGuire (eds.), *Hermeticism and the Scientific Revolution* (Los Angeles: William Andrews Clark Memorial Library, 1977), i–ii.

1980s

"Memoirs of Fellows and Corresponding Fellows of the Medieval Academy of America," *Speculum* 57, no. 3 (1982): 699–710 (with Robert M. Lumiansky, William J. Roach, Siegfried Wenzel, W. Bloomfield Morton, John F. Leyerle, George Kane, Paul O. Kristeller, et al.)

Book Reviews

1930s

Sommerfield Baldwin, "Business in the Middle Ages," *Annals of the American Academy of Political and Social Science* 193 (September 1937): 192.

Thomas Van Cleve, "Markward of Anweiler and the Sicilian Regency: A Study of Hohenstaufen Policy in Sicily during the Minority of Frederick II," *American Historical Review* 43, no. 1 (1938): 170–71.

1940s

R.P. Johnson, "Compositiones variae from Codex 490, Biblioteca Captolare, Lucca, Italy: An Introductory Study," *Isis* 32, no. 2 (1940): 350–52.
Joseph Strayer and Dana Munro, "The Middle Ages, 395–1500," *American Historical Review* 48, no. 2 (1943): 396–97.
Warburg and Courtauld Institutes (eds.), "England and the Mediterranean Tradition: Studies in Art, History, and Literature," *American Historical Review* 52, no. 3 (1946): 502–3.
"Dumbarton Oaks Papers, no. 3," *American Journal of Archaeology* 51 (1947): 345–46.
Erwin Panofsky (ed. and trans.), "Abbot Suger on the Abbey Church of St. Denis and Its Art Treasures," *College Art Journal* 7 (Autumn 1947): 66–67.
Steven Runciman, "The Medieval Manichee: A Study of the Christian Dualist Heresy," *Journal of Bible and Religion* 16, no. 2 (1947): 118.
George Boas, "Essays on Primitivism and Related Ideas in the Middle Ages," *The Journal of Religion* 29, no. 2 (1949): 167.

1950s

Christopher Dawson, "Religion and the Rise of Western Culture," *The Journal of Religion* 31, no. 1 (1951): 55–56.
"Leonard de Vinci et l'experience scientifique au XVIe siecle (Collogues internationaux au Centre national de la recherche scientifique, Paris, juillet 4–7, 1952)," *American Historical Review* 60, no. 1 (1954): 59–60.
Margaret Hogden, "Change and History: A Study of Dated Distributions of Technological Innovation in England," *Speculum* 29, no. 2 (1954): 280–82.
A.P. Usher, "A History of Mechanical Inventions (2nd rev. ed.)," *Isis* 46, no. 3 (1955): 290–93.
William Carroll Bark, "Origins of the Medieval World," *American Historical Review* 63, no. 4 (1957): 942–43.
Robert James Forbes, "Studies in Ancient Technology, vols. 1–3," *Isis* 48, no. 1 (1957): 77.
Evelyn Jamison, "Admiral Eugenius of Sicily, His Life and Work, and the Authorship of the Epistola ad Petrum and the Historia Hugonis Falcandi Siculi," *American Historical Review* 63, no. 3 (1957): 645–47.
Bern Dibner, "Agricola on Metals," *American Historical Review* 64, no. 1 (1958): 162.
Robert James Forbes, "Studies in Ancient Technology, vol. 4," *Manuscripta* 2 (1958): 50–51.
Edouard Salin, "La civilisation merovingienne d'apres les sepultures, les textes et le laboratoire, vol. 3: Les techniques," *American Historical Review* 64, no. 3 (1958): 616–17.
Charles Singer, et al. (eds.), "A History of Technology, Vol. 2: The Mediterranean Civilizations and the Middle Ages," *Speculum* 33, no. 1 (1958): 130–35.

1960s

Robert James Forbes, "Studies in Ancient Technology, vol. 4," *Isis* 51, no. 2 (1960): 227–28.
Alessandro Pratesi, "Carte latine di abbazie calabresi provenienti dall'Archirio Aldobrandini," *Speculum* 35, no. 2 (1960): 323–24.

Edouard Salin, "La civilisation merovingienne d'apres les sepultures, les textes et la laboratoire, vol. 4: Les croyances; conclusions, index general," *American Historical Review* 66, no. 1 (1960): 116–17.
C. Singer, E.J. Holmyard, A.R. Hall, and T.I. Williams (eds.), "A History of Technology," *Technology and Culture* 1, no. 4 (1960): 339–44.
Brian Tierny, "Medieval Poor Law," *The Journal of Economic History* 20, no. 3 (1960): 502–4.
M.R. Laurent and A. Guillou, "Le 'Liber visitationis' d'Athanese Chalkeopoulos," *Speculum* 36, no. 3 (1961): 491–92.
G. Smith, "The Heritage of Man," *The Asian Student* 25 (February 1961): 3.
Robert S. Woodbury, "History of the Lathe to 1850: A Study in the Growth of a Technical Element of an industrial Economy," *American Historical Review* 68, no. 1 (1962): 170–71.
Centre de documentation d'histoire des techniques, "Documents pour l'histoire des techniques, cahier no. 1," *Technology and Culture* 4, no. 1 (1963): 51.
F. Natale, "Avviamento alto studio del Medio Evo siciliano," *Speculum* 38 (1963): 389–90.
L. Saggi, "S. Angelo di Sicilia: Studio sulla vita, devozione, folklore," *Speculum* 38 (1963): 151.
Maurice Daumas (ed.), "Histoire generate des techniques, vol. 1: Les origines de la civilisation technique," *Isis* 55, no. 2 (1964): 228–30.
W.O. Hassel, "How They Lived: An Anthology of Original Accounts Written before 1485," *Speculum* 40, no.1 (1965): 141–42.
R. Kilbonsky, E. Panofsky, and P. Saxl, "Saturn and Melancholy," *Isis* 56 (1965): 458–59.
S. Borsari, "Il monachesimo bizantino nella Sicilia e nell'Italia meridionale prenormanne," *Speculum* 41 (1966): 116–17.
E.S. Hedges, "Tin in Social and Economic History," *Speculum* 41, no. 1 (1966): 144–45.
A.G. Keller, "A Theatre of Machines," *History of Science* 5 (1966): 145–46.
Joseph Needham and Wang Ling, "Science and Civilisation in China, Vol. 4: Physics and Physical Technology, pt. 2: Mechanical Engineering," *Isis* 58 (1967): 248–51.
Marc Bloch, "Land and Work in Medieval Europe,"*Agricultural History* 42 (1968): 271.
Bertrand Gille, "Engineers of the Renaissance," *Renaissance Quarterly* 21, no.1 (1968): 39–42.
Wilhelm Treue, et al. (eds.), "Das Hausbuch der Mendelschen Zwolfbrüderstiftung zu Nürnberg: Deutsche Handwerkerbilder des 15. und 16. Jahrhunderts," *Technology and Culture* 9 (1968): 480–81.

1970s

Georges de Santillana and Hermann von Dechend, "Hamlet's Mill: An Essay on Myth and the Frame of Time," *Isis* 61, no. 4 (1970): 540–41.
Joseph Needham, "Clerks and Craftsmen in China and the West," *Science* 168 (May 8, 1970): 728.
J.F.D. Shrewsbury, "History of the Bubonic Plague," *Journal of Interdisciplinary History* 1, no. 3 (1971): 545–47.
Nicole Oresme, "Le livre de politique d'Aristotle," *American Historical Review* 77 (1972): 125–26.

A.C. Leighton, "Transport and Communications in Early Medieval Europe, A.D. 500–1100," *Speculum* 49, no. 3 (1974): 577–79.

R. Bulliet, "The Camel and the Wheel," *The Middle East Journal* 31, no. 1 (1977): 101–2.

Jean Gimpel, "La revolution industrielle du Moyen Age," *Annals of Science* 34 (1977): 89–91.

Joseph Needham, et al. "Science and Civilisation in China, vol. 5, pt. 2," *Archives internationales d'histoire des sciences* 27 (1977): 324–28.

A.-D. Von den Brincken, "Die 'Nationes christianorum orientalium' *im Verstiindnis der lateinischen Historiographie von der Mille des 12. Bis in die zweite Hiilfte des 14. Jahrhunderts*," *Speculum* 53, no. 1 (1978): 201–2.

Institut for mittelalterliche Realienkunde bsterreichs, "Die Funktion der schriftlichen Quelle in der Sachkultuiforschung," *Speculum* 53 (1978): 359–61.

E. Bassani, "Gl'antichi strumenti musicali dell'Africa nera," *African Arts* 12, no. 2 (1979): 84–85.

1980s

Richard Unger, "The Ship in the Medieval Economy," *Technology and Culture* 23, no. 2 (1982): 223–27.

Donald Hill, "A History of Engineering in Classical and Medieval Times," *The Times Literary Supplement*, no. 4257 (November 2, 1984): 1247.

Chapter 2
Does the history of technology stand on the shoulders of giants?[1]

B.B. Price

> We are like dwarfs sitting on the shoulders of giants; we see more things, and more far-off ones, than they did, not because our sight is better, nor because we are taller than they were, but because they raise us up and add to our height by their gigantic loftiness.
> Bernard of Chartres (*ca.*1060–*ca.*1124),
> quoted by John of Salisbury[2]

This is a quotation well known to medievalists and undoubtedly to many others. With reference to the history of technology, it can readily evoke names, faces and, more important, writings. There were clearly historians of technology, even many great ones, before there was the history of technology as a recognized academic field. Even if one were to restrict one's search to the last three quarters of the last century, the mere question of who might be considered the "giants" of the history of technology can elicit a veritable list. This is not a hint for the need for criteria to determine who is among the pantheon; it is merely an observation that one does not have to look far to find twentieth-century historians of technology whose scholarship is still revered.

Surprisingly or not, among the names of the giants would be several who took a strong interest in things medieval. The quotation, a rhetorical device of the Middle Ages, holds thus a special attraction in the context of considering earlier study of medieval technology and its contribution to today's study of the history of technology. Three scholars, Lewis Mumford, Lynn White and Jean Gimpel, have received

---

1   This essay was originally written in 1995 for an invited talk on medieval technology at MIT and remained unpublished until now. It has been very slightly rewritten, but the historiography has not been updated. It not only stands both as a reflection of where White's influence stood three decades on from *Medieval Technology and Social Change* but also, somewhat silently, asks the reader to consider where we have gotten in the twenty years since. – *ed.*

2   Bernard of Chartres as quoted by John of Salisbury, *Metalogicon*, Ill, 4 [*Joannis cognomine Sarisberiensis Carnotensis episcopi opera omnia*, Patrologiae cursus completus, Patrologia lingua latina (PLL) 199, ed. Jacques Paul Migne (Paris: Migne, 1855), 900].

recognition and stature both for their interest in and contributions to understanding medieval technology.[3] In their light, the quotation seems to compel not only attention but also a certain breadth of perspective. The contributions to the history of medieval technology of Mumford, White and Gimpel can and arguably ought to be viewed and assessed in the larger context of the whole history of technology as it has developed and became what it is today.

One dares then to ask whether the history of technology stands on the shoulders of these giants. The question will, in fact, be posed in three different ways, by way of differing emphasis:

- "Does the history of technology stand on the shoulders of these *giants*?"
- "Does the history of technology stand on the *shoulders (i.e., theses)* of these giants?"
- "Does the history of technology *stand (as in, "go forth")* on the shoulders of these giants?"

The first two questions can and will be dealt with relatively briefly. No short, neat response presents itself, however, for the third. An attempt to answer it here focuses on our act of "standing," which is where the real issue seems to lie.

Our posture *vis-à-vis* each of the three scholars is perplexed and perplexing. At the outset of this writing my assumption was that historians of technology today [1995] do not stand on the shoulders of these three giants. As the number of scholarly citations of them added up, the hypothesis was, however, shown to require the revisions that follow. It still seems that there are plenty of reasons for doubting of any recognition of increased stature within the history of technology due to Mumford, White and Gimpel. On one hand, the research community has strongly condemned the ideas of each one. On the other, their statements can be seen being *used*, exploited by citation, and some of those who pursue this mode of research often receive a large degree of positive scholarly attention.[4] Also, while admittedly

---

3   Since this is a slightly disguised way of addressing some of the "old chestnut" theories in the history of medieval technology, I am not offering a wider survey of authors on medieval technology, including, for example, those whose chapters appeared in Charles Singer's *History of Technology*. Cf. Barton C. Hacker, "Military Institutions, Weapons, and Social Change – Toward a New History of Military Technology," *Technology and Culture* 35, no. 4 (1994): 768–834, esp. 809–10, for a useful and lengthy note to publications on retrospective and prospective looks at the history of technology.

4   One example springs to mind in which the author, while not denying his dependence upon over a dozen scholars of history of technology (although not in this case Mumford, White or Gimpel; see p. xvii), by openly citing them to construct the pieces of his whole, clearly anticipated, criticism – rightly so, for his own wrenching of supportive details from here and there in his sources: David F. Noble, *A World without Women: The Christian Clerical Culture of Western Science* (New York: Alfred A. Knopf, 1992). This statement can hardly prepare most readers, however, for the fact that throughout the entire

the ideas of Mumford, White and Gimpel are manifestly still being taught, one is led to wonder whether this is, almost as it at times appears, out of lethargy to revise the syllabus or for want of anything better to fill the void.

We might expect the appropriate reaction to be "What can be expected?" since our training seems rather deficient in fostering work forward from the ideas of these three scholars. It would appear that the few students interested in the history of medieval technology have neither the languages (*e.g.*, Latin, Greek, and medieval vernaculars) nor the skills (even elementary scientific and technical training) to grapple with the theses they advance. Mumford and those of his closer generations recognized the importance of such tools on their scholarship,[5] and we must as well, on our own potential. There was also the sense that presently we have not absorbed the desire of the giants to be superseded in height[6] nor seen that as our role, for while

---

300-page book, virtually every paragraph is intricately woven around citations, some annoyingly quoted more than once (*e.g.*, at 20 and 52, or at 131 and 146). Noble uses the literature (*e.g.*, George Ovitt, *The Restoration of Perfection: Labor and Technology in Medieval Culture* [New Brunswick, NJ: Rutgers University Press, 1986], 183) to document that women were periodically, if not traditionally, highly involved in the practical arts, in order to affirm that experience of the practical arts has been considered, at best, a lower order of learning than abstract theoretical understanding, and at worst, a subversive one (*e.g.*, Paolo Rossi, *Philosophy, Technology, and the Arts in the Early Modern Era* [New York: Harper & Row, 1970] and Richard S. Westfall, "Flood Along the Bisenzio: Science and Technology in the Age of Galileo," *Technology and Culture* 30, no. 4 [1989]: 905–7); to confirm the degrees of interaction between the worlds of the artisan and the scholar (*e.g.*, in the Middle Ages, Edward Grant, "Science and Technology in the Middle Ages," in *God and Nature*, ed. David C. Lindberg and Ronald L. Numbers [Berkeley: University of California Press, 1986]; in the sixteenth century, Rossi, *Philosophy, Technology, and the Arts in the Early Modern Era*; in the seventeenth century, Robert K. Merton, "Science, Technology, and Society in Seventeenth-Century England," *Osiris* 9, pt. 2 [1938]; and in the twentieth century, Edward D. McDonald and Edward M. Hinton, *Drexel Institute of Technology* [Philadelphia: Drexel Institute, 1942], 28–29); and to echo the characterization of women as labor capital (*e.g.*, Hugo Meir, "The Technological Concept in American Social History," PhD dissertation, University of Wisconsin, 1950; Julia S. Tutweiler, "The Technical Education of Women," *Education* 8 [1882]: 201 (one of Noble's commendable but rare direct uses of a primary source). In the introduction (xvii) he explains what he was hoping to avoid. See also the present author's review of *World without Women* in *Technology and Culture* 36, no. 2 (1995): 394–96.

5 "Without the kind of elementary scientific and technical training I received, I would never have dared later on to give at Columbia University perhaps the earliest courses offered anywhere on the Machine Age, nor could I have written 'Technics and Civilization' and 'The Myth of the Machine'." Lewis Mumford, *Sketches from Life: The Autobiography of Lewis Mumford, the Early Years* (New York: Dial Press, 1982), 101.

6 *Technics and Civilization* "has become gigantic, but the more one puts into it, the more empty somehow it gets: or rather the holes become more visible. . . . This monstrous book is but the sketch of the book I want to write: the very touch of failure that already

it is undeniable that issues for research abound in the ideas they expressed, students are not being led into their research areas. The real pity is that the stage for many challenging debates had been so beautifully set, and very early on.

To pursue the discussion of whether or not we stand on their shoulders, the three selected scholars are first briefly introduced and then their fundamental theses described. The third section is devoted to examining how we have related to their ideas right into the twenty-first century.

Giants of the history of technology

Lewis Mumford (1895–1990)

Lewis Mumford was a pioneer, renowned for having found a place for the history of technology within the issues of twentieth-century intellectual life quite generally. While his connections to academic institutions, such as Massachusetts Institute of Technology (MIT), were notoriously weak, his ideas have been honored, studied and analyzed within them.[7] More than the personage even during his lifetime, the works of Mumford attracted, and still attract, attention from virtually all stripes of historians of technology. Among those works that figure most prominently are his two-part *Myth of the Machine*[8] and *The City in History: Its Origins, Its Transformation and Its Prospects*[9] but especially *Technics and Civilization*,[10] the focus here. *Technics and Civilization*, 495 pages long, was published in 1934. Mumford describes the chronological steps in its being written in a prefatory note to the volume, where he mentions a first draft in 1930, a second in 1931,[11] and in his autobiography he notes that its final

---

hangs on my words as they reach and snatch after the thoughts that elude me is perhaps in another sense the best pledge of success." Mumford to Catherine Bauer, June 4, 1933 in Lewis Mumford, *My Works and Days: A Personal Chronicle* (New York: Harcourt Brace Jovanovich, 1979), 309.

7   See the academic essays in Thomas P. Hughes and Agatha C. Hughes, eds., *Lewis Mumford, Public Intellectual* (New York: Oxford University Press, 1990), esp. the contributions of MIT faculty Rosalind Williams, "Lewis Mumford as a Historian of Technology in *Technics and Civilization*," 43–65 and Leo Marx, "Lewis Mumford: Prophet of Organicism," 164–80.

8   Lewis Mumford, *The Myth of the Machine: Technics and Human Development* (New York: Harcourt, Brace, Jovanovich, 1967) and Lewis Mumford, *The Myth of the Machine: The Pentagon of Power* (New York: Harcourt Brace Jovanovich, 1970).

9   Lewis Mumford, *The City in History: Its Origins, Its Transformation and Its Prospects* (New York: Harcourt, Brace, and Company, 1961).

10   Lewis Mumford, *Technics and Civilization* (New York: Harcourt, Brace, and Company, 1934; rpt. 1970).

11   "The first draft of this book was written in 1930 and the second was completed in 1931. Up to 1932 my purpose was to deal with the machine, the city, the region, the group,

composition began in March 1933.[12] He seems very soon to have been haunted by the larger-than-life proportions and nature of his ideas at the time.

Not particularly obliging to my metaphor, Mumford cast the book as the giant and himself as merely its heroic author. "The book has become gigantic," he wrote to Catherine Bauer already in June 1933, a simple reference to size perhaps, until coupled with his description in August 1933 of the experience of controlling the work:

> As for Technics and Civilization it still goes: indeed "goes" is little better than Ogden's Basic English, for it pours, thunders, avalanches, tramples, and billows, knocking its poor author against the rocks as if he were shooting the Niagara, dragging him down to depths he had never suspected, whirling him through caverns measureless to man, scraping his buttocks against flinty facts and even more jagged theories, and in general knocking both wind and sense out of him, but at least leaving him with no doubt about the fact that he is living: for if Dr. Johnson vindicated reality by knocking his stick against the railing, how much more does one establish the fact of life by taking such a Niagara rapids journey![13]

With the theses that he seems to have been "propelled" to advance in *Technics and Civilization* and his other books, Mumford in 1934 was the precursor of a history of technology to come and with which he would later identify himself. At the writing of *Technics*, he has been described as "operating in something of a void" since "the discipline of the history of technology was unformed and still largely at the factgathering stage."[14] It has recently been asserted, nonetheless, that that work "more than any other single book, would serve to define the history of technology."[15] Soon, indeed, Mumford was to be among those in the first generation of the Society for the History of Technology (SHOT), along with Cyril Stanley Smith, Abbot Payson Usher, A. Rupert Hall, Jacques Ellul and Lynn White, Jr. He was present in more than one guise at the first meeting of the six founders of SHOT at Case Western Reserve in 1958: "Lewis Mumford's classic *Technics and*

---

and the personality within a single volume. In working out the section on techniques it was necessary to increase the scale of the whole project: so the present book covers only a limited area of the first draft." Mumford, *Technics and Civilization*, v.

12 "The first week in March 1933, just before I planned to start writing 'Technics and Civilization,' Catherine and I had a shattering quarrel. But despite this I doggedly began on the opening section of its first chapter." Mumford, *Sketches from Life*, 466. Williams offers a much more detailed blow-by-blow in "Lewis Mumford as a Historian," 43–44, n. 1–4 and *passim*.

13 Mumford to Babette Deutsch, August 3, 1933 in Mumford, *My Works and Days*, 176.

14 Williams, "Lewis Mumford as a Historian," 44.

15 A. Jamison, "Technology's Theorists: Conceptions of Innovation in Relation to Science and Technology Policy," *Technology and Culture* 30, no. 3 (1989): 505–33, esp. 518. Jamison was at the time a student in the Graduate Program in Science and Technology Policy at the University of Lund, Sweden.

Civilization (1934) was no doubt familiar to all [who attended] and very likely held a place of honor on their five-foot shelves."[16]

Perhaps for Melvin Kranzberg and his colleagues, it was Mumford's concluding passage to *Technics and Civilization* that resonated in their decision to name SHOT's journal *Technology and Culture*:[17]

> We have observed the limitations the Western European imposed upon himself in order to create the machine and project it as a body outside his personal will: we have noted the limitations that the machine has imposed upon men through the historic accidents that accompanied its development. We have seen the machine arise out of the denial of the organic and the living, and we have in turn marked the reaction of the organic and the living on the machine.[18]

Lynn White, Jr. (1907–1987)

Except for his graduate work at Harvard and the first years of teaching at Princeton between 1933 and 1937, Lynn White's career played itself out in California. He became, in fact, an extremely important West Coast proponent of the history of technology. His works were, however, read worldwide. Among them, the most frequently cited by historians of technology are *Machina ex Deo: Essays in the Dynamism of Western Culture*,[19] published by MIT Press, for which White was ostensibly awarded SHOT's Dexter Prize, and above all, *Medieval Technology and Social Change* (*MTSC*).[20] That book, which will be the focus of the discussion of White's ideas here, is a short volume, revealing its origin in three lectures, given at the University of Virginia in 1957. Published in 1962, the original text had been doubled to its 134 pages virtually by footnotes alone. Since the lecture series had been White's way of testing his scholarly wings again after fifteen years in administration as the president of Mills College, he was no doubt quite surprised, as reports have it, at the importance immediately attributed to the ideas.

---

16   John M. Staudenmaier, *Technology's Storytellers* (Cambridge, MA: MIT Press, 1985), 162.

17   While I acknowledge Staudenmaier's assertion (162–63) that Mumford's ideas were behind the title of the journal, to set the stage for his discussion he quotes instead from Mumford, "Authoritarian and Democratic Technics," *Technology and Culture* 5, no. 1 (1964): 6 and 8. Mumford's concluding spirit of *Technics and Civilization* (quoted here) where technics and organic culture can exist together, would seem more in keeping with the founders' hopes for the thrust of the new journal. Cf. also Staudenmaier, *Technology's Storytellers*, 121–22.

18   Mumford, *Technics and Civilization*, 433.

19   Lynn White, Jr., *Machina ex Deo: Essays in the Dynamism of Western Culture* (Cambridge, MA: MIT Press, 1968); subsequently reissued as *The Dynamo and the Virgin Reconsidered* (Cambridge, MA: MIT Press, 1976).

20   Lynn White, Jr., *Medieval Technology and Social Change* [hereafter *MTSC*] (Oxford: Oxford University Press, 1962).

Word of his ideas, even as espoused in lecture form, must have spread very rapidly, for already by January 1958, having published only one article (1940)[21] and two reviews (1954 and 1955)[22] related to the history of technology, White was a very valued member of the six founders of SHOT.[23] By 1960 he became its president for three years and prevailed upon others to use *Technology and Culture* as the only title of the society's journal. Once openly expressed, White's interest in medieval technology virtually swept him away from the roots of his training as a historian of medieval religious culture, leading him to think of himself very much as a historian of technology.[24] It did not, however, apparently change his perspective on his stature as a thinker. Like Mumford, White, too, shied away from casting himself as the metaphorical giant (neither, however, did he see himself as the hero). White was a humble innovator whose motivation came from the heart of his own "cultural atmosphere," his belief in God.[25]

Jean Gimpel (1918–1996)

Jean Gimpel was a historian of the Middle Ages interested in both its social and technological sides. His writings include the highly praised *The Cathedral Builders*,[26] as well as the work in view here, *The Medieval Machine. The Industrial*

---

21   Lynn White, Jr., "Technology and Invention in the Middle Ages," *Speculum* 15 (1940): 141–59; rpt. in Lynn White, Jr., *Medieval Religion and Technology: Collected Essays* [hereafter *MRT*] (Berkeley: University of California Press, 1978), 1–22.

22   Review of Margaret Hodgen, *Change and History: A Study of Dated Distributions of Technological Innovation in England* (New York: Wenner-Gren Foundation for Anthropological Research, 1952), *Speculum* 29 (1954): 280–82; review of A.P. Usher, *A History of Mechanical Inventions*, 2nd ed. (Cambridge, MA: Harvard University Press, 1954), *Isis* 46 (1955): 290–93.

23   "Most of the people on my committee could not come to the meeting. . . . But some important people did come: Bob Multhauf, . . . and, most importantly, Lynn White!" quoted by Staudenmaier from personal correspondence from Melvin Kranzberg, Staudenmaier, *Technology's Storytellers*, 224, n. 8. Kranzberg also writes of White as a "big name," one "whose reputation alone was sufficient guarantee of quality."

24   "The Study of Medieval Technology, 1924–1974: Personal Reflections," *Technology and Culture* 16, no. 4 (1975): 519–30; rpt. in *MRT*, xi–xxiv and "History and Horseshoe Nails," in *The Historian's Workshop: Original Essays by Sixteen Historians*, ed. L.P. Curtis (New York: Alfred A. Knopf, 1970), 47–64.

25   Staudenmaier, *Technology's Storytellers*, 184, states that "*Machina ex Deo* (1970) was recognized, no doubt in conjunction with his earlier [*MTSC*], as a genuine *innovation* in the historiography of the field" (emphasis added). Compare White's interpretation of the possible stimuli for one medieval attempt at heavier-than-air flight in his, "Eilmer of Malmesbury, an Eleventh Century Aviator," *Technology and Culture* 2, no. 2 (1961): 97–111, esp. 110 [rpt. in *MRT*, 59–73].

26   Jean Gimpel, *The Cathedral Builders* (New York: Grove Press, 1961).

Revolution of the Middle Ages.[27] While it may not be very bold to presume that both Mumford and White are known at least by name to almost everyone in the field of the history of technology, it may well be that it is a different story with Gimpel. By virtue of this contrast to the other two alone, his status as a "giant" in the history of technology might well be open to discussion.

Two factors motivate his inclusion here. Gimpel, French by birth, lived in both French- and English-language spheres, was familiar with both language's scholarly environments and published in both French and English. What this means is that he had the greatest potential of the three to bring the historiographic schools of the French and Anglo-Saxons to bear in his own work and to attract the attention of each to his ideas. Second, of the three authors, he is the only one to have chosen to survey the many different aspects in the whole of medieval technological life without sacrificing greatly in depth of detail in order to hold onto the broad hypotheses of the medieval industrial revolution. The ramifications of that presentation of ideas will be noted in what follows.

First, a few words about the importance of the two groups' historiographies are perhaps in order. While Gimpel was the only one to come by the connection by birth, all three scholars were highly influenced by the French historiography developing since 1931 under Marc Bloch, Lucien Febrve and the Annales School in Paris. Lynn White dedicated his *Medieval Technology and Social Change* to the memory of Marc Bloch, although he never met him.[28] The French historians' calls for an integrated treatment of technology within historical contexts and a recognition of nonliteral, nonverbal expressions, testimonials to a so-called *mentalité* (in which mind-sets can be not just determined but which can also be seen to be determining historical agents) were not to be ignored.[29] The Anglo-Saxon approach to history was meanwhile also undergoing changes, influenced by anthropologists, economic historians and the new sociologists. Anthropologists, such as Alfred L. Kroeber, influenced both Mumford and White. Figures particularly influential in the area of medieval history were Charles Homer Haskins, whose work in medieval science is still a landmark, and a following generation of scholars, such as Georges Sarton and Joseph Strayer, who as their mentor had, affirmed for the Middle Ages the existence of the primacy of rationality, intellectually and, most important, for its technology, also pragmatically.

---

27   Jean Gimpel, *The Medieval Machine. The Industrial Revolution of the Middle Ages* (New York: Holt, Rinehart and Winston, 1976), originally published in French as *La revolution industrielle du Moyen Age* (1975).

28   White, *MTSC*, iv and see Bert S. Hall, "Lynn White's *Medieval Technology and Social Change* After Thirty Years," in *Technological Change: Methods and Themes in the History of Technology*, ed. Robert Fox (London: Harwood Academic Publishers, 1996), 90, from whence come many of the observations of this paragraph.

29   It is interesting to note, however, that not once in *Medieval Machine* does Gimpel acknowledge any indebtedness to Marc Bloch. Georges Duby and Jacques LeGoff, Bloch's kindred spirits, were cited.

Each of the three authors, Mumford, White, and Gimpel, played an extremely supportive and formative part in the emerging field of study we know today as the history of technology. This introductory section closes with a brief vignette of one of Gimpel's experiences in the 1950s, just before the formation of SHOT:

> In 1953 when I submitted an article to *Techniques et Civilisations*, the magazine's editor, Bertrand Gille,[30] was writing the majority of its contents under various noms de plume to give the impression that there was a substantial group of scholars interested in the history of technology. Louis Delville, the publisher of the review, had to be convinced that mine was not just another of Gille's nom de plume articles. With few authors and very nearly as few subscribers, the review published its last number in 1956.[31]

Aside from their institutional roles, Mumford, White and Gimpel were thinkers and writers, and it is for these contributions that they are here labeled "giants." So we turn now to each one, to examine the shoulders they have offered us to stand on. With what ideas do they raise us up? From what theses do we gain our lofty vantage point?

Mumford: the Middle Ages and the clock

Within Mumford's *Technics and Civilization* are two very important themes related to medieval technology, an overriding, general one about the nature of technology during the Middle Ages and a specific, fundamental one concerning the significance of the medieval innovation of the clock.

The Middle Ages

Mumford was interested in both cataloging and characterizing the "inventions" of the Middle Ages (*i.e.*, from the tenth[32] to the fourteen century). His catalogue comprised technical inventions or adoptions, such as the mariner's compass, permanent rudder, glass works, cheap paper, cannon, lenses, spectacles, guns, waterwheel/watermill,[33] windmill, paper, magnetic needle, gunpowder and

---

30 In his Works and Days, Mumford thanked scholars like Bertrand Gille for their "reinforcements" in affirming that the 'new wave' in Western technology began as far back as the eleventh century, not much later, as is generally held "by one-generation minds bedazzled over our immediate successes" (468).

31 Gimpel, "Epilogue," *Medieval Machine*, 238–39.

32 Mumford was not really particular as to the first significant medieval century: he mentions at different times the tenth, eleventh and twelfth as key. Compare, for example, his "focus was the technical changes that began in the twelfth century of our era" ("Appraisal," 528) versus "the 'new wave' in Western technology began as far back as the eleventh century" (*Works and Days*, 468).

33 The watermill was used to furnish power for pulping rags for paper in Ravensburg in 1290, for the hammering and cutting machines of an ironworks near Oobrilugk, Lausitz

spinning wheel,[34] as well as "social inventions" such as the university and the medical school.[35] For Mumford, the Middle Ages was, in the context of a discussion of technological change, not significantly isolatable. It was instead a part of a much longer period, the *eotechnic* phase,[36] dated from 1000 to 1750. Mumford's periodization according to material culture, although hardly an original device, incorporated the Middle Ages into the water-and-wood complex (implicitly also including wind in the process; *Technics*, 110). The main technical characteristics of the eotechnic era – the diminished use of human beings as prime movers, and the separation of the production of the energy from its applications, and immediate control with the development of wind and water power (*Technics*, 112) – did not, "however, reach their height in most parts of Europe until the seventeenth century" (*Technics*, 117, 148–150), hence Mumford's lengthy extension of the period. Two significant weaknesses Mumford identified for the eotechnic regime were beginning to be manifest during the Middle Ages: the irregularity of power and that the new industries, such as glassmaking, mining, and printing, functioned outside the institutional controls of the old order of the guilds, and ultimately outside the institutions of Christian synthesis, that is, monasteries and the Church itself. Equally increasingly evident, Mumford asserts, were also the strengths of the Middle Ages: the absolute saving of human labor, or at least, the diminished amount and intensity of manual work and the creation of an organically ordered human landscape (*Technics*, 147–48).[37]

(Forst, on the German–Polish border) in 1320, for sawing wood in Augsburg in 1322, for beating hides in a tannery, for spinning silk, for working up the felts in fulling mills, for powering the grinding machines of armourers. Mumford, *Technics*, 114–15.

34 These are all mentioned within the text, but still more are included in Mumford's appendix itemizing technologies starting with the tenth century: "List of Inventions," *Technics*, 438. Print and the printing press, both from the fifteenth century, were to him considered postmedieval.

35 Mumford mentions the factory but does not link it directly to the Middle Ages (*Technics*, 138).

36 The eotechnic period, included apparently only by August 1933, is an addition to Mumford's original conception of the work, extending thereby its scope significantly backward in time: cf. Williams, "Lewis Mumford as a Historian."

37 As the direct precursor of the Baroque city, Mumford, "regards the medieval city as the last significant, relatively enduring societal embodiment of the organic principle; its street plans tended 'to follow nature's contours.' . . . Each medieval town developed out of a unique situation, 'presented a unique constellation of forces, and produced, in its plan, a unique solution.'" It grew, as it were, from the inside out, because the decisive determinant was "a consensus . . . so complete as to the purposes of town life that the variations in detail only confirm the pattern. That consensus makes it look, when one views a hundred medieval plans in succession, as if there were in fact a conscious theory that guided this town planning." This passage is cited from Marx, "Lewis Mumford," 170–71, in which are embedded citations from Lewis Mumford, "Principles of Medieval Town Planning," in *The City in History* (New York: Harcourt, Brace & World, 1961), 299–305.

Despite its amalgamation in the eotechnic period with later centuries, the Middle Ages was still seen by Mumford to provide its own holistic culture within which to examine technology. He identified numerous elements that formed the nature of medieval culture and considered all of them important in relation to the technology of the time:

- Spatial relations tended to be organized as symbols and values (*Technics*, 18).
- Space and time formed two relatively independent systems (*Technics*, 19).
- The external world had no conceptual hold upon the mind (*Technics*, 29).
- Discipline of the personality was essentially the province of the Church (*Technics*, 33).[38]
- In their hatred of the body, the orthodox minds of the Middle Ages were prepared to do it violence; instead of resenting the machines that would counterfeit this or that action of the body, they welcomed them (*Technics*, 36).
- The double process of naturalism and abstraction had begun to characterize the thought of Europe as early as 1300 (*Technics*, 125).
- Thanks to the menial services of wind and water, there was no need for recourse to slavery (*Technics*, 118).

The clock

Although Mumford's inclusion of an eotechnic period, with its full discussion of the Middle Ages, in *Technics and Civilization* is a late arrival,[39] his notions about the medieval clock were among the very first ideas to give shape to his work. They first took on a formalized conception in a draft of 1930 in which he wrote, "A new rhythm crept into life, the mechanical readings of *the clock supplant* the unevenness of endured time."[40] The evolution from this first to a last formulation

---

38 Mumford was influenced by the belief of his mentor Patrick Geddes, not only in the usefulness of periodization according to material culture but also in the idea that a university could leave an imprint, liberating (or otherwise) scientific and historic thinking on all the activities of a community, as the Church had once imprinted its theological and esthetic visions on the medieval city. Mumford, *Sketches from Life*, 156.

39 See n. 35, in this chapter.

40 Box 8, folder 4, 44 of Lewis Mumford Papers, Van Pelt Library, University of Pennsylvania. The reference is taken from Williams, "Lewis Mumford as a Historian," 382, as well as the following elaboration: In the margin Mumford scrawled "Expand," and in the August version the discussion had indeed been expanded into a paragraph: "gestation and growth were supplanted by the mechanical punctuation of *the clock*. . . . Time became an entity in itself, divorced from the events that were bound up with it and quantified it." Mumford then mentions how establishing hours and minutes of longitude created similar attitudes toward space (space as an abstract entity, unrelated to historical events, one place as good as another) and concludes with "Wherever this new rhythm became established, industrialism followed quickly" (4–5; former page numbers 51–52 crossed out). By the

shows Mumford's thesis concerning the importance of the medieval invention of the mechanical clock became ever more developed in his thinking. In its shortened final form in his *Works and Days*, extracted from the whole of the published passage in *Technics and Civilization*, on "The Monastery and the Clock," Mumford indicated himself what he felt was the essence of his thesis. For him its kernel was captured in five of the eleven original paragraphs in *Technics and Civilization*,[41] and its principal statement was "[t]*he clock, not the steam engine, is the key machine of the modern industrial* and scientific *age*" (italic emphasis added).[42]

The assertions about the clock had already taken on a similar form in the section dedicated to the clock in *Technics*[43] and again a little later in the work: "In mechanical invention proper, the chief eotechnic invention was, of course, the mechanical clock."[44] Rephrased elsewhere again it appears as "the *invention of the mechanical clock* in the fourteenth century did far more to advance modern science and technics than *the steam engine* or the automatic loom" (italic emphasis added).[45]

Mumford highlights the technical sophistication of the mechanical clock. Its measurement is according to the evenness of the energy flow, whose regularity affords standardization of the production and product, mechanical time. Its means of measuring served as a model for many other kinds of mechanical (geared, motion transmitting) works. He also notes the divorce of the mechanism from its context due to this technical sophistication. Thus, among the implications of its use were its increasing ubiquity and the degree to which it, by virtue of its product, "time," disassociated its followers from human events. The mechanical clock became or created a nonhuman point of reference and thereby changed thinking in relation to things human (biological, historical, etc.): "Timekeeping passed into time-serving and time-accounting and time-rationing." As one early reviewer of *Technics and Civilization* phrased it, "the clock is seen as the first automatic machine, the forerunner of the automatic factory. It also becomes the great regimenter of our daily life and foreshadows the dictatorship of the machine."[46]

Aside from affirming repeatedly that the mechanical clock of the Middle Ages was an invention more significant than the steam engine yet to come in its inevitable supplanting the uneven, biologically timed intervals of life with mechanically

---

final version of *Technics*, Mumford had separated his observations on space from those on time. The words or phrases rendered in bold in the text and notes formed the recurring core of Mumford's expression of his thesis on the clock. One could also focus on what ideas were grafted periodically to that core.

41 Five paragraphs, numbers 1–3, 5, and 11, of the original section 2 in *Technics and Civilization*, 12–18, are the only ones reproduced in *Works and Days*, 197–99.
42 Mumford, *Works and Days*, 198.
43 The opening line of *Technics*, 14, para. 5.
44 Mumford, *Technics*, 131–34.
45 Mumford, *Works and Days*, 468.
46 Review of *Technics* by W.F. Ogburn in *Saturday Review of Literature*, April 28, 1934, 10, 657.

even divisions,[47] Mumford also indicated the context of its creation: An eotechnic invention, the mechanical clock, was "born with the renewed impulse toward regularity and regimentation" (*Technics*, 131). "The spiritual routine of the monastery, if it did not positively favour the machine, at least nullified many of the influences that worked against it" (*Technics*, 35). Mumford's fundamental thesis was straightforward and basic, but as was noted by Williams, "Mumford's linkage of the clock and the monastery, of technology and occupation, results in a far more precise and powerful argument than his simple assertion in the 1930 draft that the clock is the crucial invention of modern technology."[48]

In addition to the themes and theses of Mumford, several aspects of the presentation of his ideas also must be noted, even without belaboring form following content or vice versa. One is that Mumford used pictures to illustrate his ideas in *Technics and Civilization*, a detail of presentation he felt had at least formative importance.[49] Another feature of his writing was his style, one "in which the imaginative and the subjective part is counterbalanced by an equal interest in the objective, the external, the scientifically apprehended."[50] Yet another element of Mumford's presentation of ideas is his use of metaphorical reasoning. Witness, for example, the use of Darwinian botanical law to convey the possibility of technology transfers from elsewhere into Western Europe: "Taking root in medieval culture, in a different climate and soil, these seeds of the machine [waterwheel/watermill, windmill, paper, magnetic needle, gunpowder, spinning wheel] sported and took on new forms: perhaps, precisely because they had not originated in Western Europe and had no natural enemies there, they grew as rapidly and gigantically as the Canada thistle when it made its way onto the South American pampas" (*Technics*, 109).

Between 1934 and now, Mumford's ideas have not been forgotten. His themes, theses and approach are still being laid out and paraphrased today. Mumford

---

[47] This summary is intended to reflect the passages in added italic font in the earlier paragraph and its notes, ideas common to virtually every expression Mumford made of his clock thesis.

[48] Williams, "Lewis Mumford as a Historian," 55–56.

[49] Cf. "VI Technics of Wood," in *Technics*, 122a: "When it came to helping him [Victor Branford] that summer [1920] to gather together a graphic survey of Westminster, to be demonstrated at the Summer School of Civics in High Wycombe where I was lecturing, I sometimes found Brandford capricious or arbitrary in his choice of illustrations. For all that, my own use of pictures in 'Techniques and Civilization' and later volumes owes not a little at all that I took in, against my original academic limitations, from Brandford." Mumford, *Sketches from Life*, 269.

[50] Mumford, *Works and Days*, 270.

continues to be recognized as one of technology's more learned theorists, "concerned with the long cycles of historical movement and [as one who] sought to link the development of technology to the broader movements of cultural values."[51] At the very least the character of his ideas is evoked. John Staudenmaier in *Technology's Storytellers*, for example, tries to convey how Mumford "articulated a complex technologically centered interpretation of civilization in the West," writing that "the work remains an early representative of attempts to create a historical synthesis of technology and non-technological factors."[52] Hacker writes in a 1994 article in *Technology and Culture* that Mumford was "unprecedented in focusing on technology as a subject in its own right, rather than viewing it as an aspect of economic development or social progress."[53]

Specific to Mumford's interest in the Middle Ages, Konvitz, Rose and Tarr, from their interest in technology and the city, note that as "one of the first to address the influence of medieval and early modern technology on subsequent developments, he formulated detailed analyses of the relationship between technology and urban life in both epochs."[54] Apparently, *Technics and Civilization* is used less frequently in the history of technology courses than it was in 1978 and earlier, but it does still figure pedagogically among the select "older books" in some classes.[55] In one published instance of a history of technology syllabus, Mumford's "wood-water complex" is parachuted into the course at the moment of the final exam![56]

White: stirrup, plough, and power

Within Lynn White's *MTSC*, each of its three chapters offers one or more important theses. The first group concerns the impact of the stirrup on the medieval

---

51 Jamison, "Technology's Theorists," 519.
52 Staudenmaier, *Technology's Storytellers*, 12.
53 Hacker, "Military Institutions," 785.
54 Josef W. Konvitz, Mark H. Rose, and Joel A. Tarr, "Technology and the City," *Technology and Culture* 31, no. 2 (1990): 284–94, esp. 286.
55 Cf. Lars Olsson, *Undergraduate Teaching of History of Technology – A Survey of the Teaching at Some Universities in the USA in 1993* (Gothenburg, Sweden: Chalmers University of Technology, 1995), 33 (cited from preliminary version in typescript). One small personal testimonial to the fact that Mumford is still alive and well is that when I went to locate the Hughes edition of essays about him, I found it to be placed on two-hour reserve at MIT's Retch Art and Architecture Library as part of a 1995 spring term course in which his ideas and writings figured prominently.
56 Richard F. Hirsh, "Syllabus of 'History of Technology from Prehistory to the Industrial Revolution'," in *The Machine in the University: Sample Course Syllabi for the History of Technology and Technology Studies*, ed. Terry S. Reynolds (Houghton and Bethlehem: Michigan Technological University and Lehigh University, 1987), 9, 12.

military and extended society; the second, the implications of the integration of the heavy plough into medieval agriculture, the third, the attitude of medieval culture to the harnessing of nonhuman, nonanimal power sources.

The stirrup

> The stirrup, by giving lateral support in addition to the front and back support offered by the pommel and cantle, effectively welded horse and rider into a single fighting unit capable of a violence without precedent. The fighter's hand no longer delivered the blow: it merely guided it. The stirrup thus replaced human energy with animal power, and immensely increased the warrior's ability to damage his enemy. Immediately, without preparatory steps, it made possible mounted shock combat, a revolutionary way of doing battle.
> (*MTSC*, 2)

This is, in short, White's thesis concerning the technical advantage afforded by the stirrup. It is, however, stated without reference to date, hence the immediately following question that was his catalyst to addressing the historical circumstances of its use: "What was the effect of the introduction of the stirrup in Europe?" At issue is the date at which stirrups first appeared in the West: "We must therefore return to the view of the older Germanic archeologists [noted are L. Lindenschmidt (1880), J. Hampel (1880) and E. Salin and A. France-Lanord (1943)] that stirrups first appeared in the West [noted are finds in Wurttemberg, Hesse and perhaps Bingen am Rhine] some time in the early eighth century" (*MTSC*, 24). Once he feels a date is satisfactorily established, White claims the thesis for which he is best remembered: the stirrup was, in fact, a new arrival when Charles Martel used it as "the technological basis of his military reforms" and successfully repelled the Muslims invading from the Iberian peninsula at the Battle of Tours in 732, through the primary use of cavalry and the use of the long lance as the horseman's weapon (*MTSC*, 28). Two implications of the use of the stirrup are also advanced: "The feudal class of the European Middle Ages existed to be armed horsemen, cavaliers fighting in a particular manner which was made possible by the stirrup" (*MTSC*, 28), and "the requirements of the new mode of warfare which the stirrup made possible found expression in a new form of western European society dominated by aristocracy of warriors endowed with land so that they might fight in a new highly specialized way" (*MTSC*, 38). This is White's linking of military feudalism and chivalry. "Inevitably this nobility developed cultural forms and patterns of thought and emotion in harmony with its style of mounted shock combat and its social posture" (*MTSC*, 38). Thus, "White found a technological basis for feudalism, through intervening military organizational changes that ultimately transformed social structure."[57]

---

57 Hacker, "Military Institutions," 814.

The plough

White's thesis concerning the heavy medieval plough has a number of the same ingredients: an issue of dating, the correlating of synchronous technological and social events and an assertion of the impact of the combination. He argued that a "balanced system of animal and cereal production, in conjunction with the heavy plough, was apparently developed into a normal and accepted system during the seventh century in the Frankish heartland" (*MTSC*, 56).

He establishes then the date and place of its arrival:

> As the Carolingians marched their armies into barbarian Germany, as St. Boniface and his Benedictine legions replaced pagan shrines with cathedrals and cloisters, as Teuton and Latin began to fuse their talents in the building of a new European culture, at that same moment the BalticNorth Sea spring planting was married to the Mediterranean autumn planting to create a new agricultural system far more productive than either of its progenitors.
>
> (*MTSC*, 71)

The plough, he argued, "help[ed] to account for the relative prosperity and vigour of the Carolingian Age" (*MTSC*, 56), and "the widespread replacement of oxen by horses marked an epoch in the application of power to agriculture" as well as the migration of peasants into larger centers of habitation (*MTSC*, 63, 67–68).

He then proceeds to describe the contemporaneous situation:

> Moreover, the heavy plough and its consequence of distribution of strips in the open fields helped to change the northern peasants' attitude towards nature, and thus our own. From time immemorial land was held by peasants in allotments at least theoretically sufficient to support a family. Although most peasants paid rent, usually in produce and services, the assumption was subsistence farming. Then in northern Europe, and there alone, the heavy plough changed the basis of allotment: peasants now held strips of land at least theoretically in proportion to their contribution to the plough-team. Thus the standard of land distribution ceased to be the needs of a family and became the ability of a power-engine to till the earth. No more fundamental change in the idea of man's relation to the soil can be imagined: once man had been part of nature; now he became her exploiter.
>
> (*MTSC*, 56)

The impact of the combination is thus assessed, first in light of the issue as formulated by White, subsequently via the formulation of the problem by others, if such exists. In this case, Henri Pirenne is treated in light of the earlier assertions of date, place and cohesive picture:

> A more durable solution of the historical problem of the change of the gravitational centre of Europe from south to north [addressed by Pirenne] is to be found in the agricultural revolution of the early Middle Ages. By the early ninth century all the major interlocking elements of the revolution had been developed: the

heavy plough, the open fields, the modern harness, the triennial rotation – everything except the nailed horseshoe, which appears a hundred years later. To be sure, the transition to the three-field system made such an assault on existing peasant priorities that its diffusion beyond the Frankish heartland was slow;[58] but Charlemagne's renaming of the months indicates how large the new agricultural cycle loomed in his thinking. We may safely assume that its increased productivity was a major stimulus to the north even in his day.

(*MTSC*, 78)

Sources of power

White's third section on the sources of medieval power is once again a multifaceted study. He says, at the outset that it is focused on attitude, not on technology *per se*:

Our present concern is . . . to examine the new exploratory attitude towards the forces of nature which enabled medieval Europe to discover and to try to harness other sources of power which have been culturally effective chiefly in modern times.

(*MTSC*, 89)

His summation of the medieval attitude toward power, "consciously focused, lusting, enthusiastic" is found near the end of the chapter: "The symptom of the emergence of a conscious and generalized lust for natural energy and its application to human purposes, is the enthusiastic adoption by thirteenth-century Europe of an idea which had originated in twelfth-century India – perpetual motion" (*MTSC*, 129–130). Meanwhile, however, White has provided a detailed survey of the use of power sources and powered mechanisms in the Middle Ages:

The expansion of Europe from 1492 onward was based in great measure upon Europe's high consumption of energy, with consequent productivity, economic weight, and military might. But mechanical power has no meaning apart from mechanisms to harness it. Beginning probably with the fulling mill on the Serchio in 983, the eleventh and twelfth centuries had applied the cam to a great variety of operations. The thirteenth century discovered spring and treadle; the fourteenth century developed gearing to levels of incredible complexity; the fifteenth century, by elaborating crank, connecting-rod, and governor, vastly facilitated the conversion of reciprocating into continuous rotary motion. Considering the generally slow tempo of human history, this revolution in machine design occurred with startling rapidity. Indeed, the four centuries following Leonardo, that is, until electrical energy demanded a supplementary set of devices, were less technologically

---

58 "It may be that the 300-year delay between the arrival of the modern harness and the widespread use of the horse for non-military purposes can be explained by the practical difficulties of switching a village from the biennial to the triennial rotation" (*MTSC*, 73). That is, because there was no third field to be assarted or carved out of the earlier two.

engaged in discovering basic principles than in elaborating and refining those established during the four centuries before Leonardo.

(*MTSC*, 129)

A note on archaeology

In the context of White's contributions in *Medieval Technology and Social Change* a word might also be added about his method of research. He felt that historians of technology ought to incorporate the findings of archeology into their arguments:

> One might expect that scholars exploring the sources of feudalism would have made every effort to supplement the extant documents with the archeological material which, in recent years, has begun so greatly to modify our view of the early Middle Ages. But this is not the case: the vast literature of ingenious controversy about feudal origins has been produced chiefly by legal and constitutional historians, and therefore is almost entirely a matter of textual exegesis.
>
> (*MTSC*, 2–3)

White made very detailed and exacting use of archeological results from as far back as the eighteenth century for the stirrup, horseshoe, and crank, among other technologies discussed. It would, however, be a mistake to conclude from this passage that White shunned textual analysis. Quite the contrary, he used to the fullest the offerings of texts for philological and contextual exegesis. He did, nonetheless, value artifactual and pictorial evidence just as much and considered and weighed it just as carefully. One last feature of his ideas to note here was that both his factual and hypothetical statements would be accompanied by lots of examples to illustrate them. This feature of his exposition was as much appreciated by his undergraduates attending lectures at the University of California, Los Angeles (UCLA) as by his readers worldwide.

White's death in 1987 brought a flurry of obituaries and quasi-obituaries into print. None of them had to protest very much to assert that his ideas were outliving him. "White's work has long been acknowledged as a paradigm for the 'new' approach to a contextual history of technology,"[59] said one eulogizer, a paradigm that, as we shall see shortly, was still being adhered to in 1995. Even easier to assert than his continued presence in research circles was to confirm White as a fixture in teaching. He was not far from being included in the syllabus of virtually every survey course of the Middle Ages, but even more impressive is his relative staying power within the teaching of the general history of technology. It is impressive in terms

---

59 Staudemaier, *Technology's Storytellers*, 184.

of sheer frequency of use in a field in which medieval technology *per se* is so rarely taught.[60] Lynn White is still the pedagogues' authority.

Gimpel: the medieval industrial revolution

There is one main theme and thesis to Gimpel's *Medieval Machine*, which is the book's very subtitle: *The Industrial Revolution of the Middle* Ages. Just as Mumford's bold assertion that the clock is more important than the steam engine cannot stand on its own, Gimpel offers much evidence both factual and theoretical to support his claim.

Although Gimpel's book lacks the cohesion to make it obvious, the theme of each chapter is designed to establish that all the components necessary for an industrial revolution to occur (identified in bold type) existed in the Middle Ages. In Chapter 1, Gimpel introduces mechanization as a first element: "The Middle Ages introduced **machinery** into Europe **on a scale** no civilization had previously known" (*Medieval Machine*, 1*ff*), including machines for employing natural, non-human sources of power. In Chapters 2 and 3 he identifies when and where the first machines were being integrated: "The first impact on the new sources of energy was on **agriculture**" (*Medieval Machine*, 29*ff*); a **mining** industry, with the sector devoted to stone quarrying dominating, flourished in medieval Europe (*Medieval Machine*, 59*ff*). The ecological impact of new industry is the focus of Chapter 4; the scale of industrialization in the Middle Ages was great enough to have played **havoc with the environment** of western Europe (*Medieval Machine*, 75*ff*).

An industrial society's distinction between an entrepreneur-professional group and the workers becomes part of the medieval newly mechanized culture. Gimpel identifies in Chapter 5 the growth of technology as effecting such a workforce in three major industries – mining, textiles, and construction – such as to be inevitable. So inevitable in fact that, involved as they were in the dynamics of increasing production, "**the entrepreneurs of the Middle Ages developed new attitudes toward their workmen**, and created new regulations accordingly"[61] (*Medieval Machine*, 93*ff*). **Professional men** also existed who, at the higher end of the wage scale, earned a considerable income but had as well "the benefit of a whole series of privileges attached to their professional status" (Chapter 6, *Medieval Machine*, 114*ff*). The notion of progress as a trademark of an industrializing era is highlighted in Chapter 7, "The Mechanical Clock: The Key Machine." Medieval

---

60 Cf. Olsson, *Undergraduate Teaching of History of Technology*, 23, who can note only one instance of a course treating the history of medieval technology (that of the present author at MIT). See also Ibid., 32 and Hirsh, "Syllabus," 1–12.

61 "In the medieval industrial world, the psychological drive was progressively curbed also by the introduction of legislation that favoured those already in positions of power and aimed to preserve the status quo." Gimpel, *Medieval Machine*, 250.

society **believed in progress**, a concept unknown to the classical world, as was witnessed in the spirit of inventiveness that accompanied their mechanically minded outlook, one which extended even into the realm of the angels (*Medieval Machine*, 147*ff*). Gimpel also felt that the link between technological progress and scientific thinking was well established in the Middle Ages. In Chapter 8 he asserts,

> From the first quarter of the twelfth century to the last quarter of the thirteenth century – until the year 1277, to be precise – ... before the Church had begun to dictate rigid dogmas, **men learned how to reason and dispute intellectually**, and this intellectual freedom helped lay the foundations of modern science.
> (*Medieval Machine*, 171–172*ff*)

Thus, Gimpel's

> thesis is that the early Medieval period, far from being tradition-bound and scientifically illiterate, was actually a seminal age of industry and invention. Led by progressive-minded institutions like the Cistercian monasteries, European entrepreneurs ... turned the horse into an efficient agricultural tool ... and devised the assembly line to speed up textile production.[62]

The medieval industrial revolution did for Gimpel draw nonetheless to a close, and in Chapter 9 he attempts to summarize why. By contrast to the thirteenth-century movement of enlightenment, "in the period following the condemnation of 1277 the medieval machine – the progress of technology – was checked"; it "suffered a setback, and there followed a dark and increasingly decadent age" (*Medieval Machine*, 199). In his conclusion Gimpel itemizes specific "factors from a broad spectrum of human activity – including economics, ideology, education, inventiveness, and industrialization – common to medieval France" as reflections of its era of expansion/growth, 1050 to 1254: "la Beauce (medieval wheat country), the heavy plow, faith, the cathedral, Beauvais, Cistercians, Chartres, the gold louis, the water mill, the horse" (*Medieval Machine*, 244).

Only by the "Epilogue" does the reader realize that Gimpel has adopted the criteria of R.A. Buchanan's *Industrial Archeology in Britain*[63] for the social prerequisites necessary for the successful generation or reception of technological innovation to the point of revolutionary change. With his checklist complete, Gimpel sums up the three main participants and conditions. The key medieval groups of landlords and their water mills, Cistercians and their model farms and factories and the bourgeois or self-made men and their financing of the expanding

---

62 Review by Gerald Jones in *New York Times Book Review*, January 9, 1977, 20.
63 R.A. Buchanan, *Industrial Archeology in Britain* (Harmondsworth, UK: Penguin Books, 1972).

textile and other industries all satisfy the condition of "the existence within society of key groups who are prepared to consider innovations seriously and sympathetically." The enlarged market in response to population increase, Cistercian labor-saving devices in response to labor shortage, and the new fuel, coal, in response to the rise in the price of timber, satisfied the condition of technological innovation's "being encouraged to match social needs." The estate administration of Glastonbury's investment in a new post mill, Richard of Wallingford's invention of two astronomical instruments and Giovanni di Dondi's building a clock are all testimonials to some medieval surplus productivity, with skilled personnel and some materials not having to be diverted to war efforts, meeting thus the conditions that the "social resources vital for their realization – capital, materials and skilled personnel" were also available in the Middle Ages and that "an adequate economic system" existed, which could provide "surplus capital," some in the form of surplus productivity and some diverted "into channels where the inventor can use it."

Following in the footsteps of many historians of economic thought, Gimpel also confesses his alliance with the belief that "[t]echnological progress is cyclical, as is most of history. The West," he noted apocalyptically, "has been privileged to live through two major cycles – the Middle Ages and the Renaissance" (*Medieval Machine*, 240).

In the fine French tradition of *son et lumière*, perhaps the best demonstration to show that Gimpel's thesis, at least in its boldest connection to machine technology, is alive and well is to cite from the episode "Faith in Numbers," written and narrated by James Burke in his public television series *Connections: An Alternative View of Change* (BBC). Strolling in French Provence through the ruins of the Roman milling complex at Barbegal, Burke depicts the "Dark Ages" bridge between the fall of Rome and the Middle Ages in terms of technology:

> So, put yourself in their position. The wars are all over. There's loads of productive land everywhere. You've got water coming out of your ears and an amazing machine to use to harness the power. What would you do? Yes, you'd have yourself a *medieval* industrial revolution![64]

As he voices these words, a close-up of a rapidly turning overshot wooden vertical waterwheel fills the screen. Just to confirm any suspicions of chance similarities, it might be noted that Jean Gimpel is, however, surprisingly not listed as a consultant to Burke's program.

---

64 James Burke, "Faith in Numbers," in *Connections: An Alternative View of Change* (New York: Time-Life Films, 1978).

Researching on the shoulders of giants

Now that the giants and their shoulders have been introduced, what can one say about the act of standing on their shoulders? Can one say anything about how we currently [1995] relate to the theses of Mumford, White and Gimpel? If so, can we be said to be 'standing' on their shoulders, and if so, how?

To approach these questions, the methodology adopted was quite simple. Since the intent was to answer the question in relation to both our research and pedagogical dependence in the history of technology on the ideas of the three scholars, only the production and outcome of research related to the previously mentioned published theses in the history of technology have been examined. The search for research and teaching dependence on them took the form of following up on a selection of the citations of Mumford, White, and Gimpel in the last two decades. Electronic citation indices, such as the *Arts and Humanities Citation Index* and *Social Science Citation Index*, proved very useful for citation counts for White and Gimpel but only since 1980, the beginning of the online catalogue. By 1995, of White there are 640 citations noted in all, 104 to *Medieval Technology and Social Change*. Of Gimpel there had been eighty-two recorded citations since 1980, twenty-four to *The Medieval Machine*. This survey focuses, for facility's sake, on the pertinent citations between 1990 and 1994. During these four years, there were forty-one recorded published references to White's *Medieval Technology and Social Change*. There were eighteen such references to Gimpel's *The Medieval Machine*, and six references to Mumford's *Technics and Civilization*.[65] Not all these references were citations directly relevant to the history of technology. Publications were examined in which (a) the references were to the author and the particular work of his in question and (b) the subject matter was primarily pertinent to the history of technology.[66]

Mumford, White and Gimpel welcomed discussion of their ideas and hoped for many scholars to address their concerns with seriousness. Indeed, the stage for lively exchange had been heavily crafted by each. Some of Mumford's earliest reviewers noted "technical lapses, particularly on the economic side, which would be sufficient to condemn a book with a more narrowly scientific objective."[67] They

---

65 Mumford's work is so vast and eclectic, yet I decided not to use electronic searching but to pursue finding references to his *Technics and Civilization*, by scouring the hardcopy published version of *Art and Letters Citation Index* for the years 1990 to 1994.

66 For articles, the journal of the publication provided an initial screening device. All citations in *Technology and Culture*, for example, were considered pertinent regardless of content.

67 "A work of creative imagination, stimulating and provocative despite technical lapses, particularly on the economic side, which would be sufficient to condemn a book with a more narrowly scientific objective." Review of Mumford, *Technics and Civilization*, by B.J. Thresher in *American Economic Review* 24 (1934): 542.

anticipated objections, calling *Technics and Civilization,* "a brilliant, if sometimes superficial, survey of an indefinite subject":[68] "Many will challenge Mr. Mumford's conclusions: and a detailed review could pick quarrels with some of his more hasty interpretations."[69] Yet another assessment pointed to the study's "sacrificing some depth of detail in favour of exceptionally broad hypotheses."[70] Once White and/or Gimpel were available to be considered in light of Mumford's ideas, there was apparently even more grist for the academic mill. They seem almost goaded by some of Mumford's assertions:

> The fact is, at all events, that the machine came most slowly into agriculture, with its life-conserving, life-maintaining functions, while it prospered lastly precisely in those parts of the environment where the body was most infamously treated by custom: namely, in the monastery, in the mine, on the battlefield.
>
> (*Technics*, 36)

The other option is that the will to dominate the environment and the sense of the inferiority of man faced with his religious ideals and pretensions help explain why the power motive became isolated and intensified toward the close of the Middle Ages.[71]

As for White's ideas providing intellectual fodder, there is no doubt that *Medieval Technology and Social Change* was sought out for reading. Published in 1962, by 1973 it was translated into four major European languages: French, German, Italian and Spanish. One of White's bibliographers listed thirty reviews of the work between 1962 and 1969.[72] Initial treatment was enthusiastic and criticism mild as, for example, the comments by G.C. Homans, in his 1962 review in *The American Journal of Sociology*: "In the field of agrarian history, White indulges in some unjustified speculations . . . he tends to oversimplify the effects of technological and social

---

68 Review of Mumford, *Technics and Civilization*, by Herbert Read in *Yale Review* n.s. 24 (1934): 173.

69 Review of Mumford, *Technics and Civilization*, by "H.W.S." in the *Journal of Philosophy* 31 (June 7, 1934): 331.

70 Actually, the appraisal is quite laudatory: "While his division of the stages of civilization into the eotechnic, paleotechnic, and neotechnic periods was based on technological factors, the study differed from White's and Hunter's by sacrificing some depth of detail in favour of exceptionally broad hypotheses. Even granted this limitation, the work remains an early representative of attempts to create a historical synthesis of technology and non-technological factors." Staudenmaier, *Technology's Storytellers*, 12.

71 "White raises the question of the influence of Roman Christianity on the West's style of technology – as exploitation of, rather than harmony with, nature." Staudenmaier, *Technology's Storytellers*, 247, n. 35. Indeed, in so doing he not only treats "questions that could also be considered ancillary to an exploration of Western capitalism" (ibid.) but also alters the timeframe of Mumford's analysis, potentially pushing its conclusions back several centuries.

72 Bert S. Hall, "Lynn Townsend White, Jr. (1907–1987)," *Technology and Culture* 30, no. 1 (Winter 1989): 194–213, esp. 213.

change."[73] Subsequently, however, the scrutiny became so harsh, it has been said, that a distinction between *ad hominem* and *ad argumentum* criticism seems to have had to be created.[74] Bert S. Hall, one of White's UCLA graduate students, has depicted how White must have been seen from his opponents' side, a "technical determinist," "trapped by older pre-Annales School views of technology, as something grounded in a different rationality as a logic of engagement with the natural world unmediated by culture in any serious way."[75] White was also criticized for having thought that "different cultures may express themselves through different technologies, but usually only in very simple ways," by "accepting" or "rejecting" an "innovation."[76]

White's theses were treated with viciousness, although it might be noted more so under the pens of medievalists than of historians of technology, as perhaps the following analysis will bear out. As for his arguments pertaining to the introduction of the stirrup, they have been described as "systematically destroyed."[77] Only the word *successfully* has been omitted, although as observed below, by the 1980s even military historians left his claims alone, perhaps for dead. The substance of the criticism will be addressed shortly. Concerning White on the changes the plough wrought, Hall maintains that "[i]t is not that a consensus has emerged against White; it is that no consensus has emerged at all."[78] White's ideas in his last chapter were perhaps simply by way of their formulation with cultural, if not intellectual, history less vulnerable to the same kinds of critical angst over determinism that had haunted the themes of first two chapters of his book. Critics have focused instead almost exclusively on pecking away at White's individual examples.

In the case of Gimpel, one might be able to consider the gauntlet for intellectual debate to have been thrown from the start. Right away he was dismissed by some as superfluous:

> In terms of historical content, little here is new and much on the more narrowly economic topics (agriculture, textiles, mining) is oversimplified and even antiquated. . . . As a survey of medieval techniques, it is no necessary purchase for libraries which already possess Lyn [*sic*] White, *Medieval Technology and Social Change*, Carlo Cipolla, *Clocks and Culture, 1300–1700*, Gimpel's own *The Cathedral Builders*, and the like.[79]

---

73 Review of White, *MTSC*, by G.C. Homans, *American Journal of Sociology* 68 (1962): 396.

74 White himself was aware of this distinction in the attacks. By way of describing the emotional vitriol of some of his reviewers in a retrospective article, he quoted a UCLA colleague asking him, "Lynn, why do your Birmingham critics sound as though you had raped *all* their daughters?" "Introduction," in MRT, xviii.

75 Hall, "Medieval Technology," typescript, 2–3.

76 Hall, "Medieval Technology," typescript, 2–3.

77 Ibid., typescript, 14.

78 Ibid., typescript, 16.

79 Review of Gimpel by R.C. Hoffmann in *Library Journal*, December 15, 1976, 2571.

But what has become of this field so readied for action, this collection of hoary giants' waiting to be climbed? The initial assessment of our activity as being passive and not even 'dwarf-like' has been altered, at least in the context of research. Taking account of the numerous citations of the three authors in and of itself was influencing, but even more altering was the growing realization of the many varied ways we present ourselves on the shoulders of these giants. Rather than examining each giant and analyzing our relationship to him in particular, however, each of our manners of "sitting" on the giants' shoulders are characterized. The names are meant to be catchy but also evocative of the interesting gamut of approaches currently being explored in relation to their ideas. The least exciting way will serve as an opener.

Simply sitting (using the giant's shoulders for support)

The attitude here seems to be one of "shouldering the dwarf, alone the 'giant' is honoured." With numerous instances which spring from the citation references, this posture is alas still one of the most popular. The first two examples here use a giant's details to reinforce equally detailed assertions. The latter two aim at a more abstract level but are no less derivative and passive.

In "The Appreciation of Technology in Campanella's *The City of the Sun*," Phyllis A. Hall presents the ideas of the Italian Dominican monk Tommaso Campanella (1568–1639) on technology, as found in his utopian work *The City of the Sun*, written in 1623. She uses Gimpel's description of sewage systems in medieval monasteries[80] as the "authoritative source" for comparing Campanella's utopian city's sophisticated water and sewage system with any contemporary inspiring example. "Although some medieval monasteries had sewage systems, European cities did not yet have any system such as the one Campanella outlines."[81]

In "The Origins of the Wheelbarrow," M.J.T. Lewis sets out to re-examine the assumption "that the wheelbarrow was unknown in Europe before roughly AD 1200, whereas in China it had been used (*cf.* Needham) since perhaps the 1st century BC."[82] In a portion of his arguments regarding the absence of evidence for the wheelbarrow in the Western, Latin speaking half of the ancient world, Lewis sits firmly on the shoulders of Lynn White's documentation:

> A supposedly Roman gemstone, published in 1700 and not seen since, depicts a cupid sharpening an arrow at a grindstone which he is turning by means of a

---

80 Gimpel, *Medieval Machine*, 87–91; P.A. Hall, "The Appreciation of Technology in Campanella's *The City of the Sun*," *Technology and Culture* 34, no. 3 (1993): 613–28. Gimpel is noted by Hall, "Appreciation," 627, n. 101.

81 Hall, "Appreciation," 627.

82 M.J.T. Lewis, "The Origins of the Wheelbarrow," *Technology and Culture* 35, no. 3 (1994): 453–75, esp. 453. Lewis was affiliated with the University of Hull (Kingston Hull, Humberside, UK), teaching the academic study of industrial archaeology.

treadle, connecting rod, and crank. It is mounted on a handcart which is probably two wheeled, although it is sometimes described as a "wheelbarrow." But the drive is foreign to all we know about Roman mechanics; the earliest treadle-cranked grindstone Lynn White could find dates from about 1480, and the earliest mounted on a handcart from 1589.[83]

Although it is the reference to the wheelbarrow, not the crank, that interests Lewis, nonetheless, armed with White's earliest sightings for the crank in engravings dated much later, he concludes that "the subject smacks thoroughly of a forgery." It is interesting to note that the "dwarf" does not fully use the shoulders of his giant even for sitting, for White gives his readers the name of the author and publication in which the line drawing of the reported gemstone appeared.[84]

At a much more abstract level, the same sitting posture is also adhered to. Andrew Jamison, in his look at what had been meant by technological innovation in "Technology's Theorists: Conceptions of Innovation in Relations to Science and Technology Policy," asserts that since "explicit theorizing about technological innovation is a product of industrialization," looking farther back in time is an exercise in finding the prehistory of analysis. Fortunately for the Middle Ages, he does find in its evidence from the twelfth and thirteenth centuries one ingredient that helps make the innovation process a focus of attention: signs that the status of "practitioner" was becoming elevated. He notes that sign in the form of "a privileged position in the textile cities of western Europe" for master builders of Gothic cathedrals.[85] Within his look at the 'prehistory of analysis' is Jamison's token reference to two of our giants, Gimpel and White. Gimpel, he notes, provides "an intriguing source on the industrial revolution" of the twelfth and thirteenth centuries; White's *Medieval Religion and Technology* is noted as "well worth consulting." No page numbers are offered for either author's work.

In tracing the historiography of military technology and its more recent form, Barton C. Hacker also paid homage to Lynn White's influential scholarship, in a class with that of Michael Roberts and Carlo Cipolla. He described White's qualities, as "paying attention to the possible technological sources of social change" and clearly drawing "lines linking what had formerly seemed relatively minor changes in military technology to vast consequences for the structure and organization of European society."[86] White would undoubtedly have liked being praised for his

---

83 Lewis, "Origins of the Wheelbarrow," 467, referencing White, *MTSC*, 167.
84 M.A. de La Chausse, *La Gemme antiche figurate di Michel Angelo causeo de La Chausse (Rome: G.G. Komarek, 1700)*. White, *MTSC*, 105, 167, n. 1.
85 He observes that this status antedated even the technical treatises of the Renaissance! Jamison, "Technology's Theorists," 507, esp. n. 3.
86 The fact that Hacker sees White very sympathetically as a "giant" is evidenced in his following comment that "[e]normous weight of documentation failed to deflect all criticism, but whatever the merits of the specific case for stirrups and chivalry, the larger argument for paying attention to the possible technological sources of social

attention to the minor ingenious things, for not only had he observed that they had proved able to hold the Western imagination in thrall[87] but also, he believed, like Jerome, whom he cites at the outset of his monograph: "Non contemnenda quasi parva sine quibus magna constare non possunt" ("Do not condemn as insignificant those things without which great affairs could not take place").[88] Tracing the favor White's work has found within the history of military technology, Hacker notes that it is precisely because he saw large-scale social change as the consequence of little things that his work has come under much criticism, much more so than the assertions of authors focused on the process of innovation.[89]

Standing to see things a-far-off (extending a thesis into unexpected realms)[90]

Aspects of the works of both White and Gimpel are seen to be extended into timeframes beyond the Middle Ages or into components of the medieval culture which neither of them considered directly. This is clearly a laudable form of standing on the shoulders of the giants.

In "Technology and War: The Historiographical Revolution of the 1980s,"[91] Alex Roland writes of White's book as a model followed today among historians of

---

change was strongly reinforced." Hacker, "Military Institutions," 813–14. In addition to White's *MTSC*, Hacker also references his "The Crusades and the Technological Thrust of the West," in *War, Technology and Society in the Middle East*, ed. V.J. Parry and M.E. Yapp (Oxford: Oxford University Press, 1975), 97–112.

87   Also Hacker, "Military Institutions," 834.

88   White, *MTSC*, viii. Translation from Hall, "Lynn White's *MTSC* after Thirty Years," 85. Alternately, it has been rendered that "[t]he apparently small details should not be ignored for it is only through them that the large designs are possible."

89   He lists the contrasting reception of A. Hunter Dupree, *Science in Federal Government: A History of Policies and Activities to 1940* (Cambridge, MA: The Belknap Press of Harvard University Press, 1957) and 2nd rev. ed. (Baltimore: Johns Hopkins University Press, 1989); Elting E. Morison, "A Case Study of Innovation," *Engineering and Science Magazine* (April 1950): 1–10; rpt. as "Gunfire at Sea: A Case Study of Innovation," *Men, Machines and Modern Times* (Cambridge, MA: MIT Press, 1966); and I.B. Holley, Jr., *Ideas and Weapons: Exploitation of the Aerial Weapon by the United States during World War I: A Study in the Relationship of Technological Advance, Military Doctrine, and the Development of Weapons* (New Haven: Yale University Press, 1953; rpt. Washington, DC: Air Force Office of History, 1983).

90   The posture *"Standing to see more things (collecting data)"* is another possible one which would come between *"Simply sitting"* and *"Standing to see things a-far off."* While there were no instances of this posture within the four years of cited articles, an example could be found in some aspects of D.L. Simms, "Water-Driven Saws, Ausonius, and the Authenticity of the *Mosella*," *Technology and Culture* 24, no. 4 (1983): 635–43.

91   A. Roland, "Technology and War – The Historiographical Revolution of the 1980s," *Technology and Culture* 34, no. 1 (1993): 117–34.

technology whose works are firmly rooted in viewing technology as an explanatory factor in historical development. Roland, as he reviews Daniel Headrick's *The Tools of Empire* treating *Technology and European Imperialism in the Nineteenth Century*,[92] finds Headrick following the methodology of White's *Medieval Technology* in two respects. First, his work "poses a technological answer to a question that has long puzzled historians": To what was the surge in European imperialism due in the late nineteenth century? Second, "also like White, Headrick pulls up short of technological determinism," arguing that the looking overseas "was influenced," but not dictated, by the availability of the new technologies, (*e.g.*, armed inland-going vessels in addition to gunned sailing ships) that made military expansion possible. Headrick's explanation which is seen to derive in solid White-ian fashion from "the interaction between motives and means" extends White's historiography to a much more modern era.

A more extended view of White's and Gimpel's examinations of medieval technical change can be found in Pamela O. Long's article "Invention, Authorship, Intellectual Property, and the Origins of Patents: Notes Toward a Conceptual History."[93] In it she seeks out the origin of a Western notion of "intellectual property," presently a legal term referring to various kinds of intangible property, beginning as far back as Greek and Roman antiquity. Having worked her discussion historically forward to the Middle Ages, Long refers to Gimpel and White as part of an "initial bibliography for the complex issues of labor and technology in the medieval period." They do, however, provide quite specific ideas: that the twelfth century was "a time when technological developments in agriculture and in the harnessing of power, among other factors, had led to population growth, the development of commerce and the rise of urbanism," that this represented a "technical revolution," that the "revolution" was preceded by earlier stages introducing innovations such as "the adoption of the stirrup, the improvement of the horse's harness, the development of the three-field system of cultivation, and the expansion of waterpower," that "some of these technical innovations occurred in monastic and other environments where literacy did exist" and that rewards for improvement in agricultural, military, and power technologies consisted of "more food, greater safety, and relief from backbreaking labor."[94] It is upon these ideas that Long stands to consider her own interest in intellectual property, to puzzle out the reasons for "no evidence for an [contemporaneous] interest in authorship, credit to inventors, or the appropriation of technical knowledge."[95] Elevated on the shoulders of Gimpel and White, she rejects the frequent attribution of a lack of contemporary comment on technical invention to "the widespread illiteracy of practitioners" and proposes a second explanation as the

---

92 Daniel Headrick, *The Tools of Empire* (New York: Oxford University Press, 1981).
93 Pamela O. Long, "Invention, Authorship, Intellectual Property and the Origin of Patents – Notes Toward a Conceptual History," *Technology and Culture* 32, no. 4 (1991): 846–84.
94 Ibid., 869.
95 Ibid., 869.

more probable: "that for numerous medieval practitioners, issues involving credit, invention, and authorship were of no concern."[96] From the immediate rewards of the technological changes considered by Gimpel and White, Long sees further to their making possible the extended reward of "the ability to possess luxuries, of great symbolic value to the dominant classes,"[97] a reward which predated an interest in any claim to "intellectual property" and its rights. Based perhaps more on her reading of White than Gimpel, Long represents her story as beginning, in some sense, where Gimpel and White leave off:

> 'Intellectual property' attributes did not develop as part of the technological advances that contributed to the growth of urbanism. I would propose, rather, that such an outlook emerged from the context of medieval urbanism itself. Medieval cities and the market economics that developed within and among them provided the essential context for the emergence of a fully developed concept of intellectual property.[98]

Standing to see the 'far-out' (to pursue the curiosities, idiosyncrasies of the thesis)

A few recent authors have lit upon the more curious aspects of the 'shoulders of giants' theses. Specifically, their idiosyncratic periodizations *à la* Mumford do not escape comment by their reviewers. There seems thus to be a two-faceted attention to the giants' "novelties": the one of greatest interest here, manifesting emulation and adaptation, and yet another, reflecting through the reviewer the fascination of author and reader. The attraction has been identified in at least two lengthier reviews.

Alex Roland, in his review article, noted earlier, "Technology and War," surveys what he refers to as "the unprecedented flowering of scholarly interest" in the subject in the 1980s.[99] In addition to identifying authors who stand in extending the giants' central theses, he spots as well an author who stands on a sidelight. One of the works he reviews is Martin Van Creveld, *Technology and War: From 2000 B.C. to the Present*[100] that contains a "curious periodization" like Mumford's. "As Lewis Mumford did before him" in *Technics and Civilization*, van Creveld also identifies a dominant material in each age: respectively, wood, iron, steel, and now "sophisticate alloys, ceramics and other synthetic materials." Unlike Mumford, however, Roland notes that van Creveld does not use this scheme again in the book, save to title the various parts. There is no attempt to construct from his periodization an explanation of "the evolution of military technology." Roland

---

96 Ibid., 869.
97 Ibid., 869.
98 Ibid., 869–70.
99 Roland, "Technology and War," 117–34.
100 Martin van Creveld, *Technology and War: From 2000 B.C. to the Present* (New York: Free Press, 1989).

notes in his review's conclusion that this attraction to the periodization models of earlier scholars, such as Lewis Mumford, himself indebted to the pioneering work of archeologists, is not unique to van Creveld. Given the archeological heritage of the models, however, they are, he notes, "most often developed by those who work, or at least begin, with ancient history."[101] Almost ironically, he identifies no exceptions – not even their *ur*-model in Mumford – to demonstrate that such models could help clarify studies beginning in the Middle Ages as well.

Historians of the urban environment are also engaged by Mumford's periodization. As pointed out by his reviewers, Mark J. Bouman, seeking "the meaning of street lighting and the patterns of light distribution in cities from ancient Greece and Rome to Minneapolis during the 1920s," lets Mumford's periods inform part of his study.[102]

Standing to see, without being seen (not acknowledging sources)

It has gone without saying thus far that the posture of standing on the shoulders of giants presupposes acknowledging on whose shoulders one is standing. Unfortunately, however, even in the midst of our rigorous twentieth-/twenty-first-century assault on plagiarism, not all sources are always identified. The case of not acknowledging one's standing on giants is an especially interesting one, for its detection could reflect as much on the giant as on the one standing tall. Two instances are noted here. The first is a simple case of "oversight." The second is far more interesting, for it would be a classic example of "standing to extend a thesis," identified earlier, but for the lack of connection between the presumed elevating source and its new form. In both examples, it is hard for the giant's shoulders to go undetected beneath the "dwarf."

In "The Origins of the Wheelbarrow," M. J. T. Lewis does not acknowledge Lynn White as the source for the "taken-for-granted" attitude that the wheelbarrow made its first appearance in Europe in the thirteenth century or the idea that this appearance is thought to have had some connection to China.[103] Both ideas are found in White's earliest work dedicated to medieval technology, "Technology and Invention in the Middle Ages."[104] Although it is hard to believe, for Lewis, White's shoulders may be formed only by *Medieval Technology and Social Change*. Thus, however hard he is striving to stand, Lewis's posture here is still only a sitting one.

---

101 Roland, "Technology and War," 133.

102 This analysis of Bouman derives from the review article of Konvitz et al., "Technology and the City," 292. Although helpful, their n. 15 does not provide full bibliographic information of Bouman's work.

103 Both ideas are blatantly stated as the starting point for Lewis's whole article; Lewis, "Origins of the Wheelbarrow," 453.

104 White, "Technology and Invention in the Middle Ages," 141–59, esp. 150; rpt. in MRT, 1–22, esp. 9–11.

On the other hand, one of the most interesting "unacknowledged" (or "independent") research connections is found in Phyllis A. Hall's article on Campanella's *City of the Sun*.[105] (Like Lewis's, this article was also noted earlier as manifesting really only a sitting posture.) Although Tommaso Campanella (1568–1639) and his work are postmedieval, Hall's presentation of the ideas of this Italian Dominican monk on technology as found in his utopia of 1623 are, it appears, right out of medieval historiography. The most striking example is Hall's description of one of the inventions Campanella attributes to his Solarians: "The Solarians also invented a two-headed mace, and for using the weapon they attach a new type of stirrup to the reins of a horse whereby the warrior can steer with his feet."[106] Hall goes on to give Campanella's own description of the stirrup and the explanation of "how this invention works" by the editor of the work, Daniel J. Dunno. Is this generation of scholars, however, not standing on White's model of the stirrup making possible – although not demanding – "a vastly more effective form of attack"?[107]

Standing with researcher's spectacles for enhanced seeing (using the same methods)

Occasionally the methodological pathway the giants started to walk is pursued upon their shoulders, in depth and detail, frequently, as above, without any homage to the giant's trailblazing.

M. J. T. Lewis's interest in the origins of the wheelbarrow, "so much more lowly yet so much more widely applicable" even than the crane, follows right in the footsteps of Lynn White's interest in the *parva*. To investigate his humble subject Lewis has used virtually every kind of resource evidence White would have, lamenting in his spirit that archaeology can be of no help in tracing the wooden tool through time. Terminology contextually understood proves to be his most useful source in establishing that the wheelbarrow appears as "a flash in the pan" in ancient Greece only to reappear in Western records in the 1170s.

In addition to Lewis's pursuit of an elevating posture, with the unacknowledged aid of White's methodology, he also combines his conclusions with another instance of "standing to see, but without being seen." Since the wheelbarrow "survived the fall of Rome only in the Byzantine Empire," Lewis posits that "perhaps during the Second Crusade (1147–49), it was encountered by westerners who took the idea back home with them and modified their existing handbarrow to take a front wheel."[108] Although White is not acknowledged, the idea of a relationship between the crusades and technology transfer is one he had pioneered in "The Crusades and the Technological Thrust of the West" in 1975.[109]

---

105 Hall, "Appreciation," 613–28.
106 Ibid., 621.
107 White, *MTSC*, 2.
108 Lewis, "Origins of the Wheelbarrow," 474–75.
109 White, "Crusades," 97–112.

Standing on air, too high to look down (thesis rejected)

In some instances, the "dwarfs" are standing on the shoulders of the giants if only to stand above them. In so doing, they reject at least some of their fundamental ideas.

M.J.T. Lewis rejects White's claim that *carruca* was used as the term for plough as early as the eighth century.[110] This is a question of disputing the linguistic evidence, with each citing different passages from the *Monumenta Germaniae Historica: Legum*. The homage to White is in Lewis' adopting the same historiographic techniques. His standing on White's shoulders is his independent decision about the evidence for the use of *carruca* as plough "before Charlemagne's *Capitulare de Villis* of 800 or a little before." In citing White, Lewis shows he realizes that he is by extension affecting the credibility of White's thesis that the heavy plough helped account "for the bursting vitality of the Carolingian realm in the eighth century."[111]

John Langdon provides another example of this posture in an article titled "Lordship and Peasant Consumerism in the Milling Industry of Early 14th-Century England." In endeavoring to understand more about the precise nature of aspects of the economic activity in the Middle Ages connected to the milling industry he addresses several critical points in relation to this discussion. From among his findings on landlord involvement on the English milling economy, he asserts,

> The most notable, and perhaps most surprising, aspect of milling investment by lords was their relative lack of interest in mills for non-agricultural use. Again, this is particularly obvious in the I.P.M.s [Inventories Post-Mortem], where only 55 mills (3.5 percent of the sample) were described as being for purposes other than the processing of grain, all of them for fulling.[112]

Langdon explains this fact by tying the prioritizing of investment in the various types of mills to their performance as revenue producers, nonagricultural mills being linked to relatively poor performance.

These conclusions run counter to claims by both White and Gimpel. Langdon expresses the implication of his findings as follows: "Altogether, the reluctance of English lords to invest in non-agricultural mills is very clear, and starkly contradicts those theories that would claim the mill was the linchpin of a great medieval industrial revolution."[113] Two of the most influential publications that Langdon feels fall within that category of theories are White's *Medieval Technology*

---

110 Lewis, "Origins of the Wheelbarrow," 469, n. 48; referenced by Lewis is White, *MTSC*, 50–51, 54.

111 White, *MTSC*, 54; Lewis, "Origins of the Wheelbarrow," 469, n. 48.

112 J. Langdon, "Lordship and Peasant Consumerism in the Milling Industry of Early Fourteenth-Century England," *Past & Present* 145 (1994): 3–46 at 13–14.

113 Ibid., 14.

and Social Change ("esp. 79–89") and Gimpel's *Medieval Machine* ("ch. 1").[114] Although Langdon's assertions do not cut to the quick of White's thesis about waterpower,[115] he does seem to see White's concept of a "medieval industrial revolution based on water and wind" as his target.[116] In the case of Gimpel, his objection also resides with the claim for a "medieval industrial revolution." His note refers to Chapter 1 in which Gimpel touts the theretofore unmatched scale of mechanization of the Middle Ages. Langdon's finding is, however, far more undermining of Gimpel's thesis about the role of the landlords as a "key medieval group," "prepared to consider innovations seriously and sympathetically," and unfortunately, he missed this opportunity truly to float above this giant.

Standing aloft and aloof

Those who in a slightly different way have "risen above" the shoulders of their giants assume another similar posture. It is stated beautifully by Hacker with reference to Mumford: "Widely admired but highly idiosyncratic, Mumford's work has served more as a source of inspiration than a model for emulation." [117] Unfortunately, rather than giving any specifics of the results of the inspiration, Hacker offers references to those of Mumford's works whose historiographical views have, he claims, been adopted. Among them is *Technics and Civilization*.

Standing spread-eagle (the shoulders outgrown)

In this posture the giant is surpassed. The primary stance is not the rejection of thesis, but due to its having been rejected, the platform of the giants' shoulders is seen as slightly reconfigured:

> [O]verall the result [of the criticism of White, Roberts and Cipolla] has been not so much to undercut them as to define and clarify their themes more fully, as well as to explore their broader implications. Criticism has centered less on the

---

114 The most influential publications along these lines have probably been the following: Bertrand Gille, "Le moulin à eau: une révolution technique médiévale," *Techniques et civilizations* 3 (1954): 1–15; White, *MTSC*, esp. 79–89; Jean Gimpel, *The Medieval Machine* (Harmondsworth, UK: Penguin Books, 1977), ch. 1; and Terry S. Reynolds, *Stronger Than a Hundred Men: A History of the Vertical Water Wheel* (Baltimore: Johns Hopkins University Press, 1983), ch. 2.

115 "Our present concern is not to demonstrate this astonishing rise in productivity, but rather to examine the new exploratory attitude towards the forces of nature." White, *MTSC*, 89.

116 White, *MTSC*, 89. This assumption is based on Langdon's echoing White's phrase and Langdon's extension of his reference to White through (89), when in fact White's discussion of waterwheels and watermills ends on (85).

117 Hacker, "Military Institutions," 785, esp. n. 54.

concept of military technology as motor of social change than on which technology most mattered.[118]

Hacker describes White as vulnerable in letting fortifications and siege warfare escape his notice: "Critics of White's views about the impact of stirrups have argued that siege warfare and fortifications more decisively shaped medieval society than heavy cavalry."[119] Although to the larger issue of the importance of siege warfare and fortifications he cites numerous studies, including one of his own on ancient catapults, as critics of White, he lists only the publications of Bernard B. Bachrach, the most directed being "Charles Martel, Mounted Shock Combat, the Stirrup, and Feudalism."[120] Hacker goes on to note that a great deal of revisionist attention has been paid to the military history of late medieval and early modern Europe, but he makes no reference to White's work as having undergone further scrutiny in the 1980s, the decade on which his review is focused.

In point of fact, Hacker's references would indicate that in the 1980s, White was passed over in silence, with the criticisms of the previous decade perhaps still ringing in military historians' ears.[121] Hacker's is a very curious indirect assessment of White, for while White is appraised as having survived, with his theme of technology as a possible source of social change intact, the kinds of criticism thrown at him are deemed to have been successful, regarding "the exact nature and times of changes that occurred, and the relevance of organization and ideas as well as hardware."[122] In Hacker's survey, White's theses are nonetheless highlighted as useful and applied to studies in later periods of history.[123] Here the battered giant is in a sense a testimonial to the effectiveness of the battering techniques!

The great unraised

This posture is slipped in at the last as a reminder that not everyone publishing in the area of the history of technology uses, even without acknowledging them, the three giants under discussion as their reference point. While it is here identified as the classification of *The Great Unraised*, it could also refer to those who see themselves as elevated by some successor instead. Hall, for example, refers to Mulford Q. Sibley's observation that "Bacon's idea of man conquering nature was the most

---

118 Ibid., 821.
119 Ibid., 822.
120 Bernard B. Bachrach, "Charles Martel, Mounted Shock Combat, the Stirrup, and Feudalism," *Studies in Medieval and Renaissance History* 7 (1970): 47–75. For a summary of the numerous critics of White's thesis concerning the stirrup, see Contamine or DeVries, note 130 in this chapter.
121 Hacker, "Military Institutions," 822, n. 159.
122 Ibid., 821.
123 Ibid., 821–22, esp. n. 157.

revolutionary view of technology ever formulated"[124] without realizing that White (and Mumford in his own way) attributed a view of dominating nature to the exegetically sophisticated medievals, revolutionizing thinking long before Bacon.[125]

Briefly then, in reading Jamison, Roland, Konvitz, Long, Lewis, Hall, Langdon and Hacker, not to mention Greenberg, Klingelhofer, Gorecki and Whitney,[126] among numerous others publishing within the tight four-year period under closest scrutiny, one is left with the reassuring impression that the research posture *vis-à-vis* the giants, Mumford, White and Gimpel is potentially varied, reflective and vital. Many researchers were and are still using them to stand, extend, elaborate, reject and refine the ideas they advanced. Whether or not these positions are imagined to be uplifting to them, they ought to be encouraging to us, for in going forth from their work scholars today not only acknowledge their contributions but also build on the methods and theses they espoused.

Teaching on the shoulders of giants

The focus thus far has been on our posture as researchers, but what about our posture as teachers at elevated heights? At a glance, it seems that the cohesive, directed approach of each of our giants is enough to make us comfortably well-seated pedagogical "dwarfs." Each of the authors seems to put to lie the statement quoted from Marc Bloch – "l'oeuvre de mise au point n'est presque jamais dans le déstin du premier architect"[127] – for at least two of these writers and their works in question, if not all three, are examples of extremely synthetic scholars in their own earliest pioneering phases. Their achievements make us all the more vulnerable to pedagogical passivity. A real question presents itself as to how to step away from a

---

124 Hall, "Appreciation," 628.
125 White, "Cultural Climates and Technological Advance," in MRT, 217–53.
126 Dolores Greenberg, "Energy, Power, and Perceptions of Change in the Early Nineteenth Century," *American Historical Review* 95, no. 5 (1990): 693–714, esp. 693; Eric Klingelhofer, *Settlement and Land* Use *in Micheldover Hundred, Hampshire, 700–1100*, Transactions of the American Philosophical Society 81, pt. 3 (Philadelphia: APS, 1991), esp. 45, 51; Piotr Gorecki, *Parishes, Tithes and Society in Earlier Medieval Poland*, ca. *1100–1250*, Transactions of the American Philosophical Society 83, pt. 2 (Philadelphia: APS, 1993), esp. 10; and Elspeth Whitney, *Paradise Restored: The Mechanical Arts from Antiquity through the Thirteenth Century*, Transactions of the American Philosophical Society 80, pt. 1 (Philadelphia: APS, 1990), *passim*.
127 "Synthetic work is almost never the accomplishment of the first researcher." The use here of this quotation from Bloch, *Annales d'histoire économique et sociale* 7 (1935): 102, is in strong contrast to its use also in reference to White as "pioneering scholar" by Hall, "Medieval Technology," typescript, 20 and n. 37.

body of ideas presented in a so satisfyingly pedagogical way yet on which so much justified criticism has been heaped.

Part of the answer might lie in a rethinking of their place in our history of technology syllabus. Rather than serving as representatives of the state of research in the history of technology either in terms of methodology or content, their contribution could be offered within a qualifying context.

Complementing

One quite readily accessible context is the survey text. Two in particular include some of Lynn White's ideas and provide a qualifying setting either of other approaches or of historical chronology: Burke and Eakin's *Technology and Change* and the first volume of Kranzberg and Pursell's *Technology in Western Civilization.*[128]

Another possible contextual setting for the giants might be to compliment them with newer texts of slightly different focus, from which to offset their methods and ideas. A number of books and articles by Cardwell, Casson, LeGoff, Pacey and Young have already found their way into the history of technology syllabus, although rarely sharing the stage with the giants.[129]

Rejecting

Another context that can provide even greater perspective on their ideas is the context in which critical assessments of the authors are also included in the syllabus. Again with reference to Lynn White, for example, criticism of his most famous thesis on the stirrup is readily accessible in works by Philippe Contamine or Kelly DeVries.[130]

Reflecting

A yet more radical suggestion would be for us to adopt new approaches to the whole history of technology syllabus. Many different themes and possible configurations

---

128 John G. Burke and Marshall C. Eakin, eds., *Technology and Change* (San Francisco: Boyd and Fraser, 1979); Melvin Kranzberg and Carroll W. Pursell, Jr., eds., *Technology in Western Civilization*, 2 vols. (New York: Oxford University Press, 1967).

129 D.S.L. Cardwell, *Turning Points in Western Technology* (New York: Science History Publications, 1972); Lionel Casson, "Godliness and Work," *Science* 81, no. 2 (1981): 36–43; Jacques LeGoff, "Merchant's Time and Church's Time in the Middle Ages," in *Time, Work and Culture*, trans. Arthur Goldhammer (Chicago: University of Chicago Press, 1980), 29–42; Arnold Pacey, *The Maze of Ingenuity* (Cambridge, MA: MIT Press, 1976); and P. Young, *The Machinery of War* (London: Hart Davis, 1973).

130 Philippe Contamine, *War in the Middle Ages*, trans. Michael Jones (Oxford: Basil Blackwell, 1980), 179–84; Kelly DeVries, *Medieval Military Technology* (Peterborough, ON: Broadview Press, 1992), 95–110 [A second edition, considerably revised is now available that should supersede the 1992 edition: Kelly Robert DeVries and Robert Douglas Smith, *Medieval Military Technology* (Toronto: University of Toronto Press, 2012) – ed.].

of ideas present themselves at a quick brainstorming. The titles of possible courses presented here are meant to be evocative and stimulating, although clearly as mere titles, they express little in and of themselves. In each, the giants could find a place where the strengths of his novelty, creativity, insight and so on (as well as the weaknesses perhaps of his details, the structure of argument, etc.) could be identified.[131]

In all, numerous ways have been tried in university courses to complement, reject and reflect the work of our giants. The titles of the courses, of course, need to pique undergraduate interests, so they tend to, on the whole, reflect positive assessments of the past (for a sample listing, see the Appendix).

The giants' legacy

The reason for this lengthy exploration into the place of Lewis Mumford, Lynn White, and Jean Gimpel in the research and teaching of the history of technology was not to reaffirm simply that they still figure. This was asserted and supported at the outset. It was instead to see what place they are given and how we relate to them. Their giantesque stature, albeit due to both their institutional and intellectual contributions to the field, still dominates over the substance of their arguments. For the most part they function as icons in the teaching syllabus and frequently as members of the totem pole of authorities to be cited in scholarly articles. Admittedly there is a place for simple respect and, if none of the "dwarfs" is standing, we can only hope that there are still those who climb onto the giants' shoulders to sit. Sitters, at the very least, perpetuate the historical legacy.

There is, however, happily still some serious attention granted to the ideas of Mumford, White and Gimpel. This has to a very modest degree become the realm of devotees, although none could really lay claim to a "school" in the history of technology. Nonetheless, the study of technological change and cities, for example, includes in its history the role of Mumford and his direct followers. Among them, already no longer a part of today's orthodoxy was Sam Bass Warner, Jr. This "leading urban historian" of the 1960s saw himself modestly as the inheritor of the scholarly tradition of Mumford, among others. By the late 1960s his, and with him Mumford's, bold conceptualizations and the analysis of change and periodization through the frameworks of technological systems had, however, given way to another approach: narrower studies of a single city or urban technology.[132] Historiographically, according to an appraisal by Jamison,

---

131 Apologies beforehand to anyone whose course has already captured a part of this list and to which, out of ignorance, acknowledgment cannot be given, for there are undoubtedly numerous pedagogues working actively to bring the history of technology into its most stimulating and creative light.

132 Konvitz et al., "Technology and the City," 287ff.

there are still the "radicals," forming one of three groups of current theorists of technological innovation, along with the entrepreneurs and synthesizers, who, in their focus on the social, rather than the purely technical, identify with Mumford.[133]

There are the ones who revive the themes taken up by Mumford in the 1930s: the "human values in machinery," "its psychological as well as its practical origins," "its spiritual contributions to our culture" and "the cultural motivations behind technological innovation."[134] More broadly still, those who raise a *cri de coeur* about the future of our understanding of technology, whether in historical context or otherwise, seem most frequently focused on Mumford, of the three giants, as their guiding force. Konvitz et al., for example, conclude their look at technology and the city with a Mumford-esque plea:

> One might adduce numerous periods and topics in need of their historian. Yet modern historical scholarship also has need for a renewed sense of the mind, the person, and the whole in human affairs. Such renewal would prove particularly valuable in the history of technology. . . . Perhaps the reassertion of intellectual history informed by the social sciences will help to restore a dimension to historical scholarship largely absent in the most frequently cited works since the mid-1960s.[135]

Even more propitious, however, is the fact that the ideas of the giants have *not* in any significant way been co-opted into specific schools of thought. They still stand independently untainted by association and accessible to any scholar. Nonetheless, it is affirmed here that they do stand collectively in at least one usurpable respect; they are all advocates for the importance of consideration of the Middle Ages in the history of technology. It is particularly in that light that they shall be viewed in closing. They each espouse two reasons why the Middle Ages should figure in a study of the history of technology: (1) for its own sake and (2) for the sake of perspective.

As advocates for the study of the history of medieval technology, White and Gimpel, in particular, were unabashed models for medievalists. They championed the period for its richness of technological contributions. They also championed active interest in its offerings. Their main reason for harping at its urgency is that the evidence for drawing conclusions about the period is trace, fragile and increasingly ephemeral. Konvitz et al. capture this sentiment today at the end of their

---

133 Jamison, "Technology's Theorists," 532–33.
134 Ibid., 518, quoting Mumford, "The Drama of the Machines" (1930), rpt. in Lewis Mumford, *Interpretations and Forecasts 1922–1972: Studies in Literature, History, Biography, Technics and Contemporary Society* (New York: Harcourt Brace Jovanovich, 1972), 227.
135 Konvitz et al., "Technology and the City," 293.

review. Their choice of a 1941 quotation from Siegfried Giedion is particularly relevant and ominous to historians of the technology of the Middle Ages:

> We are too unaccustomed to considering interrelationships between different realms of human activity to see clearly the points at which they are connected. The danger is that the material for reconstructing those relationships may be lost by the time their importance has been recognized.[136]

Lewis, standing on the giants, reminds us that the wooden wheelbarrow's material traces are already lost. For the history of medieval technology, time is a-wasting.

Mumford, White and Gimpel also present the importance of the study of medieval technology in the context of the whole history of technology, both in terms of method and content. For Gimpel and Mumford, in particular, its study can serve as a hedge against contemporary technological hubris. As Gimpel affirms in his epilogue to *The Medieval Machine*: "We are convinced that we are living in the first truly technological society in history, . . . The historian of technology must correct this belief.[137] Gimpel's trumpet call complements Mumford's much earlier depiction of the battlefield:

> Unfortunately, much of our thinking today in technocratic circles is being done by one-generation minds bedazzled over our immediate successes. . . – however isolated these feats are from the total historic culture that made them possible, and from man's many non-technological needs, projects, and aspirations which give meaning to the whole process.[138]

For Mumford, White and Gimpel there is a place for the history of medieval technology within the greater study of the history of technology. This statement is accompanied, however, by a sigh, to be interpreted as a sigh both of relief and of resignation. The relief stems from the fact that without such giants in the history of technology the history of medieval technology would quite probably have been left in the dust and dusty volumes of the past. Instead, it features even today in both the research and teaching of the history of technology. The sigh as resignation is, however, also present for as much as Mumford, White and Gimpel continue to serve as catalysts, in the wonderful variety of ways highlighted earlier, for the discussion and dissemination of ideas about the technology of the Middle Ages, as a subfield, the study of medieval technology by historians of technology does not seem to have outgrown the giants' definition of its bounds or applicable methods. Thus, to both our delight and our dismay the history of medieval technology has retained the place Lewis Mumford, Lynn White, and Jean Gimpel staked out

---

136 Sigfried Giedion, *Space, Time and Architecture: The Growth of a New Tradition* (Cambridge, MA: Harvard University Press, 1941), 270; cited by Konvitz et al., 294.
137 Gimpel, *Medieval Machine*, 240.
138 Mumford, *Works and Days*, 468.

for it from the beginnings of academic history of technology. At the very least to preserve that stake is to preserve some of the history of technology's most worthy giants on whose shoulders we do indeed presently stand.

Appendix: White-inspired course titles in the 1990s[139]

In a survey of scholars teaching courses in the late 1990s, the following courses were found to use *Medieval Technology and Social Change* and/or other of White's articles from *Medieval Religion and Technology* as course readings. They were taught at a diversity of universities and are grouped by theme.

"Technology and Human Values,"* "The Dream of a Perfect World," "Technological Utopias," "The Goals of Technology and Humanism," "Technology, the Environment and Human Values," "Technology and the Human Spirit."

"The History of. . . (Printing, War, etc.)," "The Machine in. . . (Europe, China, etc.)," "(Cultures of. . ., Power Sources of, etc.) . . . Earth, Air, Fire, and Water."*

"The technology and art of. . . (iron, steel, etc.)"

"Issues in. . . (pollution, hygiene, safety, etc.) in a technological society," "The culture of. . . (work, food, production, etc.)," (Farmers', Militarists', Merchants', etc.). . . . interests in technology."

"Invention and Innovation," "Literature and technology," "Art, religion and technology,"* ". . . (Christianity, Islam, Buddhism) and the technological society," "Civilizing the Machine/ the Civilizing Machine."

"Communication and Technological Change," "Technology and Community/ Cities," "Energy and Society," "The technologies -primitive, appropriate, etc.,"* "Servant Technology."

"Division of Labour," "Technology and the State," "The Social Impact of Technology," "Technology, Society and Human Beings,"* "Technology and Gender," "Invention as Technical and Social Act."

"Culture and Technology/Technology as Culture," "Technology and Leisure," "Technology and Contemporary Politics and Society."

'Technology and the Intellectual World: Personalities and Ideas," "The technological elite," "Logic and machines," "Minds and Machines," "Philosophy and Technology throughout History," "Technology as Intellectual History."

"Society and Economic Transitions," "Technology and Material Culture"

"Human Responses to Technological Change," "Technology and Critical Decisions," "Ethical Issues in Technology," "Science and Technology."

---

139 For those marked with an asterisk (*), see their syllabi in "Machine in the University," 123 and 226–47, *passim*. [This list is consolidated from the original for space considerations – *ed.*].

Chapter 3

Lynn White's "Roots" and *Medieval Technology and Social Change*

The view from outside medieval studies

Elspeth Whitney

Medieval historians know Lynn White, Jr. as one of the founders of the field of medieval technology and its cultural and social contexts. Non-medievalists know him as an environmentalist, a Christian, and a critic of the mainstream Christian tradition of human dominion over the natural world, but they knew little about Lynn White the historian. This bifurcation of White's legacy reveals much about how disciplinary boundaries such as those separating the study of culture from human material interaction with nature have hampered our understanding of human engagement with the environment in both the past and present. Environmental history and related disciplines have, of course, struggled with what it means to be "interdisciplinary."[1] The history of the reception of White's famous "Roots" article illustrates some of the perils of *not* being interdisciplinary and emphasizing perhaps artificial divisions between religion and culture, on one hand, and failing to distinguish between theology and the history of religious ideas, on the other.

If historians of the Middle Ages are well acquainted with Lynn White's achievements in the fields of the history of technology and agricultural history, White's work shaped and challenged medieval studies in myriad and important ways, and his legacy has been profound. Yet most medievalists are unaware that White has had an equally or even more enduring influence on areas outside of medieval history, namely, ecotheology, environmental ethics, and ecocriticism, as well as on the public. White's influence in these fields remains strong into the present day, has been echoed in popular versions of environmental history, and remains a living aspect

---

1 Eric Pawson and Stephen Dovers, "Environmental History and the Challenges of Interdisciplinarity: An Antipodean Perspective," *Environment and History* 9 (2003): 53–75; Sverker Sörlin and Paul Warde, "The Problem of the Problem of Environmental History: A Re-Reading of the Field," *Environmental History* 12 (2007): 107–30.

of the debate on what to do about environmental issues affecting us today.[2] Almost all of White's authority in these areas, moreover, rests on a single one of White's works, "The Historical Roots of Our Ecologic Crisis," a short article with a global reach addressed to a general audience and devoid of footnotes.[3] Initially published in 1967 in *Science*, "Roots" was subsequently endlessly reprinted and referenced as a founding work of the nascent environmental movement and related fields of ecocriticism, environmental ethics, and ecotheology. It is also the only one of White's publications in which he explicitly frames medieval Christianity in a negative light as the direct cause of contemporary environmental degradation. Outside of medieval history, therefore, White's ideas have had a second life, differing not only in their audience and disciplinary definition but also in their ideological orientation.

White's scholarly output on the cultural context of medieval technology, much of it collected in *Medieval Religion and Technology*, explicated his thesis, with nuance and a wealth of supporting detail, that the Middle Ages was a technologically innovative period largely because of the "activist" values of medieval Western Christianity. White's approach to big historical problems had often been to make bold assertions, expressed in persuasive, often ideologically charged rhetoric, which he then often subtly qualified in the fine print.[4] "Roots" was perhaps the most extreme example of this tendency, in that it asserted White's claim in its most uncompromising, negative, and simplified form but, here, accompanied by little in the way of concrete evidence. "Christianity, in absolute contrast to ancient paganism and Asia's religions (except perhaps, Zoroastrianism), not only established a dualism of man and nature but also insisted that it is God's will that man exploit nature for his proper ends."[5] White continued, "Modern science

---

2 See, for example, *Religion and Ecological Crisis: The "Lynn White Thesis" at Fifty*, ed. Todd LeVasseur and Anna Peterson (London and New York: Routledge, 2017) which contains fourteen essays, only two of which are by historians and only one of which is by a medieval historian (myself).

3 Lynn White, Jr., "The Historical Roots of Our Ecologic Crisis," *Science* 155, no. 3767 (March 10, 1967): 1203–7, rpt. in Lynn White, Jr., *Machina ex Deo: Essays in the Dynamism of Western Culture* (Cambridge, MA: MIT Press, 1968), 75–94. Henceforth, references to "Roots" will be to its rpt. in *Western Man and Environmental Ethics: Attitudes toward Nature and Technology*, ed. Ian G. Barbour (Reading, MA: Addison-Wesley Pub. Co., 1973), 18–30.

4 Bert S. Hall, "Lynn White's *Medieval Technology and Social Change* After Thirty Years," in *Technological Change: Methods and Themes in the History of Technology*, ed. Robert Fox (Amsterdam: Harwood Academic Publishers, 1996), 85–102 at 92, 94–95.

5 White, Jr., "Roots," in *Western Man and Environmental Ethics*, 25. White did offer evidence for his thesis in a follow up piece to "Roots," "Continuing the Conversation," published in *Western Man and Environmental Ethics*, 55–64, summarized from his "Iconography of *Temperantia* and the Virtuousness of Technology," in *Action and Conviction in Early Modern Europe: Essays in Memory of E.H. Harbison*, ed. T.K. Rabb and J.E. Seigel (Princeton: Princeton University Press, 1969), 197–219 and "Cultural Climates and

is an extrapolation of natural theology and . . . modern technology is at least partly to be explained as an occidental, voluntarist realization of the Christian dogma of man's transcendence of, and rightful mastery over, nature."[6] (Greek Orthodox Christianity is dismissed as "intellectualist" and therefore less committed to the conquest of nature.) The Western program of the religiously sanctioned exploitation of nature, according to White, was first realized during the medieval agricultural revolution and continued thereafter throughout Western history. If the joining of science and technology in the nineteenth century gave humankind unprecedented powers over nature resulting in "ecologic" crisis, then "Christianity bears a huge burden of guilt," he claimed. Any hope of avoiding ecologic crisis lay in transforming "the Christian axiom that nature has no reason for existence save to serve man," replacing it with St. Francis' heretical view of the "equality of all creatures."[7]

"Roots" quickly became, and continues to be, a touchstone for arguments about the causes of modern disregard for limits on human utilization of nature. Like Rachel Carson's *Silent Spring* (1962), it helped crystallize a growing public awareness of environmental issues. During the 1970s, its influence reached deeply into the popular and political discussion of environmental issues, surfacing in, for example, *The Whole Earth Catalogue*, the *Boy Scout Handbook*, *Time* magazine, and publications of the Sierra Club. Senator Alan Cranston cited "Roots" in Congress, and Pope John Paul II, following White's lead, declared St. Francis to be the patron saint of ecology in 1979.[8] "Roots" has been called "one of the most significant articles to appear in environmental studies in the second half of the twentieth century" as well as "a foundational document and a type of holy text of environmental history."[9] Since 1967, it has been endlessly reprinted and referenced in anthologies, textbooks, and scholarly work in ecology and religion, environmental

---

Technological Advance in the Middle Ages," *Viator* 2 (1971): 171–201 [both reproduced in Lynn White, Jr., *Medieval Religion and Technology: Collected Essays* (Berkeley: University of California Press, 1978), 181–204 and 217–54, respectively]. "Continuing the Conversation," however, has been rarely cited or referred to by commentators on "Roots." Two exceptions are Leslie Sponsel, "Lynn White Jr., One Catalyst in the Historical Development of Spiritual Ecology," in *Religion and Ecological Crisis*, eds., LeVasseur and Peterson, 89–102 and Christopher Cone, "Continuing the Conversation: Applying Lynn White Jr.'s Prescriptions for a Christian Environmental Ethic," 103–109 in the same volume.

    6   White, "Roots," 27.

    7   Ibid., 29.

    8   Roderick Frazier Nash, *The Rights of Nature: A History of Environmental Ethics* (Madison, WI: University of Wisconsin Press, 1989), 93, 175; Elspeth Whitney, "Lynn White, Ecotheology, and History," *Environmental Ethics* 15 (1993): 157–58.

    9   Ben A. Minteer and Robert E. Manning, "An Appraisal of the Critique of Anthropocentricism and Three Lesser Known Themes in Lynn White's 'The Historical Roots of our Ecologic Crisis'," *Organization and Environment* 18 (2005): 166; Joachim Radkau, "Religion and Environmentalism," in *A Companion to Global Environmental History*, ed. J.R. McNeill and Erin Stewart Mauldin (Malden, MA and Oxford, UK: Wiley-Blackwell, 2012), 496.

ethics, the sociology of religion, and ecocriticism. Its inclusion in numerous "readers" devoted to highlighting ecological issues in diverse fields, including literary studies, religious studies, economics, ethics, and philosophy ensured its continuing role as a focal point for discussion of how to deal with ongoing environmental damage.[10]

The most enduring influence was among those who saw religion or world views as crucial to both the genesis and solution to environmental problems. In 2010 "Roots" was singled out as "probably the most cited contribution to ecotheological debate" due to its central role in the debate about the relative importance of "dominion" and "stewardship" within the Christian tradition.[11] Since its publication, "Roots" has had a surprisingly ecumenical influence and has been variously credited with the "greening" of American Protestantism and the sparking of "an explicitly Islamic environmental ethic," as well as being one of the founding texts of Deep Ecology.[12] Partly because of its wide reach, many books on religious or cultural Western attitudes toward nature used White's argument as a useful jumping-off point and became, in effect,

---

10 To give just a few readily available examples, Susan J. Armstrong and Richard G. Botzler, eds., *Environmental Ethics: Divergence and Convergence*, 3rd ed. (Boston: McGraw-Hill, 2004), 219–24; Kai N. Lee, William R. Freudenburg, and Richards B. Howarth, eds., *Humans in the Landscape: An Introduction to Environmental Studies* (New York and London: W.W. Norton and Company, 2013), 377–79; Cheryll Glotfelty and Harold Fromm, eds., *Ecocriticism Reader: Landmarks in Literary Ecology* (Athens: University of Georgia Press, 1996); Richard C. Foltz, ed., *Worldviews, Religion and the Environment: A Global Anthology* (Belmont, CA: Thomson/Wadsworth, 2003); Rajaram Krishnan, Jonathan M. Harris, and Neva R. Goodwin, eds., *A Survey of Ecological Economics* (Washington, DC and Covelo, CA: Island Press, 1995), 36–39. White is also mentioned in 10 of the 25 articles in Roger S. Gottlieb, ed., *Oxford Handbook of Religion and Ecology* (Oxford: Oxford University Press, 2006). For earlier reprints and examples, see Paul A. Djupe and Patrick Kieran Hunts, "Beyond the Lynn White Thesis: Congregational Effects on Environmental Concern," *Journal for the Scientific Study of Religion* 48 (2009): 670–86, which cites at least twelve books and articles that directly or indirectly cite White as a focal point, and Whitney, "Lynn White, Ecotheology, and History," 158–59.

11 David G. Horrell, "Introduction," in *Ecological Hermeneutics: Biblical, Historical and Theological Perspectives*, ed. David G. Horrell, Cherryl Hunt, Christopher Southgate, and Francesca Stavrakopoulou (London: T&T Clark, 2010), 2; seven of the following twenty chapters cite "Roots." On White's influence, see also Robert Booth Fowler, *The Greening of Protestant Thought* (Chapel Hill and London: The University of North Carolina Press, 1995), 19–20, 58–59.

12 Richard C. Foltz, "Islamic Environmentalism in Theory and Practice," in Foltz, *Worldviews*, 359; George Sessions, "Ecocentrism and the Anthropocentric Detour," in *Deep Ecology for the Twenty-First Century: Readings on the Philosophy and Practice of the New Environmentalism*, ed. George Sessions (Boston: Shambhala, 1995), 101, 171–72. "Roots" has also been a focal point for Judaism and environmentalism: Martin D. Yaffe, ed., *Judaism and Environmental Ethics: A Reader* (Lanham, MD: Lexington Books, 2001), 6–11.

extended commentaries on "Roots."[13] Almost fifty years after its publication, discussion of "Roots" is alive and well on college campuses and on the web, as any cursory Internet search of White's name will show.[14] Readings of "Roots" were sometimes so broad that it has been used to argue the general point that science and environmental crisis have an ethical and moral, if not specifically religious, dimension.[15]

White was also credited with a definitive role in the formation of a religiously oriented American environmentalism.[16] Despite the fact that "Roots" is the sole publication of White's prolific output to take an environmentalist stance, its publication earned White a place in the history of American environmentalism, and White himself came to be included among the ranks of key environmental thinkers, along with such luminaries as Rachel Carson, Garrett Hardin, E.R. Schumacher, and the authors of *The Limits to Growth*.[17] Joachim Radkau, for example, who has referred to "Roots" as a "sacred" or "holy" text of environmental history, nevertheless connects "Roots" more substantively to the first generation of environmentalists such as John Muir and Aldo Leopold, rather than to early environmental historians, singling out White's recognition of the beatniks and hippies as having

---

13 See, for example, Gilbert F. LaFreniere's *The Decline of Nature: Environmental History and the Western Worldview* (Bethesda, MD: Academica Press, 2008) and Stephen Bede Scharper, *Redeeming the Time: A Political Theology of the Environment* (New York: Continuum, 2004), 23–52.

14 A few examples include Christopher Layton, "Upon Reading Lynn White's 'The Historical Roots of Our Ecological Crisis'," *Fallen into Knowledge*, September 11, 2012, online at www.christopherlayton.org/post/31346533782/upon-reading-lynn-whites-the-historical-roots-of-our; J. Lowe, "Christianity's Role in Our Ecological Crisis – Lynn White's Essay Revisited," *Daily Kos*, January 27, 2008, online at www.dailykos.com/story/2008/01/27/444470/-Christianity-s-Role-in-Our-Ecological-Crisis-Lynn-White-s-Essay-Revisited; Stephen Geard, "The Dominion of Man – A Tasmanian Perspective," *Netspace*, February 5, 2009, online at http://sdgeard.customer.netspace.net.au/dom.html; John Michael Greer, "Toward a Green Future, Part One," *The Archdruid Report*, November 6, 2013, online at http://thearchdruidreport.blogspot.com/2013/11/toward-green-future-part-one-culture-of.html. There is even a blog devoted to "Roots," admittedly not a very active one, online at http://historyofourecologicalcrisis.blogspot.com.

15 Thomas J. Sauer and Michael P. Nelson, "Science, Ethics, and the Historical Roots of Our Environmental Crisis – Was White Right?" in *Sustaining Soil Productivity in Response to Global Climate Change: Science, Policy and Ethics* (Chichester, West Sussex, UK, and Ames, IA: Wiley-Blackwell, 2011), 3–16.

16 Fowler, *The Greening of Protestant Thought*, 20; Radkau, "Religion and Environmentalism," 496.

17 Peter Hay, *Main Currents in Western Environmental Thought* (Bloomington: Indiana University Press, 2003), 26–27, 100–6; J.E. de Steiguer, *The Origins of Modern Environmental Thought* (Tucson: The University of Arizona Press, 2006), 99–109; LaFreniere, *Decline of Nature*, 304. A profile of White was also included in Michael Nelson, *Fifty Key Thinkers on the Environment* (London: Routledge, 2001), 200–5.

played a role in the early environmental movement.[18] To a lesser extent, "Roots" was also included within a backlash against environmentalism by those who saw human-centered religious values as antithetical to perceived extreme claims about the relationship of humans to nature. Steven Schwarzschild, for example, accuses White of believing that "man is part of nature, nature is sacred, and man therefore ought to serve nature rather than the reverse," yet cites White as perhaps "the most influential ideologist of this sort in the country."[19] Likewise, Thomas Sieger Derr blames "Roots" for what he describes as "the determination of mainstream environmentalism to blame Christianity for whatever ecological trouble we are in."[20]

"Roots" therefore achieved extraordinary success and readership. Yet, until very recently, this success was almost totally divorced from the recognition of White's other work among either the general public or academics that were not medieval historians. The near complete disregard for either *Medieval Technology and Social Change* (*MTSC*) or *Medieval Religion and Technology* (*MRT*) by scholars outside the field of medieval history is quite remarkable. True, White had not cited himself in "Roots," which had no notes, and some of the essays in *MRT* were published ten years or more after "Roots." Yet, given the huge volume of work written in the forty-plus years since the appearance of "Roots" that challenges or corroborates White's characterization of Christianity as inherently aggressive toward nature, it seems extraordinary that scholars did not take the trouble to find and read White's academic publications, much less other relevant work done by medievalists. Although a few scholars in the field of the history of environmental ethics have over the past several years incorporated White's *MTSC* into the discussion, most notably Robin Attfield, this attention to White's seminal work in environmental history is rare.[21] White's *MRT* is almost never cited, despite the fact that its numerous essays provide the substantive, detailed evidence for medieval framing of technology as morally virtuous that is lacking in "Roots." Indeed, White is more often identified in terms of his religious affiliation as a Presbyterian than in terms of his career as an historian of the Middle Ages.[22]

---

18   Joachim Radkau, *Nature and Power: A Global History of the Environment*, trans. Thomas Dunlap (Cambridge: Cambridge University Press/Washington, DC: German Historical Institute, 2008), 277, 326; "Religion and Environmentalism," 496–97.

19   Steven S. Scharzschild, "The Unnatural Jew," in *Judaism and Environmental Ethics*, 273.

20   Thomas Sieger Derr, *Environmental Ethics and Christian Humanism, with Critical Responses by James A. Nash and Richard John Neuhaus* (Nashville, TN: Abingdon Press, 1996), 19.

21   Robin Attfield, "Social History, Religion and Technology: An Interdisciplinary Investigation into Lynn White, Jr.'s 'Roots'," *Environmental Ethics* 31 (2009): 31–50. On early responses to *MTSC* and its influence, see Hall, "Lynn White's *Medieval Technology and Social Change* After Thirty Years," 85–101; Shana Worthen, "The Influence of Lynn White, Jr.'s *Medieval Technology and Social Change*," *History Compass* 7, no. 4 (2009): 1201–17.

22   Mark R. Stoll, "Sinners in the Hands of an Ecologic Crisis: Lynn White's Environmental Jeremiad," in *Religion and Ecological Crisis*, eds., LeVasseur and Peterson, 47–8

Nor have scholars in ecotheology, ecocriticism, and environmental ethics paid much attention to the rapidly expanding field of medieval environmental history, which has complicated and qualified White's conclusions in both "Roots" and *MTSC*. This applies even to some medieval scholars who are not historians. A 2010 article in the *Journal of Ecocriticism* that applies "Roots" to attitudes toward nature in "Sir Gawain and the Green Knight," for example, asserts that "'Roots' has received very little, if any, attention from a medieval perspective."[23] While technically correct – many ecotheologians did not apply a medieval perspective and few medieval historians critiqued "Roots," focusing instead on White's academic writings – this statement ignores the enormous body of work relating to the Lynn White thesis by historians.

Responses to "Roots" accordingly moved along an entirely separate trajectory from those by medieval historians to the rest of White's work. While scholars of medieval cultural, military and agricultural history subjected *MTSC* and *MRT* to sustained historical analysis and criticism on both interpretative and factual grounds, responses to "Roots" were largely formulated as theological arguments based on readings of biblical and other spiritual texts and focused on whether White had accurately characterized Christianity as embodying an inherent exploitative attitude toward nature. Framed as a theological controversy, and debated mostly by religious scholars, the controversy over "Roots," was heated but rarely touched specifically on historical questions. Instead, the argument focused on Christian "values" in and of themselves and the issue of whether the biblical mandate for human dominion over nature signified stewardship or exploitation rather than on the ways in which religion was embedded in a historical context. When White was accused of taking a "simplistic" approach by religious scholars, they more often meant that he had oversimplified the range of attitudes embedded in biblical or patristic texts than that he had oversimplified the historical record of human engagement with nature.[24] As a result, scholars in the fields of ecotheology and environmental history are still often surprised by the degree to which White's claims in "Roots" that medieval people were driven by Christian faith to dominate

---

and Whitney A. Bauman, "What's Left(Out) of the Lynn White Narrative?" in *Religion and Ecological Crisis*, eds., LeVasseur and Peterson, 167.

23 Michael W. George, "Gawain's Struggle with Ecology: Attitudes toward the Natural World in *Sir Gawain and the Green Knight*," *Journal of Ecocriticism* 2 (2010): 33.

24 See, for example, Sallie McFague, "An Ecological Christology: Does Christianity Have It?" in *Christianity and Ecology: Seeking the Well-Being of Earth and Humans*, ed. Dieter T. Hessel and Rosemary Radford Ruether (Cambridge, MA: Harvard University Press and the Harvard University Center for the Study of World Religions, 2000), 29. For some earlier examples, see Whitney, "Lynn White, Ecotheology, and History," 159–62. This reading of White is often replicated in anthologies; Armstrong and Botzler, eds., *Environmental Ethics*, for instance, place "Roots" in the section titled "Religious and Cultural Perspectives" rather than the section titled "Historical Contexts," 219.

and exploit the natural world have been modified, qualified, and challenged within medieval environmental history and related fields.

Why were scholars interested in developing religious and ethical perspectives on human relations with nature so fixated on "Roots" and so uninterested in White's other work or the work of medieval cultural and environmental historians? These writers, by and large, were more concerned with developing a religiously or ethically grounded defense of environmentalism in the present day rather than in past attitudes toward nature. History might provide ammunition, but historical ideas about nature, much less the history of how past societies had dealt with the natural world, were not of primary interest. If, as has been claimed, White had intended "Roots" as a lighthearted attempt to make non-medievalists take the Middle Ages seriously, the effort was a failure; the response overwhelmingly demonstrated that writers and public figures involved with environmental issues in the 1960s and after were heavily invested in Christian "values" but had little interest in exploring medieval Christianity or medieval practices as the origin of contemporary problems.[25] Instead, the history of attitudes toward nature was subordinated to the possibility of using religious attitudes as a means to deal with environmental problems. Stephen Bede Scharper, for example, described "Roots," as the "starting gun" in the "race to reevaluate and perhaps refashion Christianity in light of our ecological crisis."[26] Similarly, Willis Jenkins's subtle analysis of White's legacy addresses how multiple, overlapping ethical and moral strategies might be used to confront environmental problems in the light of the divisions introduced by "Roots" and the responses to it.[27]

For Scharper and others, "Roots" was an ideal foil in that, while it was ostensibly a historical argument (medieval Christianity caused medieval people to exploit nature), it so muddled the relationship of historical Christianity with what White termed "western values" that its historicity vanished beneath the weight of its rhetoric. "Roots," in fact, unmoored medieval Christianity from the Middle Ages. The logic of "Roots" demanded that Christianity and Western culture as defined by White were coextensive and that a drive to exploit nature was inherent in the Western mind-set; in "Roots," the medieval *was* the modern, and the modern, medieval. The rhetoric of "Roots" similarly encouraged a fundamental confusion about whether White believed an aggressive attitude toward nature was

---

25 Patricia Townshend, "White, Lynn, Jr.," in *Encyclopedia of World Environmental History*, ed. Shepard Krech III, J.R. McNeil, and Carolyn Merchant (New York: Routledge, 2004), 3: 1329–30; Thomas F. Glick, "White, Lynn, Jr.," in *Encyclopedia of Historians and Historical Writing*, ed. Kelly Boyd (London: Dearborn, 1999), 1296.

26 Scharper, *Redeeming the Time*, 15; Roger S. Gottlieb, *A Greener Faith: Religious Environmentalism and Our Planet's Future* (Oxford and New York: Oxford University Press, 2006), 27 makes a similar point.

27 Willis Jenkins, "After Lynn White: Religious Ethics and Environmental Problems," *Journal of Religious Ethics* 37 (2009): 283–309; see also Hessel and Ruether, *Christianity and Ecology*, xxiv–xxv and xxxiv–xxxv.

the "true" meaning of the biblical texts he cited or merely the normative interpretation of them in the Middle Ages.[28] By treating Christianity in terms of a timeless set of values, rather than a cultural construction that differed according to time and place, that is, as hermeneutics rather than as a cultural expression rooted in history, White in "Roots" appears to be a Christian determinist, in much the same way as he has been accused of being a technological determinist.[29] By arguing, as he did in "Roots," that "we" were still motivated by the values of medieval Christianity and that, in effect, nothing had really happened since the Middle Ages, White erased any contingency from the progression of Western history and, ironically, given his genuine interest in and admiration of, the history and culture of non-Western societies, created an implicit narrative of Western exceptionalism.[30]

"Roots," therefore, became the classic statement of what was termed the "ecological complaint against Christianity."[31] As a result, "Roots" became entangled in broad concerns about environmental issues that had little to do with historical analysis. Instead, it was read as a manifesto on religious values about nature in the

---

28   See Peter Harrison, "Subduing the Earth: Genesis 1, Early Modern Science, and the Exploitation of Nature," *The Journal of Religion* 79 (1999): 86–109 and "Having Dominion: Genesis and the Mastery of Nature," in *Environmental Stewardship: Critical Perspectives – Past and Present*, ed. R.J. Berry (London: Continuum, 2006), 17–31 for a broad discussion of this issue.

29   R.H. Hilton and P.H. Sawyer, "Technical Determinism: The Stirrup and the Plough," *Past & Present* 24 (1963): 90–100; Bert Hall's sensitive intellectual portrait of White makes the point that White was not so much a technological determinist as a cultural determinist: "Lynn White's *Medieval Technology and Social Change* After Thirty Years," 92. Hall attests to White's strong Christian background and beliefs in his obituary essays for White, "Lynn White, Jr., April 29, 1907–March 30, 1987," *Isis* 79 (1988): 480 and "Lynn Townsend White, Jr. (1907–1987)" *Technology and Culture* 30 (1989): 195. See also Townshend, "White, Lynn, Jr.," in *Encyclopedia of World Environmental History*, 1329. White's Christian beliefs are cited in Roderick S. French, "Is Ecological Humanism a Contradiction in Terms? The Philosophical Foundations of the Humanities Under Attack," in *Ecological Consciousness: Essays from the Earthday X Colloquium, University of Denver, April 21–24, 1980*, ed. Robert C. Schultz and J. Donald Hughes (Washington, DC: University Press of America, 1981), 47: Derr, *Environmental Ethics and Christian Humanism*, 19.

30   For White's thesis as "Eurocentric" see J.M. Blaut, *Eight Eurocentric Historians* (New York: The Guilford Press, 2000), 31–44. On White's interest in Asia, see Hall, "Lynn White, Jr., April 29, 1907–March 30, 1987," 480–81. Latent in White's exceptionalist view is an updated version of Max Weber's famous thesis, making the medieval monk, rather than the Puritan businessman, the pivotal figure in the rationalized use of nature and the development of capitalism: Elspeth Whitney, "Christianity and Changing Concepts of Nature," in *Religion and the New Ecology: Environmental Responsibility in a World of Flux*, ed. David M. Lodge and Christopher Hamlin (Notre Dame, IN: University of Notre Dame Press, 2006), 26–52.

31   James A. Nash, *Loving Nature: Ecological Integrity and Christian Responsibility* (Nashville: Abingdon Press, 1991; rpt. Washington, DC: The Churches' Center for Theology and Public Policy, 1991), 72.

present; what mattered in the great ecotheological debate about whether Christianity inculcated human domination of nature or careful stewardship of the natural world was not what had happened in the Middle Ages but Christianity's role in attitudes toward the environment in late twentieth-century and early twenty-first-century America. Despite White's Christian credentials, "Roots" was sometimes taken as an outright attack on Christianity *per se* by anti-Christian environmentalists.[32] Although occasionally writers from an ecotheological perspective acknowledged that historical and cultural forces might condition how basic religious ideas were interpreted, for the most part White's characterization of Christianity as inherently promoting the exploitation of nature, or the counterargument that it mandated stewardship, were implicitly treated as expressions of transcendent truth to be dealt with theologically by "defenders of the faith."[33] At the same time, writers on environmental ethics concerned with contemporary social and ecological practices critiqued "Roots" as promoting a lamentable turn away from pragmatic engagement with environmental justice and toward an unproductive preoccupation exclusively with the cosmological value of nature in the world's major religions.[34]

"Roots," therefore, galvanized debate about how to deal with environmental degradation as a moral and ethical issue while opening deep fissures about the appropriate role of religion in the environmental movement. Responses to "Roots" further illustrate the disciplinary divisions between environmental history, on one hand, and ecotheology and environmental ethics, on the other. In many ways, "Roots," like the second chapter of *MTSC* on which it was based, can be considered a very early work of global environmental history.[35] "Roots" differs from *MTSC*, however, not only in its lack of detailed documentation and supporting evidence, a function of White's intention to appeal to a general audience, but also in its claim that Christianity was the sole cause of the Western drive to control nature and in its characterization of that drive in negative terms as exploitative. *MTSC*, on the other hand, both left religion out of the picture and celebrated medieval technology and its products as innovative, progressive, and modern.

This theme was taken up by some world economic historians who used White's *MTSC*, particularly its second chapter, as a cornerstone for a narrative of Western economic progress. A 2002 article by world economic historian Jack A. Goldstone, for example, points to the "well-known" story of the medieval agricultural revolution, citing White and several social scientists and historians (but no other medieval historians) as having "confidently argued that 'modern economic growth'

---

32   Derr, *Environmental Ethics and Christian Humanism*, 19–21.

33   Nash, *Loving Nature*, 71. Nash, who rejects White's "single-cause" explanation for Western arrogance toward nature as "pathetically simplistic" (74), suggests that White and others influenced by him have neglected the influence of culture on religion, other kinds of historical factors, and evidence for ecological sensitivity within Christianity (68–92).

34   Jenkins, "After Lynn White," 292ff.

35   For a detailed comparison of "Roots" and the second chapter of *MTSC*, see Attfield, "Social History."

began in the High Middle Ages."[36] Elsewhere, Michael Mitterauer and David Levine, among others, used White's medieval "agrarian revolution" as indicative of Europe's economic dynamism and a harbinger of industrialization.[37] Although Goldstone himself rejects the notion of a unique Western modernity destined for universal success, he groups the exceptional rise in agricultural productivity of the High Middle Ages identified by White, along with the Dutch Golden Ages and Qing China, as periods of remarkable economic growth that temporarily, at least, broke localized Malthusian limits.[38]

Environmental historians of the Middle Ages took White's examination of medieval agricultural practices in *MTSC* seriously, even when they disagreed with his methodology and conclusions, yet they, too, until recently, paid little attention to "Roots." Conversely, environmental historians who were not medievalists ignored or were unaware of *MTSC* and focused almost entirely on "Roots," which they roundly rejected on the basis that religion was largely irrelevant to environmental history.[39] While White's insistence on the power of religion had stimulated debate within the field of ecotheology and environmental ethics, it seems to have shut down debate in the early decades of the development of environmental history as a field and short-circuited the integration of the Middle Ages into world environmental history. The very emphasis on religion that made White's argument so compelling to ecotheologians was cause for dismissal among many historians who viewed environmental history as closely related to the natural sciences.[40] White's idealist position did not fit easily into an environmental history that focused on material, economic, and political practices and was suspicious of "culture" ungrounded in a material substrate. As a field,

---

36 Jack A. Goldstone, "Efflorescences and Economic Growth in World History: Rethinking the 'Rise of the West' and the Industrial Revolution," *Journal of World History* 13 (2002): 346. For a contrary analysis, see Karel Davids, *Religion, Technology, and the Great and Little Divergences: China and Europe Compared, c.700–1800* (Leiden: Brill, 2013), 227 who has recently argued that "the ghosts of Lynn White and Max Weber can be laid to rest."

37 Michael Mitterauer, *Why Europe? The Medieval Origins of Its Special Path*, trans. Gerald Chapple (Chicago: The University of Chicago Press, 2010), 2; David Levine, *At the Dawn of Modernity: Biology, Culture, and Material Life in Europe after the Year 1000* (Berkeley: University of California Press, 2001), 2–6, 17–21.

38 Goldstone, "Efflorescences," 348.

39 See, for example, Donald Worster, "Transformations of the Earth: Toward an Agroecological Perspective in History," *The Journal of American History* 76 (1990): 1090–91; Alice E. Ingerson, "Tracking and Testing the Nature-Culture Dichotomy," in *Historical Ecology: Cultural Knowledge and Changing Landscapes*, ed. Carole L. Crumley (Santa Fe, NM: School of American Research Press, 1994), 46–48; Richard White, "From Wilderness to Hybrid Landscapes: The Cultural Turn in Environmental History," *The Historian* 66 (2004): 557–64.

40 Sorlin, "The Problem of Environmental History," *Environmental History* 12 (2007): 113.

environmental history originated in an attempt to understand the physical impacts of natural systems on humans and conversely the physical impacts of humans on nature, attempting to create, in Douglas Weiner's words, "a positivist predictive science."[41] Although this attempt was quickly complicated by a host of methodological and philosophical issues resulting in the recognition that a clear-cut separation of "nature" and "culture" was impossible, environmental history remained committed to the concrete and particular expression of humans in an interactive relationship with the physical world. Some environmental historians, therefore, found White's emphasis on culture largely irrelevant to a discipline they saw as grounding human motivation in material and biological causes. J.R. McNeill, for example, who describes himself as most at home in materialist environmental history, in a 2003 overview of the field, references "Roots" as a representative of the sort of cultural/intellectual environmental history that he finds least convincing. Still he acknowledged that other environmental historians accord more weight to culture and ideas as conditioning human behavior.[42]

Environmental historians with a global perspective also were quick to point to the historical record of environmental degradation in non-Western societies as a clear and simple proof that White was wrong to emphasize a distinctively Western and Christian ideology of domination of nature. William McNeill, for example, in the course of a discussion of the convergence of world history and environmental history remarked that White's view was "exaggerated" in the light of Asian, and particularly, Chinese, impacts on nature.[43] The record of Chinese environmental degradation documented in the work of Yi-fu Tuan and Mark Elvin has become a stock response to White's claims of a uniquely Christian drive for control over nature.[44]

---

41 Douglas R. Weiner, "A Death-Defying Attempt to Create a Coherent Definition of Environmental History," *Environmental History* 10 (2005): 406.

42 J.R. McNeill, "Observations on the Nature and Culture of Environmental History," *History and Theory* 42, no. 13 (2003): 8; for McNeill's general observations on cultural/intellectual environmental history, see pp. 6–8; Richard W. Unger, "Introduction: Hoffmann in the Historiography of Environmental History," in *Ecologies and Economies in Medieval and Early Modern Europe: Studies in Environmental History for Richard C. Hoffmann* (Leiden: Brill, 2008), 15–16. For discussion of a biological basis for human manipulation of the environment, see Dan Flores, "Nature's Children: Environmental History as Human Natural History," in *Human/Nature: Biology, Culture, and Environmental History*, ed. John P. Herron and Andrew G. Kirk (Albuquerque, NM: University of New Mexico Press, 1999), 11–30.

43 Marc Cioc and Char Miller, "William R. McNeill," *Environmental History* 15 (2010): 134.

44 Yi-Fu Tuan, "Discrepancies between Environmental Attitude and Behavior: Examples from Europe and China," in *Ecology and Religion*, ed. David and Eileen Spring (New York: Harper & Row, 1974), 91–113; Mark Elvin, *The Retreat of the Elephants: An Environmental History of China* (New Haven: Yale University Press, 2004); for uses of these sources in response to White, see Radkau, "Religion and Environmentalism," 497;

Nor did global environmental historians pick up on White's arguments in "Roots," that had been more fully explicated in *MTSC*, characterizing medieval agriculture as an unprecedented "attack" on the environment and emblematic of medieval aggressiveness toward nature. This is more surprising in that *MTSC* made no mention of Christianity as an explanatory force behind the environmental transformation of the landscape through farming. Part of the reason for this neglect may lie in the more general neglect of the Middle Ages until recently within global environmental history. Large-scale environmental history has often focused on the broadest categories of human ecological or environmental regimes, namely, the discovery of fire, the invention of farming, and the transition to fossil fuels.[45] J. Donald Hughes pointed out in 2006 that within environmental history as a field, "more work is needed in chronological periods that have been largely missing until recently. Generally speaking, this means anything before about 1800."[46]

A quick look at some recent overviews of global environmental history supports Hughes's assessment with respect to the Middle Ages. A 2010 collection of essays on the "turning points of environmental history," for example, gives a nod to "Roots" on p. 2, yet then discusses no event between the rise of cities and the Columbian Exchange and no date between 200 CE and 1492, subsuming even these under the rubric of "the first hundred thousand years" in the first chapter.[47] I. G. Simmons's *Global Environmental History*, similarly subsumes medieval history into one chapter titled "Pre-Industrial Agriculture" that begins in prehistory and ends in the early eighteenth century. *The Environment and World History*, edited by Burke and Pomeranz, includes only a few references to the medieval Middle East and the index has an entry for the Renaissance but not one for the Middle Ages.[48] Max Oelschlaeger sandwiches the Middle Ages into a few pages between much fuller discussion of the ancient and early modern periods, with the explanation that "the Middle Ages is perhaps best understood more as a

---

McNeill, "Observations," 7–8; Michael Williams, *Deforesting the Earth: From Prehistory to Global Crisis* (Chicago: The University of Chicago Press, 2003), 165–66.

45 See, for example, F. Spier, *The Structure of Big History: From the Big Bang until Today* (Amsterdam: University of Amsterdam Press, 1996) and Vaclav Smil, *Energy in World History* (Boulder, CO: Westview Press, 1994). On periodization in global environmental history, see Robert B. Marks, "World Environmental History: Nature, Modernity, and Power," *Radical History Review* 107 (2010): 209–24.

46 J. Donald Hughes, *What Is Environmental History?* (Cambridge, UK and Malden, MA: Polity Press, 2006), 74.

47 Frank Uekoetter, "Thinking Big: The Broad Outlines of a Burgeoning Field," in *The Turning Points of Environmental History*, ed. Frank Uekoetter (Pittsburg: The University of Pittsburgh Press, 2010), 2 and J.R. McNeill, "The First Hundred Thousand Years," in *Turning Points*, 13–28.

48 I.G. Simmons, *Global Environmental History* (Chicago: The University of Chicago Press, 2008), 52–109; Edmund Burke III and Kenneth Pomeranz, eds., *The Environment and World History* (Berkeley: University of California Press, 2009).

continuation of previous ideas and techniques than as a sociomaterial revolution."[49] Sverker Sörlin and Paul Warde in a recent review of the field include no synthetic works substantively dealing with the Middle Ages.[50] J.R. McNeill goes further, remarking in a 2003 overview of the field that "[e]ven medieval history, for which the sources are scant and rarely oriented towards environmental themes, can with enough imagination, be recast in an ecological light," and he cites only two studies.[51] From another perspective, it is striking that John F. Richards's magisterial *The Unending Frontier: An Environmental History of the Early Modern World* includes virtually no data from before 1500, enshrining what to many medievalists appears to be an artificially sharp division between the late Middle Ages and the early modern period.[52]

White's linkage of Christian values and environmental aggressiveness can, of course, also be reframed not as cause and effect (*i.e.*, Christianity caused Christians to exploit the environment) but as simply showing how, in particular times and places, Christianity could provide a useful justification for aggressive use of the natural world. Much of the early criticism of "Roots" from a historical perspective had seen this point as a fatal blow against White. Peter Harrison, for example, pointed out in 1999 that an explicit interpretation of Genesis as mandating human control of the natural world emerged only in the seventeenth century:

> If White was fundamentally correct to identify in specific Christian ideas and in particular biblical texts powerful determinants of Western attitudes toward the natural world, he was, for all that, mistaken in attributing to these an influence that predated the rise of science in the early modern period. Whatever evidence there may be of human impact on the natural landscape during the Middle Ages, only in the early modern period do we encounter the explicit connection between the exploitation of nature and the Genesis creation narratives.[53]

Writers in the areas of environmental ethics have been more resistant to this argument against White, but they too have increasingly voiced the idea that societies may use religious ideas to validate actions undertaken for non-religious reasons. James A. Nash, for example, has recently suggested that cultural forces

---

49 Max Oelschelaeger, *The Idea of Wilderness: From Prehistory to the Age of Ecology* (New Haven: Yale University Press, 1991), 73.

50 Sörlin and Warde, "The Problem of the Problem of Environmental History," 115–18.

51 McNeill, "Observations," 20.

52 John F. Richards, *The Unending Frontier: An Environmental History of the Early Modern World* (Berkeley: University of California Press, 2003); for the argument for continuity, see Richard C. Hoffmann, "A Longer View: Is Industrial Metabolism Really the Problem," *Innovation* 14 (2001): 143–55.

53 Harrison, "Subduing the Earth," 107. For other examples of criticism of White from this perspective, see Whitney, "Christianity," 38–46.

"often adopt and distort religious concepts, and use these honorific ideas as rationalizations or "justifications" for their projects."[54] Willis Jenkins, in particular, has traced a recent shift within the fields of environmental ethics and religion and ecology away from the pervasive influence of White's premise that "religious cosmology [alone] produces environmental behavior."[55] Thomas Sieger Derr, one of White's most ardent defenders as both a Christian and a colleague, has even claimed (despite all the evidence to the contrary) that this was the position of White himself, who had explained in private conversation that he (White) had only meant to describe how the Christian tradition could be misappropriated and that blame lay not with Christianity itself but with those using it for their own selfish ends.[56]

Among the challenges of environmental history, then, are the problems of interdisciplinarity and scale. How to do a history that incorporates both scientific and historical perspectives? How to do a history that recognizes both the global and the local scope of human interaction with the environment, while still including the middle ground? Furthermore, how to do environmental history that incorporates the full range of human engagement with nature, including not only the technological transformation of the physical world and the material impacts of natural events and conditions on human societies but also how humans understood these processes in cultural terms? The questions of what environmental history is and how it integrates perspectives from different fields are now almost a field unto itself.[57] The field of global environmental history has only in the first decade of the twenty-first century started to find room for both medieval environmental history and a more historically grounded treatment of religion and culture as part of how humans understood and framed their sense of engagement with nature. As J. Donald Hughes has put it, "[e]nvironmental history refuses to cut culture from nature."[58] These shifts have provided a new context for White's work and its influence even as they also demonstrate the ways in which current research has moved beyond initial responses to "Roots" and, to a lesser extent, his *MTSC*.

Medieval environmental history itself quickly moved beyond White's view of medieval Christianity as monolithically aggressive toward nature, whether this is viewed in primarily a negative or a positive way. David Herlihy in 1980 suggested that there were four distinct categories of responses to nature among medieval

---

54 Nash, *Loving Nature*, 72 and 77–78.
55 Jenkins, "After Lynn White," 287.
56 Derr, *Environmental Ethics and Christian Humanism*, 19–22.
57 Hughes, *What Is Environmental History?* 8–15; J.R. McNeill and Erin Stewart Mauldin, "Global Environmental History: An Introduction," in *Companion to Global Environmental History*, ed. McNeill and Mauldin, xvi–xxiv; *The Globalization of Environmental Crisis*, ed. Jan Oosthoek and Barry K. Gills (London: Routledge, 2007); McNeill, "Observations."
58 Hughes, *What Is Environmental History?* 118.

writers: the "eschatological" (the bounty of the earth was in decline), the "adversarial" (fear and awe of nature), the "collaborative" (man, like nature, could shape the environment), and the "recreational" (nature as a source of psychological and spiritual renewal).[59] Richard C. Hoffmann and John Aberth have more recently pointed to a dynamic interplay between a medieval perspective that emphasizes nature's cooperation in human rule over and use of nature and one that emphasizes a more hostile relationship between humans and nature. Aberth finds a connection between more negative attitudes about human interactions with nature and the environmental catastrophes of the late Middle Ages.[60] Hoffmann points to contrasting views in the Middle Ages of human collaboration with an autonomous Nature and a second tradition of mutual hostility between humans and the Earth.[61] Although he emphasizes the degree to which medieval people did sometimes transform their environment, Hoffmann finds the White thesis unconvincing: "the leap is simply too great from reading Genesis to making gunpowder or from ploughing a furrow in the tenth century"; moreover, "White and his critics easily lapse into simple determinism, and both the materialist and the idealist position raise genuine problems, even within the limits of the history of ideas."[62] Hoffmann therefore rejects White's abstract linkage of Christianity and medieval attitudes with respect to their environment in favor of a much more developed model of interplay among nature, culture, and humans, in which both nature and people are agents and objects of history (a model, of course, unavailable to White).[63] The most substantive exploration of the interaction between religious attitudes and practices is Ellen F. Arnold's *Negotiating the Landscape* (2013). Arnold's careful, thorough, and sensitive study of a Benedictine monastic community's engagement with nature over six centuries finds that the monks understood the natural environment variously as a desert wilderness; a productive, domesticated landscape

---

59 David J. Herlihy, "Attitudes Toward the Environment in Medieval Society," in *Historical Ecology: Essays on Environment and Social Change*, ed. Lester J. Bilsky (Port Washington, NY and London: Kennikat Press, 1980), 100–16; Peter Coates, *Nature: Western Attitudes since Ancient Times* (Berkeley: University of California Press, 1998), 40–66. Herlihy points out that a medieval belief that mankind could shape the world according to human needs appears only in the twelfth century, in Herlihy's view a response to an expanding economy, not a theological imperative, "Attitudes," 112.

60 John Aberth, *An Environmental History of the Middle Ages: The Crucible of Nature* (London: Routledge, 2013), 8–9, 41–49, and 76.

61 Richard C. Hoffmann, "*Homo et Natura, Homo in Natura*: Ecological Perspectives on the European Middle Ages," in *Engaging with Nature: Essays on the Natural World in Medieval and Early Modern Europe*, ed. Barbara A. Hanawalt and Lisa J. Kiser (Notre Dame: University of Notre Dame Press, 2008), 11–38.

62 Richard C. Hoffmann, *An Environmental History of Medieval Europe* (Cambridge: Cambridge University Press, 2014), 87; for Hoffmann's discussion of the White thesis, see pp. 87–91.

63 Hoffmann, *Environmental History*, 1–20.

offering economic opportunity; and a site for the demonstration of saintly power and virtue. "The Ardennes helped the monks of Stavelot-Malmedy to explore and explain such things as the human control (or lack therefore) of nature, the morality of resource use, the relationship between humans and other species, and the ways in which religious salvation was tied to nature."[64] Arnold, who begins her study by pointing out that the study of religious history and medieval interactions with nature "has been for far too long framed around the well-known and provocative article by Lynn White," concludes that there was "no single 'monastic' attitude toward nature in the Middle Ages, and there was definitely not a universal Christian one."[65] At the same time, most scholars agree that Christianity did provide a possible set of powerful, even if often contradictory, responses to the natural world during the medieval period and after.

Scholars of medieval agriculture and medieval technology have also toned down White's more extreme claims about the speed and universality of medieval technological development while still incorporating White's primary observation that the medieval period exhibited dynamic changes technologically and environmentally. Like scholars of environmental ethics, many recognize the need to "get beyond" the Lynn White thesis yet also recognize that the effort to do so has prompted decades of fruitful research. The work of Richard Holt and Adam Lucas has established that the diffusion of mills during the Middle Ages was far more uneven than White had suggested.[66] The work of Richard C. Hoffmann, Richard Unger, Ellen Arnold, Petra J. E. M. van Dam, Steven A. Walton, and Constance H. Berman, among others, has documented the consistent interest of medieval people

---

64   Ellen F. Arnold, *Negotiating the Landscape: Environment and Monastic Identity in the Medieval Ardennes* (Philadelphia: University of Pennsylvania Press, 2013), 211.

65   Ibid., 4–5, 211.

66   Richard Holt, "Medieval Technology and the Historians: The Evidence for the Mill," in *Technological Change: Methods and Themes in the History of Technology*, ed. Robert Fox (Australia: Harwood Academic Press, 1996), 103–21; Holt, "Mechanization and the Medieval English Economy," in *Technology and Resource Use in Medieval Europe: Cathedrals, Mills, and Mines*, ed. Elizabeth Bradford Smith and Michael Wolfe (Aldershot: Ashgate, 1997), 139–57; Adam Robert Lucas, "Industrial Milling in the Ancient and Medieval Worlds: A Survey of the Evidence for an Industrial Revolution in Medieval Europe," *Technology and Culture* 46, no. 1 (2005): 1–30; Lucas, "The Role of Monasteries in the Development of Medieval Milling," in *Wind and Water in the Middle Ages: Fluid Technologies from Antiquity to the Renaissance*, ed. Steven A. Walton (Tempe, AZ: ACMRS, 2006), 89–128. Michael Toch also questions White's emphasis on technological change as a driver of agriculture in the Middle Ages in "Agricultural Progress and Agricultural Technology in Medieval Germany: An Alternate Model," in *Technology and Resource*, ed. Smith and Wolfe, 158–69. This work has been summarized in Adam Lucas, "Narratives of Technological Revolution in the Middle Ages," in *Handbook of Medieval Studies: Terms – Methods – Trends*, ed. Albrecht Classen (Berlin and New York: Walter De Gruyter, 2010), 3: 967–90.

in managing the natural world and the dramatic transformation of the medieval landscape through technology, while also emphasizing the complexity of cultural motivations behind the use, and nonuse, of available technologies.[67] The picture that has emerged, while severely qualifying White's claim in "Roots" that medieval Christianity supplied the only, or even the primary, reason for medieval "aggressiveness" toward nature, also tends to at least partially confirm White's second claim that the Middle Ages set a precedent for later Western economic productivity linked to efforts to control the natural world. Richard Hoffmann's most recent work demonstrates the multiple ways in which medieval people transformed their environment, including through the technological innovations discussed by White in *MTSC*, while making the Columbian encounter with a new world a decisive break with modern environmental history.[68] However, the language in some of his earlier work more closely mirrored White's emphasis on medieval aggressiveness in manipulating nature: "medieval Europeans anticipated many of the environmental relations now wrongly thought peculiar to a capitalist and post-industrial age," including a tendency to put aside an awareness of the social and environmental costs of satisfying consumer demand, and "medieval peasants thus ruptured a long-standing balance between humans and woodland and set an irreversible break in the history of Languedoc's environment."[69]

The work of medievalists has also gradually come to have an increasing impact on global environmental history, which has recently expanded to include both medieval Europe and religion more generally into its purview. The Wiley-Blackwell *Companion to Global Environmental History* (2012), for example, gives the Middle Ages its own chapter in the chronological section and includes five other chapters – those on forests, fishing and whaling, war, technology, and climate change – each of which discusses the European Middle Ages at some length.[70] The Blackwell *Companion* is also an index of a new attention to religion. Joachim Radkau writes that "religion has not yet received its due within environmental history" in that the literature has lacked a properly historical and empirical focus.[71] Both Radkau and J.R. McNeill, in the introduction to the same volume, reach back to Clarence J. Glacken's *Traces on the Rhodian Shore: Nature and Culture in Western*

---

67 For medieval technology, see n. 64 and for bibliography and a review of the field of medieval environmental history, see Hoffmann, *Environmental History*, and Ellen F. Arnold, "An Introduction to Medieval Environmental History," *History Compass* 6 (2008): 898–916.

68 Hoffmann, *Environmental History*, passim.

69 Richard C. Hoffmann, "Frontier Foods for Late Medieval Consumers: Culture, Economy, Ecology," *Environment and History* 7 (2001): 155; Hoffmann, "A Longer View," 145. Hoffmann notes in this article that Lynn White "never documented the causal links in his hypothesis" that Genesis 1:27 granting Adam "dominion" over Creation "released medieval Christian exploitation of Nature," 154, n. 2.

70 McNeill and Mauldin, *A Companion to Global Environmental History*.

71 Radkau, "Religion and Environmentalism," 493.

Thought from Ancient Times to the End of the 18th Century (1967), the same year as "Roots," as an example of what cultural medieval environmental history should look like.[72]

These separate trends – a new attention to the Middle Ages and a "cultural turn" within environmental history that includes religion – has offered a new opportunity to adapt White's insights to a more historically grounded examination of religious values as they interacted in concrete, often contingent, ways with environmental practices in specific times and places. This more nuanced approach goes beyond a simple rejection or acceptance of the argument of "Roots" to a closer look at White's more scholarly writings as well as that of other scholars of medieval technology and medieval environmental history. Michael Williams's *Deforesting the Earth: From Prehistory to Global Crisis* (2003) provides such an example.[73] Williams adopts White's language, celebratory tone, and much of the content of White's 1971 article "Cultural Climates and Technological Advance in the Middle Ages," using the idea of "cultural climates" as a framing construct, not only for his chapter on the Middle Ages but throughout the volume.[74] He thus shifts away from the environmentally conscious tone of "Roots" toward White's more typical emphasis on the creativity, energy, and aggressiveness represented by the massive land clearance of the high Middle Ages. Williams, following White, highlights medieval technological development, most clearly put into practice in the "agricultural revolution" of the Middle Ages, as the beginning of Western interest in the transformation of nature for human use and reiterates the link drawn by White and others among monasticism, piety, and land clearance.[75] At the same time, he avoids much of the reductionist element in White's work, emphasizing that an attitude of stewardship existed alongside an "ethic of appropriation" in the Middle Ages and warning against a too-easy acceptance of scholarly "heroic rhetoric" that "heighten[ed] the contrast between the natural and the newly humanized landscape."[76]

We are now at a considerable distance from the initial uproar created by "Roots," and it may now be possible to appreciate White's insistence that Christian views

---

72 McNeil, "Global Environmental History," in *Companion to Global Environmental History*, xxi, n. 3 calls Glacken "remarkably the most comprehensive work in this vein as regards the western world was written over 40 years ago"; Radkau, "Religion and Environmentalism," 494, describes Glacken's book as "unique in its quality." J. Donald Hughes also lauds Glacken's work, *What Is Environmental History?* 12.

73 Williams, *Deforesting the Earth*. The volume is also available as *Deforesting the Earth: From Prehistory to Global Crisis, An Abridgment* (Chicago: The University of Chicago Press, 2006).

74 Ibid., xxii. Like White, Williams regards cultural beliefs as largely unarticulated (147); for this aspect of White's thought, see Whitney, "Lynn White, Ecotheology, and History," 156.

75 Williams, *Deforesting the Earth*, 104–5, 110, 112–15, and 152.

76 Ibid., 118 and 166.

of nature promoted human use of nature while also resisting his causal premise and ideological baggage. This approach requires acknowledging that Christian values encompassed a range of attitudes toward the natural world that might be drawn upon with different emphases depending on historical circumstances, as well as recognizing the complex interactions between theoretical constructs and "values" and practices. James Beattie and John Stenhouse, for example, take this approach in their exploration of the intersection of religion and environmental history in the context of nineteenth-century colonial New Zealand. As Beattie and Stenhouse demonstrate, a storehouse of possible Christian approaches to nature might interact in diverse and complex ways with environmental practices. They conclude that White was indeed partly correct: British "ecological imperialism" was often legitimized by a "dominion theology" that promoted land improvement projects as a God-given duty to make the land more productive.[77] At the same time, Protestant community leaders often also used religious imagery and teachings to criticize environmental degradation, express a love of nature, and mobilize against the environmental consequences of colonization, thus complicating any simple view of Christianity as monolithically anti-environment.[78]

Environmental history, especially medieval environmental history, therefore, offers a corrective to "Roots" by anchoring the story of human interaction with nature in the concreteness of a specific time and place and by contextualizing religious attitudes relevant to environmental ethics. "Roots," on the other hand, and its continuing influence provide a reminder of the power of religion to motivate, rationalize, and justify human behavior toward the natural world. Only by seeing religious values as both cause and effect of human engagement with the natural world can we get beyond the impasse created by responses to "Roots" that single-mindedly focused on Christianity as either the sole cause of environmental damage or as entirely irrelevant.[79] Similarly, the Middle Ages must be recognized as neither coextensive with modernity nor wholly antithetical to the modern but as complex, differentiated, and multifaceted as any other period of history. Medieval historians have already "gotten beyond Lynn White" while still appreciating his enormous contributions to the field; it is time for everyone else to catch up.

---

77 James Beattie and John Stenhouse, "Empire, Environment and Religion: God and the Natural World in Nineteenth-Century New Zealand," *Environment and History* 13 (2007): 414 and 431.

78 Ibid.

79 A comparable point was made by Todd Levasseur and Anna Peterson, "Introduction," in *Religion and Ecological Crisis*, eds., LeVasseur and Peterson, 1–17.

Chapter 4
Determined disjunction
Lynn White's *Medieval Technology and Social Change* then and now

Steven A. Walton

Lynn Townsend White, Jr.'s short book *Medieval Technology and Social Change* (*MTSC*) was published by Oxford University Press just over fifty years ago, and the trajectory of its popularity over half a century helps shed light on the study of medieval technology, a discipline it, and he, largely helped create. It is a short volume of only 40,000 words in 140 pages, and of those, some nearly half are references and apparatus. As one of the early reviews noted, it was "a trail-blazer rather than a monograph," and perhaps it is that brevity that contributed to how quickly its inherent points were absorbed.[1] It gave medievalists a reason to be proud of their own period and region by showing how important it was, by 'rescuing' the Middle Ages from the benign tyranny of the classicists and modernists. More broadly, it became a core argument for many broader occidentalists such as those teaching "Western Civ" at the time and since to make the point that there was indeed something special about Europe and that its 'takeoff' (in the Rostowian economic and especially technological sense) could be traced to the Middle Ages. That many of *MTSC*'s conclusions have been shown to be less than entirely durable in the last half century has certainly diminished its stature, although even with that seemingly damning baggage, it has remained quite enduring. White's densely argued little tome, with dual footnotes and material drawn from political, military, church, and art history, as well as archaeology, anthropology, linguistics, and numerous other fields, has enlivened, encouraged, and even enraged scholars since its publication. It is that influence that needs to be understood.

MTSC put the study of medieval technology on the map in the English-speaking world, and although it has been somewhat eclipsed over time – one recent survey of late antique technology only invokes his work once to note that most scholarship has moved away from White's and M.I. Finley's views that saw the ancient

---

1 M.A. Hoskin, "[Review] Medieval Technology and Social Change," *The English Historical Review* 79, no. 310 (1964): 139.

world as stagnant technologically[2] – it is fitting to reflect on how far the field has come since 1962 and to ask where it is going (recalling, of course, that of all the muses, Clio was the only one without the gift of foresight). White has been an entrée for many scholars into the various technical studies in the Middle Ages, but rather than center them in a self-defined field of 'medieval technology,' many have moved outward toward other fields, orbiting only in his gravitational well.

To continue this entirely extraterrestrial comparison – one that White himself would approve of, given his own predilection for ambitious metaphors (see the conclusion of this chapter) – we might well ask whether medieval technology is a nebula or a neutron star. Both have a gravitational field, but the nebula is a centrifugal system, flinging its matter outward: sometimes connected yet forming hazy, indefinable patterns of an interstellar cloud and sometimes channeled into well-defined and distinguishable arms like the currents in the sea of the (intellectual) galaxy. Neutron stars, on the other hand, have a dense gravity well that draws everything near them into their mass. This very metaphor, relying as it does on a comfort with astrophysics of at least a level like that of Carl Sagan's *Cosmos*, suggests the level at which White was hoping to have a societal conversation. In the age of the Space Race when he was writing, that particular metaphor resonated widely; today he might have resorted to the metaphor of DNA. Indeed, White was one of those scholars of the 1960s and 1970s who deeply believed that historians of any period could be relevant contributors to policy debates of his day. His publications also reflect a society then ready to attend to new technologies of spaceflight, supersonic aircraft, computers, or the new technologies of war (Vietnam) or peace (electronic music), as well as the growing awareness of the limits of technology, as in *Silent Spring*, the Organization of Petroleum Exporting Countries' oil crisis, or antinuclear protests.[3] Regardless, White's willingness to merge multiple fields of study into one was ambitious at the time, and one wonders whether the same could work today. These concerns, properly addressed, may help us understand where the field came from in order to understand where it is going. It will stand or fall on its own merits, of course, but as Jefferson said, an unexamined life is not worth living; who better to examine one's own academic life than historians?

MTSC is divided into three chapters: one on the stirrup revolutionizing mounted shock combat and feudal warfare and hence the feudal system; one on the agricultural revolutions of the plow, horse harnessing, and field rotation; and one of the growth of Western machines and the harnessing of mechanical power sources. Each

---

2 Luke Lavan, Enrico Zanini, and Alexander Constantine Sarantis, *Technology in Transition: A.D. 300–650* (Leiden: Brill, 2007), xvi.

3 See Lynn White, Jr., "Technology Assessment from the Stance of a Medieval Historian," *The American Historical Review* 79, no. 1 (1974): 1–13, as well as Norman F. Cantor, "Medieval Historiography as Modern Political and Social Thought," *Journal of Contemporary History* 3, no. 2 (1968): 55–73.

drew on textual, archaeological, and philosophical ideas for support. These chapters have each spawned their own industry and very few scholars have tried to take on White's whole synthetic (or implied) thesis as a whole. Perhaps this is not surprising, since the three chapters are quite distinct in the original work; those who work on one are less likely to work on one of the others. White's other studies were also eclectic and ranged across time and space, tying the European Middle Ages to such far-flung eras as the expansion of the American West and reflections on classical Buddhist technology in the Himalayas. That disjunction helps explain both the broad reach of the then nascent field of medieval technology studies and its subsequent diffuse institutional existence. It would be rare even in today's academic climate of global studies to find someone who works on military history, agricultural history, and engineering history, even if under one chronological and geographical umbrella. For a scholar in the second third of the twentieth century, however, such an approach was pregnant with possibilities. Comparing some of the immediate reactions to the work through reviews of *MTSC*, we can *see* how it entered the citation literature and popular context and see what White did, perhaps how he was able to do what he did, and where the field might go from here.

The 1962 book was translated into Italian, German, and French reaching those audiences rather quickly; Spanish and Japanese editions followed in the 1970s and 1980s. The book has remained in print continuously since its release by Oxford University Press and they have sold over 30,000 copies to date, with hundreds sold every year still today.[4] In a nod to modern concern for metrics, its sales rank at Amazon over four recent years has been increasing from nearly 400,000 to now nearly 80,000. By comparison, Gies and Gies's popular textbook, *Cathedral, Forge and Waterwheel*, has also seen a rise in sales from a rank of 330,000 to 44,000, and Gimpel's *The Medieval Machine* has always remained a distant competitor with a rank in the 800,000 to 900,000 range (a similarly brief, pregnant work, Carlo Cipolla's *Guns, Sails and Empires*, had been in the mid-200,000 range but has recently fallen to 1.2 million). These numbers probably also have some correlation to course adoption choices and the recent uptick may presage a slight revival in that regard. Still, the field of medieval technology has a long way to go to catch, for example, Jared Diamond's best-seller, *Guns, Germs, and Steel*, which has a sales rank in the upper hundreds.[5]

The fortunes of *MTSC* are a combined function of its value as scholarship and its value as a teaching tool. Its value for the latter is more relevant today, while its

---

4 Elyse Turr, Humanities Marketing Dept. Oxford University Press, pers. comm., May 8, 2012.

5 The sales ranks at Amazon can be quite volatile, as the following comparison shows. For each book, the three numbers are for May 2012, January 2014, and January 2016: White: #394,218/#194,661/#82,862; Cippola: #228,731/#251,200/#1,258,311; Gies and Gies: #332,556/#148,618/#44,201; Gimpel: #969,138/#827,200/#878,606; and Diamond: #2,650/#637/#716. We might take some solace in the growth in rankings of medieval technology books in general.

direct role for furthering scholarship now seems more limited. Furthermore, it is a product of an era whose scholarship is now in a digital shadowland. Because *MTSC* came out in the 1960s, the generations of scholars initially influenced by it came of academic age in the 1960s and the 1970s (and thus their careers mostly ran their course in the profession by the turn of the century). Separately and subsequently, a possibly tectonic shift occurred in both historiography and historical methods. While White's concerns were always tied to intellectual history, they were also very much compatible with the turn to social and cultural history that arrived in the 1960s and 1970s,[6] although his polymathic and eclectic reading and ability to bring together truly diverse sources of support for a thesis became less appealing as academic disciplines pushed for more and more internal rigor at the same time. On the other hand, his reach to archaeology and art historical sources does resonate well with the 'material turn' in history in the last decade or so.

One other subsequent shift may both explain some of the recent eclipse of *MTSC* yet could also presage a revival of its broad methodology. *MTSC* has in some ways not made the transition to the digital age. Its citation rate probably also understates the problem we find ourselves in now. Because *MTSC* is such a broad, sweeping text, dense with disparate data points from which White wove a pattern, it has fallen into the category of pre-internet production that our culture has assigned to the midden of knowledge in our headlong rush into what we call progress in the digital age (but which others might call knowledge suicide). That is, we are developing a sort of selective historical memory due to online deposition of information (as in archaeology and the stratigraphy of knowledge) in which copyrighted products of the mid-twentieth century that were not produced digitally are considerably less visible. On the other hand, the twenty-first-century shift toward approaching a preconceived topic and deductively researching it through keyword searching and following threads of information through digital sources rather than the more inductive pattern recognition from systemic reading as White practiced (with no doubt then specialized searching after that) may well revitalize the sort of polymathic sourcing that White was so good at. We certainly see this eclecticism forming in undergraduate information literacy practices, although whether the academic disciplines will recognize it or police it remains to be seen.[7]

On the teaching side, those historians who witnessed the arrival of *MTSC* and medieval technology studies first- or even secondhand used the volume and some or all of its case studies as one foundation stone for many undergraduate classes on the Middle Ages. A generation taught about the dynamism of an age and could tell the romantic tale of the stirrup and shock combat and of the less exciting but 'scientific' three-field system, and this helped them revivify as well as re-legitimate

---

6 Harvey J. Graff, "The Shock of the " 'New' (Histories)": Social Science Histories and Historical Literacies," *Social Science History* 25, no. 4 (2001): 483–533.

7 For just one just glimpse at this characteristic, see Carey Jewitt, "Multimodality and Literacy in School Classrooms," *Review of Research in Education* 32 (2008): 241–67.

the misnamed 'Dark Ages.'[8] Although the overall strength of medieval studies as a whole today seems to make that struggle less necessary and we might see *MTSC* as being able to say, "my work here is done" (*pace* Lone Ranger), though classics have certainly lost cultural capital today and even Renaissance gold shines slightly less brightly.[9] At the same time, the generational change as scholars retire, not always to be replaced with like for like, means that courses that might have used *MTSC* as a staple for introducing undergraduates to medieval technology and society may themselves have been retired for more global history courses. For those courses that remain, *MTSC* may disappear as supplemental reading lists shift to more contemporary works.

Early reviews of *MTSC*

When *MTSC* was published, it was sent to all the important journals of the day, and over the next two years, received reviews from a full dozen of them.[10] It was reviewed by *the* big names in medieval science and economic history: Thorndike, Needham, Claggett, and Herlihy. It is also noticeable *where* it was reviewed: in the historical journals as you would expect, including the *American Historical Review*, the *English Historical Review*, the *Economic Historical Review*, and *Speculum*, as well as in specialist history of science, technology, and agriculture journals such as *Isis*, *Technology & Culture*, and *Agricultural History*. But it was also reviewed in anthropology and sociology journals and even in the *American Scientist*.

The reviews themselves are fascinating to read and some are mostly quite effusively positive. Just over half the reviews were glowing, three were mixed, and two were decidedly damning. The work is called "readable, epigrammatic, and

---

8   Even though the whole historiography of the Middle Ages is fraught, that usually does not deter a good undergraduate lecture that uses the shorthand for the period. See for example, Elizabeth A.R. Brown, "The Tyranny of a Construct: Feudalism and Historians of Medieval Europe," *The American Historical Review* 79, no. 4 (1974): 1063–88.

9   Paula Findlen and Kenneth Gouwens, "Introduction: The Persistence of the Renaissance," *The American Historical Review* 103, no. 1 (1998): 51–54.

10   R. Bridbury in *The Economic History Review* 15, no. 2 (1962): 371–72; James Lea Cate in *American Scientist* 50, no. 4 (1962): 454A–456A; George C. Homans in *American Journal of Sociology* 68, no. 3 (1962): 396–97; Lynn Thorndike in *The American Historical Review* 68, no. 1 (1962): 93–94; Robert Reynolds in *Manuscripta* 6, no. 3 (1962): 172–73; Malcolm F. Farmer in *American Anthropologist* 65, no. 4 (1963): 982–83; L. Carrington Goodrich in *Journal of the American Oriental Society* 83, no. 3 (1963): 384–85; David Herlihy in *Agricultural History* 37, no. 1 (1963): 43–45; Joseph Needham in *Isis* 54, no. 3 (1963): 418–20; Joseph R. Strayer in *Technology and Culture* 4, no. 1 (1963): 62–65; Marshall Clagett in *Speculum* 39, no. 2 (1964): 359–65; and M.A. Hoskin in *The English Historical Review* 79, no. 310 (1964): 139. For full list, see the bio-bibliography of White and his works at the opening of this volume, pp. 17–18.

humorous,"[11] "an almost perfect example of what work in the history of technology should be",[12] and reviewers flagged White's learning as "breath-takingly impressive."[13] Even criticisms are muted: "If the book is one-sided in its approach, it is because it is the work of a missionary [that] will breathe life into what is often an antiquarian and isolated pursuit."[14] Some reviews are "a product of their time," which is to say downright strange: Joseph Needham wrote that ever since White's 1940 *Speculum* article on medieval invention,

> [e]veryone knew that . . . [he] could some day produce a glorious enlargement of [that article], but so long as the attendant nymphs of Mills College swelled his train this was not possible. Now from his ca-the-dra-tical seat in California he has given us the most stimulating book of the century on the history of technology.[15]

Some reviewers were convinced by the overall arguments White put forth, even if they found reason to argue with each and every one of them, an interesting view of simultaneous preconceptions on the part of the author and reader.[16] The same review that noted White's breath-taking impressiveness then countered by saying that the "unsurpassed bibliography of the subjects with which he deals is unfortunately the best that can be said of Mr. White's book. There are three chapters of steadily declining quality".[17] Needham made an oblique mention of White's tendency to state, clearly, a testable hypothesis, rather than "a quantity of vague ideas mixed up with a mass of facts in confused uncertainty," which had – amazingly – "been enough to incense some reviewers of the present book, notably, . . . on the eastern shores of the Atlantic." Some reviewers falsely (or mistakenly) accused *MTSC* of being based solely on secondary sources, others chided White for cherry-picking or seeing causality where only correlation existed, and others complained that such a short book held mere ideas rather than a proven argument.

MTSC came out just at the same moment that the massive *Oxford History of Technology* (5 vols. 1954–78), edited by Charles Joseph Singer, was rolling off

---

11   Lynn Thorndike, "[Review] Medieval Technology and Social Change," *The American Historical Review* 68, no. 1 (1962): 93–94.

12   Joseph R. Strayer, "[Untitled]," *Technology and Culture* 4, no. 1 (1963).

13   A.R. Bridbury, "Review of *Medieval Technology and Social Change*," *The Economic History Review* 15, no. 2 (1962): 371–72.

14   Hoskin, "[Review] Medieval Technology and Social Change."

15   Joseph Needham, "[Review] Medieval Technology and Social Change," *Isis* 54, no. 3 (1963). referring back to Lynn White, Jr., "Technology and Invention in the Middle Ages," *Speculum* 15, no. 2 (1940). White was president of Mills College in Oakland, California, from 1943 to 1958 and Mills remained all-female until 1990. The "ca-the-dra-tical seat" Needham refers to is White's position at UCLA.

16   George C. Homans, "[Review] Medieval Technology and Social Change," *American Journal of Sociology* 68, no. 3 (1962): 396–97.

17   Bridbury, "Review of *Medieval Technology and Social Change*."

the same press. Marshall Claggett recognized that White was "not satisfied merely to examine the historical development of each of the technological innovations within the sphere of technology alone" but rather wanted to "assay the importance of these innovations for the growth of mediaeval institutions."[18] Thus, he explicitly suggested that White's slim third section on mechanical invention should be read in conjunction with the chapters on 'power' and 'machines' in the medieval volume of Singer's *History of Technology*.[19]

The most damning of the review was P.H. Sawyer and R.H. Hilton's 10-page review in *Past & Present*, a review that was *so* damning it got its own title: "Technical Determinism: The Stirrup and the Plough."[20] Put briefly, they took White to task for arguing that a change in technology *caused* a change in society and for implying that such changes were the inevitable consequence of those technologies. Suffice to say that their well-merited criticisms spawned a whole industry contemplating the distinction between hard determinism (technology *causes*) and soft determinism (technology *predisposes*), but despite strong avowals of human autonomy and denials that we are *ever* determined *by* technology, we still quite casually speak and act as if we are.[21] Even those who do not take White explicitly to task for deterministic arguments do place him within the "functionalist" camp, where "culture is primarily a means of adapting to environment with technology as the primary adaptive mechanism."[22]

The second-most damning review appeared in the *Economic History Review*, where A.R. Bridbury said the "fundamental defect" of *MTSC* was that White "blithely ignored the devastating implications of his own remarks." He turned White's famous line, "a new device merely opens a door; it does not compel one to enter," on its ear, to say that White himself had not gone through the door to see what he himself was arguing. But Lynn Thorndike quite rightly noted that "White [had] said the last word on nothing," knowing full well that he had never intended to do so in such a short work. Thorndike then proceeded to quite congenially agree to disagree about specifics on Danish horse collars, seventeenth-century steam power,

---

18   Marshall Clagett, "Nicole Oresme and Medieval Scientific Thought," *Proceedings of the American Philosophical Society* 108, no. 4 (1964): 298–309.

19   R.J. Forbes, "Power," 589–628 and Bertrand Gille, "Machines," 629–62, both in Charles Singer, E.J. Holmyard, A.R. Hall, and Trevor I. Williams, eds., *A History of Technology, Vol. 2: The Mediterranean Civilizations and to the Middle Ages c. 700 B.C. to c. A.D. 1500* (Oxford: Oxford University Press, 1956).

20   P.H. Sawyer and R.H. Hilton, "Technical Determinism: The Stirrup and the Plough," *Past & Present*, no. 24 (1963): 90–100.

21   For the debate, see, in general, Merritt Roe Smith and Leo Marx, eds., *Does Technology Drive History? The Dilemma of Technological Determinism* (Cambridge, MA: MIT Press, 1994), and especially the two articles by Heilbronner therein that also take a relatively determinist position. Heibronner's first article was written the mid-1960s, as was *MTSC*, suggesting that perhaps technological determinism was more acceptable to scholars in that era, whereas by the 1980s it had become objectionable.

22   Thomas J. Schlereth, "Material Culture Studies and Social History Research," *Journal of Social History* 16, no. 4 (1983): 122–23.

Cambodian crossbowmen, and the crank in Han China, all of which White had cited as evidence of technological innovations and attitudes. That White ranged across all of Eurasia and the tenth to the seventeenth centuries shows the kind of breadth White tossed out in *MTSC*, but this may also explain why his effect has been so broad and diffuse.

It was this diffuse approach that seems to have gotten up the nose of many 'traditional' historians of the time. Reviewers noticed that while many were excited about *MTSC*, others were having "anguished responses",[23] difficulty with White's "curious and rather contradictory" phrasing (*e.g.*, semi-feudal intuitions being "scattered thickly"),[24] or "rather peculiar" organization of the book.[25] In other cases, even general medievalists picked up on the fact that archaeologists would take immediate issue with White's limited examples. In the end, however, that ultimately has been less of a problem, as more archaeological evidence, either pro or con, has been slow to appear. One case in point is that of the cranked automatic marble sawmills in the Byzantine world which have only come to light in the last decades.[26]

Frequency analysis

Today, digital data for all forms of scholarship are increasing at an exponential rate and a number of repositories allow us to find indications of older works' staying power and diffusion. These and more traditional indices allow for citation analysis of *MTSC* and medieval technology in general and provide a curious but fairly positive picture of its impact. *MTSC* has a respectable 1,956 re-citations in Google Scholar as of the end of 2017, but while White does have entries in the *Science Citation Index* (*SCI*), oddly none of them are for *MTSC* or his other medieval technology (or even science) writings, Instead, *SCI* only captures some of his (and his father's) broader policy writings for specific journals in education and library studies from 1939 to 1955.

Another digital repository of the written word, Google Books, can be visualized using n-grams, a concept from computational linguistics that looks at the frequency of occurrences of a word or phrase in a textual corpus. Using the many, many books digitized by Google (currently it has crested 25 million), Google programmers have parsed the data so that words' and phrases' relative frequency of occurrence in each year can be graphically displayed, thus showing the rise and fall in relative popularity – quite literally showing how much attention is being

---

23 Clagett, "Nicole Oresme and Medieval Scientific Thought," referring to those who saw the "development of mediaeval institutions in a more conventional perspective."
24 Ibid.
25 Thorndike, "[Review] Medieval Technology and Social Change."
26 See George Brooks, "Of Cranks and Crankshafts: Lynn White, Jr. and the Curious Question of Mechanical Power Transmission," this volume, pp. 106–32.

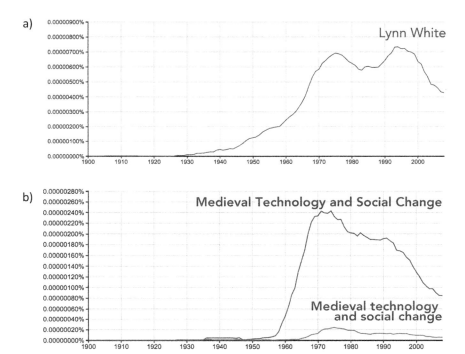

Figure 4.1 Frequency of use of terms linked to the study of Lynn White and *Medieval Technology and Social Change*, 1900–2008

Source: From Google Books N-gram Viewer (http://books.google.com/ngrams).

Note: All searches show a five-year moving average.

paid to a topic at any given time.[27] If one searches for "Lynn White," for example, one can see that his name (or, strictly speaking, *that phrase*, which, in a relatively unique case like this, can be taken as representative of the medievalist) grows in increasing popularity (*i.e.*, citation frequency) from the 1930s (clearly referring to his father) to the mid-1970s, experiences a slight flagging, and then resurges into the early 1990s, and then falls away rather precipitously in the early twenty-first

---

27 Jean-Baptiste Michel, et al., "Quantitative Analysis of Culture Using Millions of Digitized Books," *Science* 331, no. 6014 (2010): 176–82. More recent scholarship has tempered this optimism, although for the qualitative trends noted here, their caveats are not too damning: E.A. Pechenick, C.M. Danforth, and P.S. Dodds, "Characterizing the Google Books Corpus: Strong Limits to Inferences of Socio-Cultural and Linguistic Evolution," *PLoS ONE* 10, no. 10 (2015): e0137041.

century (Figure 4.1). When one searches for the (case-sensitive) title of *MTSC*, its meteoric rise in popularity in the 1960s becomes manifestly evident (Figure 4.1).[28] Its fate, however, after 1970 and especially after 1990, is clear: *MTSC* is being talked about less and less every year.

N-grams also illuminate the appearance of the concept of 'medieval technology' (Figure 4.2a). The phrase is not to be found before the twentieth century (recall that 'technology' itself is a nineteenth-century neologism, and it was not until the twentieth century that the phrase 'medieval technology' stopped being an oxymoron to many people) and is only incidentally found before the middle of the century. Beginning about 1930, the phrase starts to appear and climb steadily to about 1980. In fact, it is worth noting that the appearance of *MTSC* in 1962 is not apparently recorded in the frequency of the term overall. This data is smoothed with a 5-year running average, so individual years may have considerable variability (*e.g.*, 1963 shows an individual spike, which likely *is* a reaction to the publication of *MTSC*), but the overall trend is clear that medieval technology came into its own quite smoothly in the middle of the twentieth century. Why it peaked about 1990, or was more volatile in the 1980s, on the other hand, is less clear. Figure 4.2b helps explain a bit more. The frequency of *medieval* and *technology* over the twentieth century shows that in ways, 'medieval' technology's overall n-gram is merely a reflection of the overall appearance of the term *technology*, *medieval* having remained fairly constant (or, if anything, slightly more popular in the 1960s than in 1980) throughout the century. Terminologies change over time, and the individual bits of medieval material culture and writings about mechanical things studied as 'technology' in the late twentieth century would have been more likely to have been referred to as 'manual arts' (popular *ca.*1900–50) or 'industrial arts' (a term appearing in the 1840s and used broadly until 1910, when it became phenomenally more common until the 1970s).[29] *Technology*, however, as a general term for all these matters, proportionally eclipses both these phrases in the 1930s. In some ways, then, White was responding to growing concept within his own chronological and geographical field more than creating it in talking about the 'technology' *of* the Middle Ages.

To bring the analysis back to White and his influence, however, a comparison of the frequency of *medieval technology* against *medieval science* demonstrates the field's place in the relatively narrow band of academia known as the history

---

28 That the title seems to exist before 1962 when the book was published is due to cataloguing errors or peculiarities in Google Books, such as indexing the 1988 second edition of C.C. Gillispie's, *The Edge of Objectivity*, which cited *MTSC* as being from 1960, the date of the first edition (which obviously did not cite it).

29 For example, Thomas Benfield Harbottle, *The Industrial Arts of the Anglo-Saxons* (London: S. Sonnenschein & Co., 1893). The latter usage is likely for the idea of 'shop class' which arose in the 1920s and '30s: Patrick N. Foster, "The Founders of Industrial Arts in the U.S.," *Journal of Technology Education* 7, no. 1 (1995): 6–21.

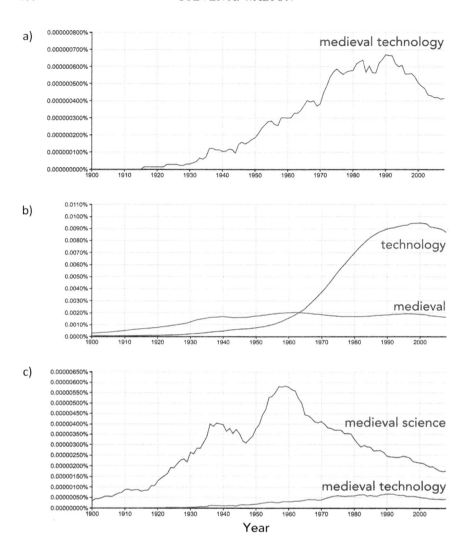

Figure 4.2 Frequency of use of terms linked to the study of medieval technology and science, 1900–2008

Source: From Google Books N-gram Viewer (http://books.google.com/ngrams).

Note: All searches show a five-year moving average.

of science and technology (Figure 4.2c). The use of the term *medieval science* grows steadily from the late nineteenth century to its peak just before 1960, after which it suffers a rather steady decline (the slow decline from 1935–45 seems to be a smoothing artifact of the general decline in scholarship during World War II; the phrase 'history of science' shows the same trend). That peak was the golden age of medieval science writing in the 1950s and 1960s, often connected to the strong research program and publications emanating from the University of Wisconsin. Medieval technology has always been a small cousin to medieval science, although that also reflects the general priority that the West and, in particular, the Cold War West and, especially, America, has put on science over technology.

Again, comparing the exponential growth (and yet again, leveling off) of the word *technology* compared to the word *medieval* alone (Figure 4.2b), one can begin to see how 'medieval technology' in general (and *MTSC*, specifically) is something like a mirror of *its* own time, as well as a window into the Middle Ages. The historiographical lesson one can derive from this parallels that which White himself derived about the Middle Ages: He argued that it was in the West just after the year 1000 (or maybe in selected places, a bit before) that people started consciously noticing and appreciating technology in their own culture. Similarly, the second half of the twentieth century seems to have done the same. It is worth noting here that the Society for the History of Technology (SHOT) was spun off the History of Science Society (HSS) in 1951, and not, as SHOT's mythology often had it, because HSS was ignoring technology but because SHOT's founders specifically wanted to separate studies of technology from studies of science.[30] And on this note, it is worth pointing out here that White was a founding member and then president of SHOT from 1960 to 1962, just as *MTSC* was in preparation. Thus, in both the early second millennium and in the mid-twentieth century, people *chose* to start paying attention to technology. And in that, White's *MTSC* can be seen as both a groundbreaking analysis of the Middle Ages and a reflection of the era in which it was written.

International medieval bibliography

Moving to a more academic data source, by 2012, fifty years after the publication of *MTSC*, the *International Medieval Bibliography* (*IMB* online) offered only four hits on later works referencing "Lynn White" and only captures one of White's own works, the collection of essays from 1968, *Machina ex Deo*. The *IMB*'s earlier print version, however, records dozens of White's own writings, though its indexing does not lead straight to secondary works which responded to *MTSC* (thus showing another tradeoff between the new technology and the old). The bibliometric search of the print volumes between 1968 and 2003 demonstrates some intriguing trends (Figure 4.3). Bibliographies are constructed entities and their use, particularly in the pre-digital age, reflected the choices and methodologies of their construction. Items have to be categorized, but bibliographers cannot indulge

---

30 Bruce E. Seely, "SHOT, the History of Technology, and Engineering Education," *Technology and Culture* 36, no. 4 (1995): 739–72 and Steven W. Usselman, "From Sputnik to SCOT: The Historiography of American Technology," *OAH Magazine of History* 24, no. 3 (2010): 9–14.

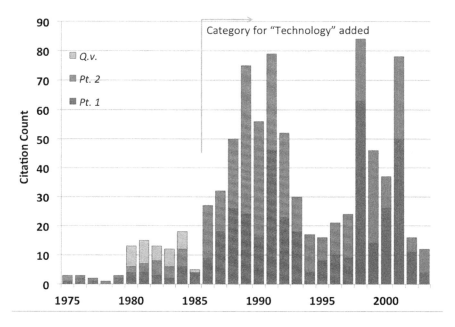

Figure 4.3 Count of entries related to 'Technology' in print version of the *International Medieval Bibliography*, 1968–2003

Note: there are no entries for 'Technology' from 1968–74.

in an infinite number of categories, so the evolution of an annual bibliography over time reveals how new categories affect the perception of the corpus of knowledge and can possibly show when groupings that received category status became self-evident or, alternately, became fragmented and faded away.

In 1968 the *IMB* had no category or entry for 'Technology.' There are citations on technological subjects such as architecture, mills, industries, transport, and so on, some as their own division within the bibliography or a named subdivision. Many of the papers on technological subjects also get subsumed under 'Economics,' 'Military,' or 'Daily Life.' At this time and until 1970, there was also no heading for 'Science', its content being subsumed under the category 'Intellectual', which also included philosophy and theology. Papers on medieval topics from SHOT's journal *Technology & Culture*, for example, were indexed under 'Art, Architecture, & Archaeology.' At various points, the *IMB* reorganized its categories, reflecting in ways not only the shifts in the wider field but also the proclivities of the editors.[31] It took until 1975 for an entry to appear in the index for 'Technology'; there were only two entries.

---

31 For example, in 1970, 'Science' became its own category, and 'Art' was divided into 'Art – general,' 'Art – painting,' and 'Art – sculpture.'

Lynn White's papers were indexed under 'Economics, social,'[32] 'Economics – General,'[33] 'Science – General'[34] or '– Italy,'[35] 'Art – Painting – Italy,'[36] 'Daily Life – General,'[37] and Historiography – General.'[38] Somewhat amazingly, his 1969 paper, "Keyser's *Belefortis*: The First Technological Treatise of the Fifteenth Century," with the word *technology* explicitly in the title, was indexed under 'Intellectual', whereas the next year his collected essays from *Machina ex Deo*, were mostly listed under the new category 'Science' (they did admittedly put his "The Necessity of Witches" under 'Social – General'). The categorization as 'Science' made sense for his article on "The Context of Science," but then both his "The Contemplation of Technology" and "Iconography of *Temperantia* and the Virtuous of Technology," both from *Machina ex Deo*, also came under that heading, as did his "The Study of Medieval Technology, 1924–74, Personal Reflections" from a few years later. Technology studies well into the 1970s were subsumed under science, a feature of post–World War II intellectual history and one from which the history of technology would not break free until the 1980s; it still persists in popular imagination to some degree and also highlights why SHOT was so desperate to separate from HSS.[39]

The relationship of technology to medieval studies as a whole is also evident in the structure of the *IMB* and its evolution over time. 'Technology' appeared for the first time in 1975 with a handful of entries for the first few years, but then the editors added a 'see also' notation. With that, the aggregate numbers jumped so that by 1985 there were just over 100 citations for articles on technology in the *IMB* to date. Then the numbers suddenly dropped to nearly zero by 1995, begging the

---

32 "The Life of the Silent Majority," in *Life and Thought in the Early Middle Ages*, ed. Robert S. Hoyt (Minneapolis: University of Minnesota Press, 1967), 85–100 (IMB 1968.1 #1725).

33 "The Origins of the Coach," *APS Proceedings* 114, no. 6 (1970): 423–31 (IMB 1971.1 #1243).

34 "The Study of Medieval Technology, 1924–1974: Personal Reflections," *Technology and Culture* 16, no. 4 (1975): 519–30 (IMB 1975.2 #3299).

35 "The Flavor of Early Renaissance Technology," in *Developments in the Early Renaissance*, ed. Bernard Levy (Albany: SUNY Press, 1972), 36–57 (IMB 1974.2 #3972).

36 "Indic Elements in the Iconography of Petrarch's *Trionfo della Morte*," *Speculum* 49, no. 2 (1974): 201–21 (IMB 1974.1 #645).

37 "Death and the Devil," in *The Darker Vision of the Renaissance: Beyond the Fields of the Reason*, ed. Robert S. Kinsman (Berkeley: University of California Press, 1974), 25–74 (IMB 1975.2 #757).

38 "Technology Assessment from the Stance of a Medieval Historian" (IMB 1974.1 #1277).

39 For this very question being asked by the founders of SHOT, see Derek J. de Solla Price, "Is Technology Historically Independent of Science? A Study in Statistical Historiography," *Technology and Culture* 6, no. 4 (1965): 553–68 and Otto Mayr, "The Science-Technology Relationship as a Historiographic Problem," *Technology and Culture* 17, no. 4 (1976): 663–73.

question of whether the field collapsed, a new editor did not believe technology deserved its own heading, or some other factor was at work. There are currents in scholarship which led their appearance in such things as bibliographic indexing: medieval technology runs in waves just as other fields. Who, for example, could have predicted the twenty-first-century resurgence of magic studies in the Middle Ages or the cross-fertilization of disability studies into medieval studies?

In fact, the editors of the *IMB* believed in 'Technology' so strongly that they split it out as separate section in the serial's overall organization. From this point onward, the number of entries exploded. An annual count of at most two dozen now zoomed to nearly a hundred (and this does not count all the cross-references to 'see also' in these years). And yet this constant new organization showed a continued increase from 1985 to 1991 but then an apparent collapse of citations in the next six years. Then for the last six years of the *IMB*'s print existence the citation count went back up and down again. When the *IMB* went online, categorization ceased altogether in deference to keyword searchability.

It is hard to know whether the data should be read as a large interest in medieval technology from the late 1980s through 2000 with a lull in the mid-1990s, or two anomalous spikes of interest in the topic just before and after the year 2000 in an otherwise declined field after the early 1990s. And to confound such an interpretation, spikes such as those in 1998 and 2001 are often caused by a collected volume of a dozen or more essays coming out in that year – as, for example, D.R. Hill and D.A. King (eds.), *Studies in Medieval Islamic Technology* (Aldershot: Ashgate Variorum, 1998) – whose numerous individual articles seriously impact the counts. Such sources (*e.g.*, the series in which this volume appears) are just the sort of things that *IMB* is good at capturing and are a major and increasing publication venue within medieval studies in general. Individual spikes and troughs, then, may reflect more the volatility in the small baseline numbers for the field, as well as the vagaries of academic publishing. At any rate, the arrival of an *IMB* index term for 'Technology' in the 1980s very likely does reflect White's influence (recall that his larger collection of essays, *Medieval Religion and Technology*, appeared in 1978), though it is not as though no work was being done on medieval technology until the category 'Technology' itself was enunciated.[40]

Conclusion

There are times where Lynn White made statements that are fascinatingly philosophical but that transgress the boundaries of scholarly disciplines and especially chronologies. How many medievalists of the 1960s were willing to claim that "[t]o

---

40 In Figure 4.3, the average total citation count for 1975–1985 is 8.0, while that for 1986 to 2003 is 41.8, over five times as much, even with the troughs after 1993.

use a crank, our tendons and muscles must relate themselves to the motion of galaxies and electrons"? Or immediately follow that statement with a totalizing pronouncement that "[f]rom this inhuman adventure our race long recoiled"? White was willing, and he did so in *MTSC*.[41] One of the initial reviews seems to obliquely chide White for this sort of excess (and for shifting to administration for 15 years as having strayed outside the profession of real historians – although it positively did "welcome the author all the way back into the profession").[42]

It remains, then, to take final stock where White and *MTSC* stand for medievalists and medieval studies 50 years on from its publication. The book is accorded a formative place in the study of medieval technology, more esteemed for its original and lateral insights between disparate slivers of evidence than as broad amalgamation of the field of medieval technology.[43] Pamela Long calls it "massively influential" and emphasizes his impact on "numerous other historians of technology as well as the perceptions of the general public."[44] Yet at the same time it is often more recognized for its pioneering syntheses than its lasting research. It is very much cited in summary studies medieval military technology, even if its concise story of the stirrup and feudalism is imparted to students on one breath only to be dismissed as too simplistic in the next. It has become the poster child – derided, sometimes, unfairly – in the study of technological determinism, yet it resists decades of attempts to dismiss it.[45]

---

41 White, *MTSC*, 118.

42 Robert Reynolds, "[Review] Medieval Technology and Social Change," *Manuscripta* 6, no. 3 (1962): 172–73. This seems to be referring to White's publications while president of Mills College, where he was more interested in contemporary education concerns: L. White, "The School Library and the Gifted Child," *Library Journal* 78, no. 16 (1953); Lynn White, Jr., "The Changing Context of Women's Education," *Marriage and Family Living* 17, no. 4 (1955); and Lynn White, *Educating Our Daughters: A Challenge to the Colleges* (New York: Harper & Row, 1950).

43 Here I am thinking of the more textbook-like Jean Gimpel, *The Medieval Machine: The Industrial Revolution of the Middle Ages* (New York: Holt, Rinehart and Winston, 1976) and the explicit textbook by Frances and Joseph Gies, *Cathedral, Forge, and Waterwheel: Technology and Invention in the Middle Ages* (New York: HarperCollins Publishers, 1994). This is not to deny the insights of Gimpel nor the direct debt White owed to Marc Bloch and Lefebvre des Noettes (see Pamela O. Long, "The Craft of Premodern European History of Technology: Past and Future Practice," *Technology and Culture* 51, no. 3 [2010]: 698–714 at 701, esp. 699–702), but White pitched his work more firmly at an academic readership than Gimpel or the Gies did.

44 Long, "The Craft of Premodern European History of Technology," 701. Still, Long found no place to cite it or speak of White's historiographical position in her booklet, *Technology, Society, and Culture in Late Medieval and Renaissance Europe, 1300–1600*, AHA/SHOT Historical Perspectives on Technology, Society and Culture 1 (Washington, DC: Society for the History of Technology and the American Historical Association, 2000).

45 Smith and Marx, eds., *Does Technology Drive History?*

White's other works spawned continuing discussion (notably his "Historical Roots of our Ecological Crisis" article), while *MTSC* seems to have achieved a sort of emeritus status. Long put it nicely in noting that "the history of technology in medieval and late medieval Europe remains a flourishing field of study, or, more accurately, a thriving *aggregate* of fields."[46] That she had to rephrase that is a cue to where *MTSC*'s legacy lies. The insights that White imparted and that inspired now at least three generations of scholars are indeed thriving but in separate areas that too infrequently talk to one another. This has already been recognized for the interface between classical and medieval studies of technology,[47] but it needs to be recognized for other areas as well. Whether scholars can capitalize on this cross-fertilization between the myriad subgenres that make up this "aggregate of fields" remains to be seen, but if White's work has value, it should be in showing us that specialization breeds myopia and while daring to link disparate fields and methodologies into an argument may run the risk of overstating one's hypothesis on occasion, we should not fear the attempt.

Marshall Claggett was quite right that *MTSC* was a "book will generate excitement and controversy for some time to come,"[48] and even if its direct citation is indeed waning, the long shadow of its influence continues to frame medieval technological studies and undergraduate medieval surveys alike. *MTSC* and White's other essays are worth rereading, and his footnotes worth re-mining, even in this day and age of digital searching. This is true not only for appreciating his achievement of gathering and interpreting remarkably diverse source material but also for the numerous insightful comments White made that would be well worth pursuing again today.

---

46 Long, "The Craft of Premodern European History of Technology," 707, emphasis added.

47 Steven A. Walton, "Review Essay: The Greeneian Reappraisal of the Context of Medieval Technology," *AVISTA Forum Journal* 14, no. 1 (2004): 25–28, referencing numerous articles by Kevin Greene on the topic.

48 Clagett, "Nicole Oresme and Medieval Scientific Thought."

Chapter 5

Of cranks and crankshafts
Lynn White, Jr. and the curious question of mechanical power transmission

George Brooks

It seems incredible to most people that such a seemingly simple and useful device as the crank was not invented early in human history. Rather, it seemed that it was not until the so-called medieval mechanical revolution that some practical person attached one stick at a right angle to the axle of a rotary device, and another at a right angle to the first for a handle, and the crank was born. Historians puzzled over its absence in the ancient world, and since the field of history of technology came into existence have tried to explain that absence. The evidence available to historians during most of the twentieth century included no clear examples of the use of either hand cranks by individuals or the mechanical crank-and-connecting-rod arrangement in any ancient machine. But then evidence of hand and mechanical cranking appeared in the early Middle Ages and subsequent examples slowly multiplied in their number and in their variety of applications until, by the close of the medieval period, the crank had become firmly established among the elements of machine design.

Arguably the strangest explanation for the seeming lack of ancient cranking and the subsequent adoption of this method in the Middle Ages is found in Lynn White, Jr.'s *Medieval Technology and Social Change* (1962). In the third and final chapter on "medieval exploration of mechanical power," White surveyed the evidence that was then available for medieval industrial mechanical devices and then turned to the question of "the development of machine design." This section begins with thirteen pages exploring the problem of the mechanical crank in antiquity and the Middle Ages. At the outset of this discussion, White alerts the reader to the unorthodox conclusion to which he was building: "[t]he crank is profoundly puzzling not only historically but psychologically: the human mind seems to shy away from it."[1] And, after rehearsing the evidence, he draws this final, grand conclusion:

---

1 Lynn White, Jr., *Medieval Technology and Social Change* [hereafter *MTSC*] (Oxford: Oxford University Press, 1962), 104.

> Continuous rotary motion is typical of inorganic matter, whereas reciprocating motion is the sole form of movement found in living things. The crank connects these two kinds of motion; therefore we who are organic find that crank motion does not come easily to us. . . . To use a crank, our tendons and muscles must relate themselves to the motion of galaxies and electrons. From this inhuman adventure our race long recoiled.
>
> (115)

This conclusion, surely among the most far-reaching utterances made by a historian of technology, was an attempt to address part of the larger and most vexing problems brought to light by White's research: *Why* did industrial technology come to a robust maturity in the medieval era, and why was such enthusiasm for mechanical solutions to basic human concerns lacking in the ancient world?

The collective impact of the work of Lynn White was to popularize the idea that medieval people possessed a uniquely enthusiastic attitude toward technological innovation, an attitude he found rooted in certain special qualities of Latin Christendom: *dynamism* is the term that he often returned to in his descriptions, and there is some justification for this. The Romans had been astute enough to adopt the obviously useful water-powered corn mill developed by Hellenistic engineers, but although they made widespread use of this device, there seemed to be little evidence of further innovation beyond its original application. Medieval builders, by stunning contrast, inherited these machines and not only kept them in operation even during the early medieval period but also presided over the adaptation of corn mills into a variety of more complex mechanisms that brought technological power to a multitude of industries: sawmills, fulling mills, mash mills, water-powered bellows and forge-hammers, bark mills, hemp mills and more. These were not just a surprising number of industrial machines, but a family of interrelated devices that had sprung from what appeared to be an ancient, but sorely under-diversified, parent machine.

The dynamism of medieval builders did not end with the development of varied forms of hydraulic industrial technology. It also led them to tap the wind as a source of power, and once introduced sometime in the twelfth century, windmills quickly filled the landscapes of northern Europe and England. Even the force of gravity was harnessed in the triumphant climax of medieval fine engineering: the mechanical clock. By the close of the medieval period, the technology of the magnetic compass, gunpowder, and printing, all borrowed from the Orient but eagerly embraced and further developed in Europe, would empower the Occident to embark on voyages of discovery and conquest that would circle the globe. It is beyond debate that Western civilization, for better or worse, was able to achieve the unquestioned global dominance it would enjoy for centuries because of the industrial foundation established during the Middle Ages. Lynn White, Jr., over the course of his career, labored to explain why medieval society was able to do what the ancients had not.

The belief in the unique dynamism of the medieval West saturates White's *MTSC*, but the essence of his belief was neatly stated in an essay published four years earlier in *The American Scholar*, with a title that itself seems to be a distillation of

White's thinking: "Dynamo and Virgin Reconsidered."[2] Reexamining the metaphors of the early twentieth-century intellectual historian, Henry Adams, who had elucidated the distinction between medieval and modern times by means of the contrasting images of gothic structures dedicated to the Virgin Mary and twentieth-century machinery, specifically the great electric dynamo on display at a World's Fair, White endeavored to show that these were not at all contrasting symbols but that mechanical dynamism emerged from uniquely medieval mental patterns. Beginning with the observation of the virtuous role of labor promulgated by the Benedictine monastic order – in contrast to the ancient attitude of work being demeaning and fit only for slaves – White provided an explanation for why, although the waterwheel was clearly known to the Romans and described by Vitruvius, it was "not until after the disintegration of the Western Roman Empire [that] it become common" (p. 66). His conclusion, couched in the stirring prose that readers of Lynn White, Jr. come to expect, attests that,

> [t]he humanitarian technology which in later centuries has grown from medieval seeds was not rooted in economic necessity; for such "necessity" is inherent in every society, yet has found expression only in the Occident, nourished in the tradition of Western theology. It is ideas which make necessities conscious. The labor-saving power machines of the later Middle Ages were harmonious with the religious assumption of the infinite worth of even the most seemingly degraded human personality, and with an instinctive repugnance toward subjecting any man to a monotonous drudgery which seems less than human in that it requires the exercise neither of intelligence nor of choice. The Middle Ages, believing that the Heavenly Jerusalem contains no temple, began to explore the practical implications of this profoundly Christian paradox. Although to labor is to pray, the goal of labor is to end labor.
>
> (72–73)

This is the grand and beautiful vision of the Middle Ages that Lynn White spent his academic career expounding. It has provided both inspiration and frustration to those who have subsequently ventured into the field of medieval technology.

Once attached to this view of a technologically dynamic medieval culture that actively promoted industrial mechanics to alleviate the drudgery of human toil, White seemed strangely blind to evidence that could undermine it. Perhaps the most glaring example of this is that the lives of medieval workers were hardly eased by the appearance of industrial mills. Many scholars have taken pains to demonstrate just how onerous the presence of the landlord's mill was to the peasants who were compelled to use it and render a fee for the privilege.[3] That the mill was used as a new and efficient means of extracting taxes from tenant farmers never enters into White's

---

2 Lynn White, Jr., "Dynamo and Virgin Reconsidered," *The American Scholar*, 27, no. 2 (1958): 183–94, republished in *Machina ex Deo: Essays in the Dynamism of Western Culture* (Cambridge, MA: MIT Press, 1968), 57–73.

3 See, among others, Richard Holt, *The Mills of Medieval England* (Oxford: Basil Blackwell, 1988) and more recently, Adam Lucas, *Wind, Water, Work: Ancient and Medieval*

studies, nor the reality that laboring over a mill is often no less arduous than laboring by hand, or at least that it trades laborious hand milling in a quern for laborious transport of the grain to the mill and flour home and shifts grain storage and grinding from as-needed to batch production with attendant worries about spoilage. Furthermore, the application of hydraulic mills to new types of manufacturing allowed for an increase in scale and intensification of industrial production that could just as easily increase the burdens for the workers who labored over them.[4]

White provided much for later historians to argue about. At this moment, we shall focus on the vexing issue of the mechanical crank. Although merely one component in the repertoire of mechanical devices required to launch industrialization, this particular device seemed a barometer of mechanical aptitude to White. It also seemed, unlike the gears associated with watermills, to be a uniquely medieval device. Despite his exhausting trawl through the sources available in his day, White found that "no representation of any form of crank survives directly from the Greeks or Romans."[5] He did not find them in the writings of any of the Hellenistic engineers, nor was there then any machine that springs from their tradition known to archeology that employed a crank. In *De architectura* (ca. 25 BCE), Vitruvius makes no mention of any cranked mechanism in his review of the machines with which an architect should be familiar. There are no casual mentions of any form of crank in other writings from antiquity, nor is any cranked device pictured among the many dozens of technological images that survive in paintings, mosaics, or sculpture. At the end of the twentieth century, scholars still could not report any clear evidence for a crank before the medieval period.[6]

Milling Technology (Leiden: Brill, 2006) and *Ecclesiastical Mills in High Medieval England: Instruments of the Lord* (Farnham, UK: Ashgate, 2013).

4 I have elsewhere argued that industrial mills are more appropriately termed "*labor-enhancing*" devices rather than "labor-saving," at least for the medieval situation: George W. Brooks, "Monks and Machines: The Lewis Mumford Thesis Revisited," *AVISTA Forum Journal* 23 (2013): 60–69.

5 White, *MTSC*, 105.

6 In the extensive encyclopedic collection of Greek and Roman sources for technology compiled by John W. Humphrey, John P. Oleson, and Andrew N. Sherwood, *Greek and Roman Technology: A Sourcebook* (London: Routledge, 2003), there are only two glossary entries under "crank" but both of them are mentioned only to be rejected. The first reports the suggestion by A.G. Drachmann (*The Mechanical Technology of Greek and Roman Antiquity, A Study of the Literary Sources* [Madison: University of Wisconsin Press, 1963; mistakenly dated to 1973]) that Archimedes' device to lift a boat from the water as recounted in Plutarch's *Life of Marcelllus* must imply a crank handle but concludes that this "interpretation probably is incorrect" (50). The other is a short note making the standard correction to the engineers and illustrators of the Italian

Confident that the ancient world had not conceived of cranking, Lynn White refuted each of a handful of scattered classical references that vaguely implied the possibility of a mechanical crank. With the benefit of an additional fifty years of archeological discovery than White had at the time of his work that clearly show that the (late) ancient world did in fact have the crank, we can perceive more clearly the ideological bent of his arguments: a half-dozen suggestions of ancient cranking should have given him more pause and call into question the entire picture of uniquely medieval dynamism that he had constructed.

White's refutations of ancient cranks

The quern, a simple device for grinding grain into flour, consists of small round upper and lower millstones that are rotated to sheer grain into flour. During much of early human civilization, the arrangement of the stones' handles and its wear patterns indicate that they were operated with a reciprocal rather than full rotary motion. As White noted, human muscles are admittedly best suited for reciprocation, not rotation, and so this is the "natural" way for a human to work.

The exact shape and design vary across cultures and centuries, but the essential function of grinding grain between the stones remains the same. Most of these querns do not survive intact, and we usually have only the stones themselves, but many types have sockets in the upper stone where it is assumed a wooden peg handle would have been inserted. The oldest querns usually have peg holes on each side of the upper stone, indicating that it was gripped simultaneously with both hands and moved back and forth like a steering wheel to effect the grinding. This method seems unchanged when we note a transition during the classical age to a pair of peg holes on the top, perhaps indicating a bar across the entire device that could be gripped in more than one place, but wear patterns of stones still indicate a reciprocating motion was employed.[7] Only in the late antique period are querns found with a single peg hole on the top of the upper stone, near the outer edge. These may be plausibly reconstructed with a wooden handle that would allow the user to revolve the upper stone against the lower and qualify as the first appearance in the archeological record of cranked motion.

Renaissance who imagined the Archimedean screw described in Vitruvius to have been turned by a hand crank, whereas all ancient depictions and literary references make it clear that they were turned by treading (317). Richard Holt, "Medieval Technology and the Historians: The Evidence for the Mill," in *Technological Change: Methods and Themes in the History of Technology*, ed. Robert Fox (Amsterdam: Harwood Academic Publishers, 1996), 103–21 at 106–7 noted that "the crank arm was *at least known* by the Romans" (emphasis added).

   7   White, *MTSC*, 108.

White was extremely cautious in dealing with quern evidence, noting that many of them had been excavated without scrupulous attention paid to their stratification layers. For example, a quern found at Dura Europos, and thus implying a date before 256 CE, features the characteristics of a cranked quern, but White was not ready to accept even this relatively late ancient date for a quern that could have been much later "left in Dura by travelers camping among the ruins."[8] Despite his cautions, many scholars came to accept that rotary hand querns did, in fact, represent the earliest form of work accomplished by cranked motions but that it was the only kind known to the ancients. At the end of the twentieth century, scholars were comfortable with the assertion that "the principle of the crank was used in the hand-driven querns with vertical handle that was present in most rural households from the third century BCE onwards."[9]

A second possibility for evidence of the crank in the ancient world comes from several written sources, none of them particularly clear, and all from later antiquity. The word χειρολαβη (*kheirolabe*) appears in several mechanical treatises by Hero of Alexandria to indicate some type of handle. Its literal meaning of "plough tail" has led some scholars to see a crank handle in this description.[10] Linguistic appeal, however intriguing, is not enough to decide such a matter, and within the technological context of the devices described a T-shaped handle makes more sense. The handle was meant to be fitted like a socket over the squared end of an axle and turned by its crossbar, merely as an alternative to the usual windlass method of turning an axle, whereby rods are inserted through the end of the axle and turned hand over hand. A similar term, χειρολαβίς (*kheirolabis*), appears just once in Hero's *Pneumatica*, and the oldest accompanying diagram in the manuscript tradition shows not a crank but a T-handle.[11] More plausible is the reference to a crank used in resetting broken limbs, which comes from Oribasius, physician to the emperor Julian (r. 361–363 CE), but again we are confronted with the difficulty of interpreting words without diagrams. In this case, a crank handle is not the only possible reconstruction. It is perhaps more sensible to imagine a T-handle than a crank for a device requiring intense hand-powered torque under fine control, as would be required in forcing a broken limb back into place.

Finally, there is the late antique poem "Mosella," written by Ausonius in the fourth century CE. Among the descriptions of the Moselle River in Germany, there is mention of the incessant shrieking noise from a stonecutting watermill. We have no other hints at the configuration of this mill other than the comment that the furious turning of millstones (*cerealia*) dragged (*trahens*) the saw through the stone. This

---

8   Ibid., 109.
9   Humphrey et al., *Greek and Roman Technology: A Sourcebook*, 50.
10 Although this rendering may be unduly suggestive, as it could be rendered simply as "hand-hold" and thus not be indicative of any particular shape. Tracy Rihll, pers. corr., May 28, 2014.
11 White, *MTSC*, 107.

must imply a straight reciprocating saw powered by a rotating wheel. This further implies a mechanism to transfer rotary power from the watermill to a reciprocating motion – from the spinning of the wheel to the back-and-forth action of the saw – something Lynn White was convinced had not happened during antiquity.

This transference can be accomplished in two ways: the first is with a combination of camshaft and spring return; the other is with a crankshaft. Both of these methods, as specifically applied to sawmills, appear clearly only in the thirteenth and fifteenth centuries, respectively. If either method were known in the fourth century, it would predate known developments in this area by over half a millennium. When viewed against the other surely known devices before and after this time, this crankshaft sawmill appears to be too much, too complex, all at once, to belong to this early age. White therefore rejected it, arguing that this passage was a tenth-century addition to the "Mosella," by which time such industrial mechanical developments were taking place all over northern Europe.[12] White's dismissal of this part of Ausonius's poem as genuinely fourth century was called into question by D.L. Simms in the 1980s, and his argument for its authenticity has been accepted by most.[13] Others proposed that in the absence of any actual description or depiction of a cranked mechanism, the lines from the "Mosella" should perhaps be interpreted as another type of machine: a wire saw or circular saw could just as easily be imagined. But these theories also run up against the problem of positing other technological elements to an early period that only indisputably appear many centuries later.[14] Some type of water-powered sawmill apparently existed in the fourth century in the northern regions of the Roman Empire, but it would be another two decades before archeology would provide the evidence to clarify this picture.

The only actual artifacts known to White that could claim to be part of a mechanical crank are some wooden pieces found by Italian archeologists at Lake Nemi. The tiny lake was drained in 1929 and two first-century CE pleasure ships, perhaps built under Caligula, were exposed and excavated. Each ship was equipped with a chute for draining bilge water, indicating that each was equipped with some kind of bailing device or pump. On one ship archeologists found the remains of an endless chain of cups, while on the other they found a peg handle and wooden disk with a central and an eccentric square hole.[15] The archeologists combined the elements from each ship and reconstructed a bilging chain of cups powered by the cranked disk. If this reconstruction is correct, then we have a simple machine powered by hand cranking created by

---

12   Ibid., 82–83.

13   D.L. Simms, "Water-Driven Saws, Ausonius, and the Authenticity of the *Mosella*," *Technology and Culture* 24, no. 4 (1983): 635–43.

14   Norman Ball, "Circular Saws and the History of Technology," *Bulletin of the Association for Preservation Technology* 7, no. 3 (1975): 79–89; John O. Curtis, "The Introduction of the Circular Saw in the Early 19th Century," *Bulletin of the Association for Preservation Technology* 5, no. 2 (1973): 162–89.

15   White provided a picture of the disk and apparent peg handle in *MTSC*, fig. 5.

Roman engineers in the first decades of the Common Era. White, however, presents three arguments against validating this claim. First, the obvious problem that the bailing device is a synthesis of finds from two different boats, so it is not at all clear that these remnants were intended to be used together as a cranked bilge pump. Second, the item identified as the peg handle is a mere one third of an inch at its thinnest point and would have easily snapped under a heavy load. Third, the dating of the device cannot be certain, as it may have been added many years after the ships themselves were built. Coins found on board dated as late as 164 CE, and the ships may have sunk as late as the third century. As attractive as it may be to reconstruct a clever cranked bilge pump out of the Lake Nemi remains, it is quite possible that the chain of cups was a later addition to the aging boat and worked by a simple hand-over-hand windlass and that the disk and peg remains were part of some other simple device on the second ship. Thus, another contender for ancient cranking found itself dismissed by White.

Nevertheless, the squared shape of both holes in the Nemi disk and the seeming fit of the peg into the eccentric hole seem to indicate that some type of rotary motion was involved in its use, and for the personal pleasure yachts of the emperor all sorts of technical innovations might be expected. Elsewhere on the ship was found clear evidence of caged bronze ball bearings, another technological first appearance, which were part of a pedestal on which, it is believed, statues of deities were made to turn. It further accords with our ideas about the process of invention that the crank, if we are correct in calling it that, does not take the standard appearance of our modern version, formed after centuries of modification. Instead, we are faced with a circular disk with eccentric handle, closely resembling the top stone of a quern, perhaps suggesting the source of inspiration. Only after some period of its use would it be realized that the entire disk was unnecessary and that the same cranking effect could be accomplished by fastening three sticks together at appropriate right angles (admittedly a challenge for achieving sufficient strength in wood, but metal readily solved that problem). Such a streamlined crank would only slowly displace the older, and easier to construct, cranked wheel. Whether or not the remnants of the Lake Nemi ships constitute a hand-cranked device may never be resolved, and the artifacts themselves were destroyed by fire in 1944, so no further direct study is possible. Earlier this century, historians of technology were comfortable proclaiming the Lake Nemi finds as the first appearance of the mechanical crank in the West.[16] Since then, opinion has fluctuated between regarding them with Lynn White as "archeological fantasy" to "the most likely solution" for how the Nemi ship bilge pump was operated.[17]

In contrast to the paucity of evidence for the ancient crank, the medieval crank makes an early and intellectually stunning first appearance in a Carolingian

---

16 See, for example, the enthusiastic interpretation of L. Sprague De Camp, *The Ancient Engineers* (Garden City, NJ: Doubleday, 1960), 156.

17 John Peter Oleson, *The Oxford Handbook of Engineering and Technology in the Classical World* (Oxford: Oxford University Press, 2008), 354–55.

manuscript, and then resurfaces sporadically, but then with increasing frequency, across the high Middle Ages. The Utrecht Psalter, illustrated in the second quarter of the ninth century, depicts a scene with soldiers sharpening a sword on a rotary grindstone turned by a hand crank (Figure 5.1). White found this figure to be extraordinary not only for attesting the existence of the crank in the early medieval era but also for a discernable new attitude towards advanced technology. The scene accompanies Psalm 64 and illustrates the battle between the righteous and the wicked. The camp of the righteous is smaller in number, but they are disciplined, standing at the ready with weapons in hand. The band of the wicked is larger in number but disorderly and thus seemingly undisciplined. The interest is in the two swords being sharpened, one in each camp. The wicked continue to sharpen the sword the old-fashioned way, by setting the sword on a low bench and dragging a whetstone along the blade. But in the camp of the righteous, advanced technology in the form of the cranked rotary grindstone is accomplishing the task much more quickly and efficiently. White declared that this amounts to "a moral enthusiasm for engines [which] is peculiar to the West."[18] In the image, the hand of God reaches down from a cloud to bless the band of the righteous who are smart enough to employ advanced technology to do the Lord's work, expressing eloquently in symbols a notion that medieval writers never put into words. This notion is expressed, again and again, in the differences between Byzantine and Latin Christianity: while the Byzantine Church forbade the use of pipe organs and mechanical clocks in churches, the medieval West embraced the use of organs in church and proudly displayed mechanical clocks not only on the exterior faces of church towers but within as well, "less to tell the time than to demonstrate visually the orderliness of God's cosmos."[19]

There is a space of several centuries between the Utrecht Psalter crank and the next appearance in medieval documents. The dissolution of the Carolingian Empire and the ravages of Vikings and Magyars help account for the paucity of documentary evidence between the ninth-century Utrecht Psalter and the twelfth century when manuscript images again provide depictions of cranks, and again in a mystical, symbolic setting. The image of *Fortuna* turning her

---

18   This image had been discussed earlier by White, in "Technology and Invention in the Middle Ages," *Speculum* 15, no. 2 (1940): 141–59, and in *MTSC*, 110, but the implications leading to his statement about "moral enthusiasm for engines" is not found until "*The Iconography of* Temperantia *and the Virtuousness of Technology*," in *Action and Conviction in Early Modern Europe: Essays in Memory of E.H. Harbison*, ed. Theodore K. Rabb and Jerrold E. Seigel (Princeton: Princeton University Press, 1969), 197–219, quoted in Lynn White, Jr., *Medieval Religion and Technology: Collected Essays* (Los Angeles: University of California Press, 1978), 186. White credits this insight to Bruce Spiegelberg of Colby College. See also Steven A. Walton, "The Virtuousness of Technology: *The Battle of Brunanburh* and Anglo-Saxon Sword Manufacture," *Technology and Culture* 36, no. 4 (1995): 987–99.

19   White, "*The Iconography of* Temperantia," 187; *MTSC*, 124–25.

Figure 5.1 The first unambiguous depiction of a hand-cranked mechanism from the Utrecht Psalter (ninth century)

Source: Reproduced by permission of University of Utrecht.

wheel was popular in moralizing manuscripts of the High Middle Ages. One such image, found in the *Hortus Deliciarum* of Herrad von Landsberg, features her not just turning but also cranking her wheel (Figure 5.2). As it is highly unlikely that the illuminator invented the clever device merely for the purposes of decoration, we may assume that cranked devices had become relatively common, at least in some parts of Europe, by the latter half of the twelfth century. But what devices would these be? The cranked grindstone might well have remained in use during the intervening centuries, although we don't see another one depicted until the fourteenth-century Luttrell Psalter shows one cranked from both sides (Figure 5.3). This justly famous and beautiful manuscript also shows another use for the crank in the workings of the hurdy-gurdy, a musical device that engages strings by means of a wheel that is turned by the performer with a hand crank and that developed from the earlier *organistrum* by at least the late twelfth century (Figure 5.4). Cranks both practical and fanciful are found with relative frequency by the end of the medieval era in the form of more cranking *Fortunae*, an image of angels rotating the heavens with cranks,[20] and in a prominently placed hand hoist in a construction scene of the Bedford Hours from the early fifteenth century (Figure 5.5). Medieval people, it would

---

20   See Jean Gimpel, *The Medieval Machine: The Industrial Revolution of the Middle Ages* (New York: Holt, Rinehart and Winston, 1976), 148.

Figure 5.2 " Fortuna" cranking her wheel from Herrad von Landsberg, *Hortus Deliciarum*, folio 215 (twelfth century)

Source: Reproduced from Christian Moritz Engelhardt, *Zwölf Kupfertafeln zu . . . Herrad von Landsperg Hortus deliciarum* (Stuttgart and Tübingen: Cotta, 1818). Redrawn by author from digital image from Special Collections, Heidelberg University Library.

seem, finally learned, as White posited, to "relate themselves to the motion of galaxies and electrons."

Archeology versus the written record

Historians of technology have long been aware of the disconnect between the technological activities of past ages and their appearance in written records. Many of the early assumptions about the limitations of the technical knowledge and capabilities of ancient and medieval times were only refuted when actual artifacts were unearthed that forced a reconsideration of long-held beliefs. Perhaps the most famous of these incidents was the discovery and eventual recognition of the

Figure 5.3 Hand-cranked rotary grindstone from the Luttrell Psalter, B.L. Add MS 42,130 (fourteenth century)

Source: Courtesy of the Trustees of the British Library.

significance of a strange object discovered in an ancient shipwreck off the coast of the island of Antikythera in the Aegean Sea. Along with an immediately recognizable and exciting collection of ancient statues which had gone down with an ill-fated ship in the early first century BCE was a small bronze object so encrusted and corroded by two millennia in the sea that it would take decades for scholars to take a closer look. Under X-ray photography they discovered that the object was a highly complex astronomical computer employing thirty-two finely cut metal gears. The Antikythera Mechanism, as it came to be known, immediately exploded generations of assumptions concerning the ancient world's lack of complex geared devices.[21] But until it was found, how could scholars have known? After all, the

---

21 Derek J. De Solla Price, "Gears from the Greeks: The Antikythera Mechanism – A Calendar Computer from ca.80 B.C.," *Transactions of the American Philosophical Society* 64, pt. 7 (1974): 1–70.

Figure 5.4 Hurdy-gurdy operated by hand crank from the Luttrell Psalter, B.L. Add MS 42,130 (fourteenth century)

Source: Courtesy of the Trustees of the British Library

written records had failed to mention such masterpieces.[22] Had it not been stumbled on by Greek sponge-divers and been part of a wreck unambiguously datable to the first century BCE, we might never have understood that the ancients were capable of such advanced mechanical wizardry.

Vitruvius, writing in the same century as the Antikythera mechanism's disappearance under the sea, provided only a few examples of large machines with gears, such as the hodometer and the water-powered mill for grinding grain, providing clear evidence that such developments had at least occurred by that time.[23] But because the textual appearance of watermills was so rare, and archeology had yet to unearth physical evidence of their widespread use in Roman society, they were considered a novelty. It was thought that the Roman engineer had recorded them, but that the Roman Empire must have made only occasional use of them.

---

22 Recent work on the Antikythera Mechanism has now gone back to the texts to reinterpret passages that may well refer to geared planetaria, but, much like the references to classical cranks that were dismissed because the crank "didn't exist," those texts had been interpreted differently since such planetaria also "did not exist."

23 Steven A. Walton, "ReCOGnition: Medieval Gearing from Vitruvius to Print," *AVISTA Forum Journal* 19, no. 1/2 (2009): 28–41.

Figure 5.5 Hoisting device operated by hand crank from the Bedford Hours, B.L. Add. 18,850, folio 17v detail (fourteenth century)
Source: Courtesy of the Trustees of the British Library

The astonishing fact that Vitruvius provided a careful enough description of the engaged crown gears to allow historians the rare occasion of being able to reconstruct an ancient machine based on a written account led to it being named the "Vitruvian Mill."[24] The fact that we call what we now know to be a common Roman industrial machine after the only writer who happened to describe one should be a constant reminder of the long indebtedness historians have had to written words, as well as to the distorted picture they provide of the work of builders who rarely leave them to posterity. As Richard Holt noted, "when the charter references [to mills] are mapped, the result does not show the distribution of mills so much as the geographical distribution of surviving charters."[25]

---

24 George Brooks, "The 'Vitruvian Mill' in Roman and Medieval Europe," in *Wind and Water in the Middle Ages: Fluid Technologies from Antiquity to the Renaissance*, ed. Steven A. Walton, Medieval and Renaissance Texts and Studies, 322 (Tempe, AZ: ACMRS, 2006), 1–38.

25 Holt, "Medieval Technology and the Historians" (note 6, above), 107.

When Lynn White was studying the subject in the mid-twentieth century, archeology was just beginning to look for, or had only rarely stumbled on, objects that reveal how mundane chores were accomplished. It seemed as if the medieval era had experienced a sudden burst of mechanical activity and apparently novel enthusiasm for machines, because the evidence for watermills "suddenly" exploded in the centuries after the fall of Rome. Already by the eleventh century, *Domesday Book* (1086) indicates somewhere in the neighborhood of 6,000 watermills in England alone.[26] Obviously, then, one accounts for this difference in water-milling intensity by positing a new attitude toward industrial machines emerging in medieval society. Jean Gimpel, in the most popular general study of medieval technology, summed up the opinion of Lynn White, which had become accepted by most historians in the field: "medieval society gave itself wholeheartedly to mechanization, while the classical world adopted it to only a limited extent."[27]

The view that held that the ancients had been somehow ill-equipped to realize the potential of industrial machinery or were socially unable to employ it because, as was often supposed, the widespread availability of slave labor prevented them from seeing its benefits, only came under sustained attack in the last decades of the twentieth century and only when archeological evidence made the continuation of the idea untenable.[28] Mindful of the example of the Antikythera Mechanism's discovery, an object – indeed, *class* of object – completely unattested in surviving writings from antiquity, some suspected that the historical view of other aspects of technological history was similarly skewed by the fickle nature of surviving written evidence. Premodern industrial machines were made almost exclusively of wood with bits of iron, both of which have much lower survival rates over centuries except in certain optimal conditions. Archeological evidence also suffers from the vicissitudes of fate in the fact that certain regions are better able to preserve artifacts than others – there are so many documented horizontal mills in Ireland, for example, not because they were necessarily more prevalent there but because the peat bogs preserve them so well (*and* because the Irish continue to cut peat for

---

26 Holt, *The Mills of Medieval England*, 5f. Holt reviews the many attempts at cataloging and enumerating the number of mills indicated in *Domesday Book*, rejecting the oft-cited value of 5,624 by Margaret Hodgen, "Domesday Water Mills," *Antiquity* 13, no. 51 (1939): 261–79, in favor of the 6,082 figure reached by Sir Henry Darby, *Domesday England* (Cambridge: Cambridge University Press, 1977), 361.

27 Gimpel, *Medieval Machine*, 7.

28 M.J.T. Lewis, *Millstone and Hammer: The Origins of Water Power* (Hull: University of Hull, 1997), was the opening volley in the reassessment of ancient industrial activity; and while Lewis discerned no cranks in his trawl through the evidence, he makes a compelling argument for multiple forms of trip-hammer mechanisms employed around the ancient Mediterranean.

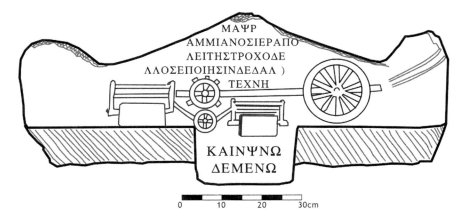

Figure 5.6 The Hierapolis gravestone showing marble sawmill, after *Journal of Roman Archaeology* 20 (2007): fig. 3

fuel and thus are more likely to stumble upon them). The Antikythera Mechanism was an assemblage of gears made of bronze, a material that, unlike iron, happens to survive well for many centuries, even in saltwater.

Historians of ancient and medieval technology have always been faced with these impediments to finding evidence: the people who left writing to posterity rarely took an interest in technological subjects, the people who built machines rarely left a written account of their activities, the artifacts of technological activity themselves rarely survive, and the artists who might have depicted such devices rarely did so, having been usually more inclined towards traditional subjects like mythology, allegory, literary characters, and decorative flora and fauna.

It has only been in the last decades of the twentieth century that incontrovertible evidence of the use of the crank in an industrial machine in antiquity was realized and published – or, more accurately, that the scattered evidence has come to the clear attention of historians of (medieval) technology. What had not survived as artifact, artistic depiction, or written description managed to travel the centuries in the form of a funerary image rendered in relief on a fragment of a limestone sarcophagus cover found outside the walls of ancient Hierapolis, an ancient Roman spa city founded around 190 BCE (now modern Pamukkale, Turkey, 450 km south of Istanbul). The discovery was unearthed during excavations done in the 1980s but took over two decades to be published.[29] When it was finally and fully deciphered, it was recognized as a representation of a stone-cutting sawmill that used

---

29 T. Ritti, K. Grewe, and P. Kessener, "A Relief of a Water-Powered Stone Saw Mill on a Sarcophagus at Hierapolis and Its Implications," *Journal of Roman Archaeology* 20 (2007): 138–63.

a form of mechanical crank and connecting rod to drive the saws (Figure 5.6). The rest of the lid and the sarcophagus itself were not found, but the lucky survival of this piece of the lid has provided investigators of the history of mechanical cranking a singular piece of evidence that forces a thorough rethinking of long-held assumptions – an "Antikythera moment."

The sarcophagus's inscription, announcing the owner as one M(arcus) Aur(elius) Ammianos (in Greek), also provides a fascinating window into the personality of the machine's builder. Ammaianos was a "citizen of Hierapolis, skillful as Daedalus in wheel-working [who] made [the device] with Daedalean craft." The relief image depicts a water wheel with an inclined chute to direct water to the impact blades. A long axle connects the water wheel to a gear with a few teeth visible. Below this toothed gear is another gear fitted with connecting rods that lead outward to the left and right and whose ends connect with saws that cut the stone. These frame saws have two reinforcing pieces at the top, very much resembling the frame or sash saws known to traditional carpentry. There is, however, no visible depiction of how the wheels convert rotary motion into the necessary reciprocal motion required to operate the saws. As is so often the case, the essential bit of mechanical linkage is the very thing omitted from the diagram. But in this case, there is enough of the machine depicted to conclude that a mechanical crank linkage must have been used to effect the conversion of power from rotary to reciprocal motion. Unlike earlier suggestions – the "Mosella," the Lake Nemi ship bilge pump, the hand quern – here there can be no reconstruction that does not involve the crank. The actual shape of the crank cannot be determined, but there are two possibilities, as have already been discussed: one is a disk with eccentric peg (such as the Lake Nemi excavators reconstructed); the other is a combination of three iron rods at right angles to each other to form the shape the modern world readily recognizes as a crank. As there were two saws attached to the gears through connecting rods, the authors had a convenient means of showing both possibilities in their reconstruction of the machine (Figure 5.7). Regardless, the style of the sarcophagus lid places the image in the mid-third century CE, and thus, we have finally and certainly found the crank in antiquity.[30]

With the existence of one ancient mechanical crank irrefutably established, it becomes easier to accept the existence of others even when the evidence is circumstantial. In the same article announcing the Hierapolis sawmill, the authors also point to evidence of two other water-powered mechanical saws, both from Asia Minor and both from around the sixth century. The stone sawmill from Gerasa is not attested by any part or image of the machine itself but by the evidence of the mill housing and the remains of a pair of partly sawn stone drums.[31] Surviving

---

30 Ibid., 139.
31 Ibid., 149–51. These finds were originally published by their discoverer, J. Seigne, in several journals: "Une scierie méchanique au VIe siècle," *Archéologia* 385 (2002): 36–37; "Sixth-Century Water-Powered Sawmill," *Journal of the International Molinological*

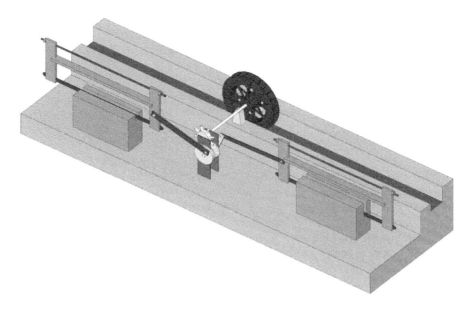

Figure 5.7 Reconstruction of the Hierapolis sawmill mechanisms

Source: Rendering by Steven A. Walton, based on *Journal of Roman Archaeology* 20 (2007): fig. 4.

within the structure were indications that water was directed via channel over the rear wall to the mill wheel. Also evident were the wheel race walls that still show the wear patterns of spinning wheels; square indentions in these walls indicate the placement of the central axle's support points. Two partially cut limestone drums, each with rows of parallel saw slits, were found on either side of the room – apparently the last pieces worked by the saw and left, unfinished, near where the blades of the machine had worked them. That the pieces had been cut by a machine is

---

Society 64 (2002): 14–16; "A Sixth-Century Water-Powered Sawmill at Jerash," *ADAJ: Annual of the Department of Antiquities of Jordan* 26 (2002): 205–13; and Jacques Seigne, "Scierie hydraulique de Gerasa/Jarash: Restitution théorique et restitution matérielle d'une machine hydraulique du vi[e] siècle de notre ère," *Studies in the History and Archaeology of Jordan* 10 (2009): 433–42. And see the open access edition of three articles in Jean-Pierre Brun and Jean-Luc Fiches, eds., *Énergie Hydraulique et Machines Élévatrices d'eau dans L'antiquité*, Nouvelle édition [en ligne] (Naples: Publications du Centre Jean Bérard, 2007 [2018]) online at http://books.openedition.org/pcjb/397: Klaus Grewe and Paul Kessener, "A Stone Relief of a Water-Powered Stone Saw at Hierapolis, Phrygia: A First Consideration and Reconstruction Attempt," 227–34; Fritz Mangartz, "The Byzantine Hydraulic Stone Cutting Machine of Ephesos (Turkey): A Preliminary Report," 235–42; and Jacques Seigne and Thierry Morin, "Une scierie hydraulique du VIe siècle à Gerasa (Jerash, Jordanie): Remarques sur les prémices de la mécanisation du travail," 243–57.

further indicated in that the saw slits occur in groups of four, one set on one of the stones and two sets on the other, and all cut to the same depth. The size and configuration of the room preclude the possibility that a grain mill or other type of known machine was housed in it. Given the dimensions of the room and the evidence of the partly cut stones that remained, a sawmill with connecting rods attached directly to crank disks mounted at the ends of the water wheel's axle seems probable.

The other example comes from Ephesos and similarly consists of a mill house and two partly sawn drums left *in situ*, each with saw slits indicating a saw frame with two parallel blades. In this case there is even less physical indication of the type and shape of the machine once housed within, but its location at the end of a row of five or more watermills arranged along a slope of a hill indicates an industrial complex that utilized a single source of waterpower. Although discovered in the 1980s and understood almost immediately to be the housing for a stone-cutting machine, the entrenched notion that cranked mechanisms were unknown at this early period induced T. Schiøler to reconstruct a far more mechanically complex mill with an unattested sliding mechanism to effect the reciprocation of the saw blades. Later, F. Mangartz produced a reconstruction of the Ephesos mill with a crank wheel and connecting rod system similar to that of the Gerasa mill reconstruction, choosing the mechanically simpler yet historically more confounding solution. These two collections of evidence, along with other partly cut stones found in the area, argue for the continuity of stone sawing mechanisms employing crank and connecting rod configurations in the Eastern Mediterranean from at least the third to the sixth centuries.

The process of technological advance evidenced in these examples may also be partially reconstructed. The third-century Hierapolis sawmill image depicts two saws connected through intermediate gearing to the drive wheel; both sixth-century examples are more plausibly constructed by having the connecting rods attached directly to wheels on the ends of the drive axle. This reduces the number of moving parts and thereby reduces the number of potential breakdowns and repairs. The fact that the earlier mill employed an unnecessary gear train may hint at the source of inspiration for the Hierapolis mill in the ubiquitous corn mills found throughout the Roman world. If we can accept that rotary hand querns were in existence in the Eastern Empire before this time, then perhaps the inventor of the stone saw with a crank-and-connecting-rod system was inspired by it and reversed the direction of energy, attaching connecting rods to eccentric points on the gear of the Vitruvian mill that would normally have powered the millstones and thus make it push and pull on a saw blade. It makes sense that the first innovative step would be to attach connecting rods to eccentric points on the gear, and only later would it be realized that a more direct and reliable connection was possible that avoided gears altogether.[32]

---

32 Ibid., 159.

The Hierapolis sarcophagus image and the evidence of stone sawmills at Gerasa and Ephesos were extraordinarily lucky finds. But fortune has done historians of technology one better. Very recently come to light is an actual Roman crank.[33] The crank, which is 82.5 centimeters in length, takes the appearance readily recognizable to modern eyes: three extensions at roughly right angles forming a zigzag shape. It was found in a refuse heap in the cellar of the Roman Curia Basilica at Augst (Augusta Raurica), Switzerland. The refuse found with it allowed archeologists to date its manufacture to the second century CE, predating all the evidence for Roman industrial cranking discussed earlier by a century or more. The square axle is made of iron and the crank is cast in bronze around it, using the lost wax method. The very short offset of the handle to the axle indicates it was built for low torque and possibly high speed and, Schiøler argues, was certainly a component in a stone sawmill. Although Schiøler's article was only published in 2009, ironically, this irrefutable piece of evidence that obliterates White's argument against ancient cranking was found in 1962, the very year in which *MTSC* was published. This certainly argues for the need for greater communication between classicist and medievalist students of technological history.[34]

The collective impact of these recent archeological finds has been to demolish the long-held belief that the industrial crank was a medieval invention unknown to the ancients. Similar to the reconsideration of the widespread nature of Roman watermill activity, clearly established by Roman archeology a few decades ago, now we have expanded the Roman repertoire of industrial machines to include those that employed the crank-and-connecting-rod system. With one example clearly established for the third century, and a pair of examples featuring similar improvements to the reliability of the machine in the sixth century, plus the actual crank that has recently come to light, historians can now posit the existence of complex mechanical technology and some larger-scale industrial activity in later antiquity for more than grinding grain. Given the Roman enthusiasm for architecture and the subsequent need for a steady supply of stone surfacing material, it should come as no surprise that they would apply their mechanical ingenuity to the cutting of stones for monuments just as they had the grinding of grain to feed their legions and citizens. Ausonius's screeching saw blades alluded to in the fourth-century "Mosella" can now be imagined comfortably as a reference to a class of industrial machines of similar design to the Hierapolis, Gerasa, and Ephesos mills.

---

33   Thorkild Schiøler, "Die Kurbelwelle von Augst und die römische Steinsägemühle," *Helvetia archaeologica* 40, no. 159/160 (2009): 113–24.

34   A sentiment that has been repeatedly argued by Kevin Greene, "Technology and Innovation in Context: The Roman Background to Mediaeval and Later Developments," *Journal of Roman Archaeology* 7 (1994): 22–33.

Hand cranks

With the evidence for industrial machines employing cranks pushed back to at least the second century CE, the related question of hand-cranked devices must be considered anew. There are potentially a great many applications for a hand crank, one of the most common being a hoist for loads that can be raised by human muscle alone. A modern person imagining the method of lifting a bucket from a well or lifting a load on a construction site is likely to imagine an axle with a cranked handle that winds a rope attached to the center of the axle as the crank is turned. This simple cranked hoist is also difficult to find in antiquity and, like other technological evidence, appears slowly but with increasing frequency as the medieval period progresses. All ancient and most medieval references to a device for lifting loads, both written descriptions and visual depictions, indicate that the preferred method was the windlass: stout pegs set at 90 degrees to each other through the axle to create four evenly spaced handspikes that the operator pulls in a hand-over-hand fashion. When the turning needs to be wound on a horizontal plane around a vertical axle the device is called a capstan, a term which often refers to a device on sailing ships for applying tension to the rigging. Vitruvius describes both windlass and capstan in conjunction with several devices, but no ancient depiction has been found such as we have for the medieval period in manuscript images depicting construction techniques.

For heavier loads the ancients and their medieval successors built similar devices, including a treadwheel crane that allowed one or more operators inside a large wheel to turn the central axle by walking ever up the curved interior surface of the wheel, winding the hoisting rope around its axle. One famous ancient depiction is an often-reproduced relief sculpture found in the tomb of the Haterii and dating to the early second century CE, a period of intense building activity by the Romans.[35] Many are known from the latter half of the Middle Ages, such as the famous treadwheel crane in the spire of Salisbury Cathedral that, although it was likely rebuilt several times over the centuries, seems to have been there since the cathedral's construction in the thirteenth century.[36]

The principle of powering a device by hand cranking was clearly in existence by the ninth century when the Utrecht Psalter image of the rotary-powered grindstone was drawn (Figure 5.1). Why should there have been such a lag between the inception of the hand crank and evidence of its seemingly obvious application as a small-load lifter? J.G. Landels makes the very useful observation that the only real advantage of

---

35 Image and clarified redrawing from front and side can be found in Henry Hodges, *Technology in the Ancient World* (London: Allen Lane, 1970): figs. 215 and 216.

36 Cecil Hewett, *English Cathedral and Monastic Carpentry* (Chichester, UK: Phillimore, 1985), 188–98, depicts this as well as several others powered by hand and by treading.

a crank over a windlass is speed.[37] A crank can be turned in a rapid, continuous action whereas a windlass must be moved in slower, halting movements, as the grip on the handspikes must be changed every quarter turn. On the other hand, there are positions in cranking where it is much more difficult to apply a turning/resisting force to the crank, so in most cases in lifting of a heavy load, one is better off with the windlass. It is not easy to make a sturdy crank handle like that depicted in the Utrecht Psalter using traditional carpentry techniques. Three straight poles must be affixed at right angles to each other, and these joints have to endure the stress of the load without giving. It takes an expert joiner to do such work, who would need a compelling reason to craft such an implement. It was much safer, simpler, and sturdier – and a proven method – to employ handspikes attached through the axle to lift in a hand-over-hand fashion. This allows users to maintain steadiness and put their entire body into the action. Even with a sturdy crank, one must do more of the work with shoulder and arm muscles alone, and anyone who has tried quickly learns that cranking wears out shoulder muscles far more quickly than the alternative method.

To have made the transition from windlass hoists to cranked hoists the ancients would have had to voluntarily choose more exhausting labor done with flimsier machines and with an increase in the chances of an accident. The potential increase in the speed of lifting loads was surely not worth such an investment of time, resources, or risk. Even in the Gothic period, by which time the crank had definitely been known for centuries, every depiction of cathedral construction shows just such a windlass hoist used to lift loads that can be managed by one operator. Only with the Bedford Hours, illuminated in the early fifteenth century, does a hand-cranked lifter appear (Figure 5.5). The gray color of this crank handle, clearly distinct from the brown wood tones of the rest of the hoist, implies that it was made of iron. By this time the crankshaft had made its appearance in large machine designs, beginning with the battle tanks rendered by Guido da Vigevano in his *Texaurus* of the fourteenth century and followed by multiple examples in the notebooks of Italian and German Renaissance engineers.[38] One suspects that improvements in

---

37 J.G. Landels, *Engineering in the Ancient World* (Berkeley: University of California Press, 1978), 10.

38 The literature on Renaissance engineering is extensive, and a full bibliography is far beyond the scope of this chapter. For an early general treatment, see Bertrand Gille, *Engineers of the Renaissance* (Cambridge, MA: MIT Press, 1966). For Guido da Vigevano, start with A. Rupert Hall, "Guido's Texaurus, 1335," in *On Pre-Modern Technology and Science: A Volume of Studies in Honor of Lynn White, Jr.*, ed. Bert S. Hall and Delno C. West (Malibu: Undena Publications, 1976). For Brunelleschi, see Frank D. Prager and Gustina Scaglia, *Brunelleschi: Studies of His Technology and Inventions* (Cambridge, MA: MIT Press, 1970). For Taccola, See Frank D. Prager and Gustina Scaglia, *Mariano Taccola and His Book* De Ingeneis (Cambridge, MA: MIT Press, 1972). For Leonardo Da Vinci, the bibliography explodes, but one could start with Ladislao Reti, *The Unknown Leonardo* (New York: McGraw-Hill, 1974). Beyond our scope here, but of direct interest to this topic, see Feng Lisheng and Tong Qingjun, "Crank-Connecting Rod Mechanism:

metallurgy during the later Middle Ages, as well as the great availability of iron in Europe, allowed for the advent of reliable metal cranks by the end of the medieval era such as depicted in Biringuccio's wire-pulling mill.[39] The Utrecht Psalter's rotary grindstone is the kind of device that would benefit from the increased speed and smoothness of operation that a crank permits; and notably, the crank does appear in the hurdy-gurdy, a musical organ similarly requiring steady, controllable, and subtly adjustable speed, which was developed in the High Middle Ages.

White tended to see such evidence as pointing to the growing enthusiasm for machines that was unique to the medieval period, but enough evidence for Roman mechanical ingenuity has surfaced to force a reconsideration of this assumption. It would appear that the type and variety of applications of any technology are largely determined by the specific perceived needs of a society, and this would have been much different for medieval people than what it was for their ancient forebears a millennium earlier.

The crank: hiding in plain sight?

Since the method of operation of ancient querns cannot be reconstructed with certainty and thus cannot be used to establish a prior use of hand cranking leading up to the innovation captured in the Hierapolis sawmill depiction, perhaps Landel's insight about the usefulness of cranks – as devices for speed (and control) rather than strength – can help determine other places to look for their existence in Antiquity. Among the collection of classical Greek painted vases in room 73 of the British Museum is a red-figured volute-*krater* dated to *circa* 350–340 BCE (Figure 5.8). Made in Apulia, and attributed to the Lycurgus painter, it depicts an abduction of the priestess Oriethyia from a temple by the north wind deity, Boreas. To the right of this scene, as museum curators accompanying the vase put it, "an aged priestess flees in terror, dropping the temple key in her haste." Below her left hand we see the thin chain, which the curators interpreted as being attached to a key that has the unmistakable shape of a crank. A handful of similar images exist from Hellenistic vase painting, and one actual example of such a key is found in the collection of the Museum of Fine Arts in Boston (Figure 5.9).[40] If we may indeed think of these

---

Its Applications in Ancient China and Its Origin," in *International Symposium on History of Machines and Mechanisms. Proceedings of HMM 2008*, ed. Hong-Sen Yan and Marco Ceccarelli (Dordrecht: Springer, 2009), 235–50.

39 Reproduced in many texts on historical technology, such as Terry S. Reynolds, *Stronger than a Hundred Men: A History of the Vertical Water Wheel* (Baltimore: Johns Hopkins University Press, 1976; rpt. 2002), 93, figs. 2–32.

40 The provenance of the Boston artifact is very unclear. The inscription declares that it is the key to the temple of Artemis at Lusoi, in Akadia (ΤΑΣ ΑΡΤΑΜΙΤΟΣ: ΤΑΣ ΕΝ ΛΟΥΣΟΙΣ), but its date is unknown, and the records of the museum in Boston only indicate that it was

Figure 5.8 Hellenistic vase painting with a possible crank in the British Museum, room 73 (fourth century BCE)

Source: Photo by author, 2010.

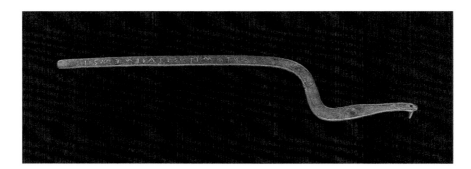

Figure 5.9 Greek temple key, MFA acc. 01.7515 (bronze, date and provenance uncertain)

Source: Courtesy of the Museum of Fine Arts, Boston.

images as depictions of cranks – or perhaps we should call them "cranked keys" – they are extraordinarily significant as they predate all other known evidence by half a millennium and carry the presence of cranks from Imperial Rome back to Hellenistic Greece.

The small handful of images of similar type have led to the generally accepted conclusion that these were large temple keys, usually carried over the shoulder by a priestess in a ceremonial fashion.[41] No ancient corresponding lock or door exists to compare them with, but we must imagine that the point of the key was either to slither in beyond the range of a straight tool and release the lock, which would make it an offset key.[42] Alternately, it could have been inserted with a genuine cranking motion to engage the locking mechanism, an interpretation bolstered by the recent consideration of a cranked winding mechanism on the first-century CE Antikythera Mechanism.[43] The slender and curved shape of the key in the Boston Museum suggests the former theory, while the vase images suggest the latter. In either case, it would have been the need to safeguard the temple valuables that triggered the innovation that would later be applied as the mechanical crank – a fascinating moment in the history of invention.

If this vase painting depicts not a key but a crank handle, then the question raised is what device it operated. The British Museum curators read their vase painting as a key that has been dropped, but it could also be a crank jutting out from the side of the rectangular base to the left. If so, there is no depiction of what it is attached to

---

purchased by Edward Perry Warren in Athens from a man living near Sicyon, and then subsequently purchased by the Museum of Fine Arts in 1901. Any archeological context in which it may have been found is unrecorded. Given these circumstances, and noting the differences in its shape compared with the few vase images available, extreme caution must be used in making any claims regarding it. Online at www.mfa.org/collections/object/key-153281, accessed October 8, 2014.

41 Such a key is depicted in this fashion on another Hellenistic vase also depicting a satyr play, this time involving Ajax attempting to abduct Cassandra from a temple; Margaret Bieber, *The History of the Greek and Roman Theater* (Princeton: Princeton University Press, 1961), 136 and fig. 494.

42 This interpretation is lent some credence by the fact that in the Roman world, a 'twice-bent baffled' gate in a city wall or fortification that caused anyone entering to zig to one side and then zag back to the other – thereby making any direct attack through the gate difficult – was known as a *clavicula*, or "little key"; Lawrence H. Keeley, Marisa Fontana, and Russell Quick, "Baffles and Bastions: The Universal Features of Fortifications," *Journal of Archaeological Research* 15 (2007): 55–95 at 62. Thanks to Steven A. Walton for bringing this to my attention.

43 See M.T. Wright, "Understanding the Antikythera Mechanism," *Proceedings of the 2nd International Conference on Ancient Greek* Technology (Athens: Technical Chamber of Greece, 2005), 49–60; Alexander Jones, *Portable Cosmos: Revealing the Antikythera Mechanism, Scientific Wonder of the Ancient World* (Oxford: Oxford University Press, 2019).

inside. The only other contextual clue is that classicists believe the abduction scene, taking place above the device, was inspired by a satyr play. If our vase painter had been at the theater, then perhaps he saw and recorded a piece of stage equipment. In the later fifth century BCE, Euripides arranged for complex and marvelous devices to lower an actor, playing the role of a god, from on high. This is the quite literal *deus ex machina* that has become the derisive term for a last-minute introduction of some character or revelation that suddenly, and improbably, brings the story to a close. In *The Clouds*, Aristophanes spoofs the wisdom of Socrates by having his character elevated in a "cloud-mobile" talking down to *hoi polloi* beneath him.[44] There must have been considerable thought given by ancient playwrights on how best to raise and lower the actor quickly and smoothly. Here is just the type of application for which a cranked mechanism is suited – and, indeed, hardly the first time when interesting and complex machinery was adopted or perhaps invented for the pleasures of the theater. The satyr play depicted on the Apulian vase features Boreas swooping down to abduct the priestess, perhaps depicting such a clever device used to move the actor and thus associate it with this type of theatrical event.

A second possibility is that the device is a component of a small automaton that depicted a theatrical scene. The Hellenistic period saw advances in gearing and mechanical simulacra that led to such devices as the Antikythera Mechanism, and Hero of Alexandria described many such devices in great mechanical detail in his *Pneumatika*. These included applications to what might be called "mechanical theater" in which a story was depicted on stage by automated figures powered by weights according to a program controlled by the precise release of ropes from pegs on a drive axle.[45] The mechanical devices involved would not have required a crank, but if the Hellenistic period saw a rising fascination with mechanical theater and at the same time witnessed the advent of complex geared mechanisms on a small scale, clever technicians building a miniature automaton of a theatrical scene to impress a patron would have been entirely unsurprising, even if evidence for such a construction would be unlikely to survive. Regrettably, most of the ancient Hellenistic builders have not enjoyed the survival of their writings, and Vitruvius, to whom we are grateful for recording as much technological information as he did, was focused on the practical engineering of construction and warfare and thus did not include any detailed descriptions of devices of fine technology dedicated to science and pleasure. Given the lack of written corroboration and the paucity

---

44 The stage directions only indicate that when Socrates's "Thinkery" is wheeled about to show the interior to the audience that Socrates is held high overhead supported by a crane. William Arrowsmith, Richmond Lattimore and Douglass Parker, *Four Plays by Aristophanes* (New York: Meridian, 1984), 35.

45 Richard Beacham, "Heron of Alexandria's 'Toy Theatre' Automaton: Reality, Allusion and Illusion," in *Theatre, Performance and Analogue Technology: Historical Interfaces and Intermedialities*, ed. Kara Reilly (London: Palgrave Macmillan, 2013), 15–39.

and inconsistencies of images identified as Greek keys, the vase may equally be interpreted as depicting a crank-operated automaton.

None of these possibilities can be conclusively argued at this time, but perhaps this suggestion will provide historians of ancient technology a fruitful direction to continue their trawling for evidence, where a bit of luck may turn up another splendid find such as happened with the Hierapolis sawmill sarcophagus. If nothing else, this investigation should remind us to check our assumptions before issuing conclusions. If these devices are indeed all merely temple keys, then at the very least historians should regard them as the earliest appearance of a tool that incorporates the essence of a cranked operation.

Conclusion

In one of his more hortatory essays, which explored the nature of doing history, Lynn White warned against the temptation of constructing models out of the patterns of evidence one is studying and of holding to them too zealously. Of course, without constructing some kind of model, then there is little for the historian to do but play chronicler of events. The historian must attempt to make sense of the evidence, White notes, but he also cautions that

> [i]f a model embraces two sets of events, it must disregard the unique elements in each. As the model expands in scope, it is necessarily removed further and further from more and more of the actualities in concrete situations. Such constructs often have great elegance, but their beauty may be both intellectually and practically perilous if it leads us to forget the factual data, which were necessarily discarded as the model emerged.[46]

White may be forgiven for not having perceived the use of cranked mechanisms in antiquity, as most of the evidence was unknown when he was working. The medieval evidence, by contrast, was for him both unambiguous and intriguing. But in constructing his model of explanation, the "inhuman adventure" of cranking, which he saw as taking so long a time for humanity to accept, he constructed the very type of exclusive model about which he cautioned. The result was that the evidence of Ausonius's "Mosella" was explained away because such evidence, in clear violation of his otherwise well-posited model, must have been somehow flawed. Historians who have taken up his work are well advised to remember the lesson of the Augst crank and the Antikythera Mechanism when constructing their own pictures of the history of technology. As Lynn White put it in the same essay, "[l]ike Ulysses, the historian binds himself to the mast of the ascertainable facts, both repetitive and unique, lest the siren song of models draw him overboard into a sea of too arbitrarily achieved theory" (9).

---

46 Lynn White, Jr., "Then and Now," in *Machina ex Deo* (note 2, above), 1–10.

Chapter 6

A Romanesque box hoist in Liège
A possible precursor of medieval tower-clock frames?

C.R.J. Currie

When it appeared in 1962, Lynn White, Jr.'s *Medieval Technology and Social Change* became a best seller. Within 11 years it had appeared in Italian, German, French and Spanish translations. Nevertheless, as Bert Hall records, medieval historians were less impressed, and the book immediately received critical reviews, denouncing White's alleged naivety and technological determinism. His theories of the impact of the stirrup on "feudalism," and of heavy ploughs and their relation to medieval agriculture, were not only not wholly new but were heavily attacked and have since been largely refuted. Yet his third chapter on mechanical power was less controversial and "is the one that has stood the test of time best."[1] It is an aspect of that chapter that this paper revisits.

The book's immediate impact and the controversy it aroused were not restricted to the university community. It is possible to recall the effect White had on medieval-history teaching to a class of 14- and 15-year-olds in a southern English school in the autumn of the year of publication. White's ideas about the stirrup in chapter I, and on the plough in chapter II, were laid out, in two senses: expounded and then knocked down, probably following the criticisms of the reviewers. It appeared, to those new to the class, to be assumed that everyone was already familiar with the book. Older members of the class, perhaps, would have been told about it earlier in the year or were supposed to have read the reviews. Nevertheless, as far as this writer recalls, nothing was said about White's chapter on mechanical power, including his perceptive observations on clocks. White gave a succinct summary of what was known about the development of clocks, from twelfth- and thirteenth-century water-clocks through

---

1   Bert S. Hall, "Lynn White's *Medieval Technology and Social Change* After Thirty Years," in *Technological Change: Methods and Themes in the History of Technology*, ed. Robert Fox, Studies in the History of Science, Technology and Medicine 1 (Amsterdam: Harwood Academic Publishers, 1996), 85–101.

the early experiments with mechanical clocks, referring to Robert the Englishman's treatise of 1271 to show that clockmakers were then actively trying to design a weight-driven clock but had as yet failed to produce a working escapement. White went on to discuss the differences between trans- and cisalpine clock technology in the fourteenth century. That was perhaps not new, but White placed his account in the context not only of civic culture but of other changes in mechanical technology and of the academic development of impetus theory in the fourteenth century.[2] His stress on the significance of clocks in the interface of technology and culture preceded Cipolla's in *Clocks and Culture* by five years; Cipolla followed White's emphasis, even though he also took a sideswipe at White's account as "recent enthusiastic literature."[3]

Also in 1962, however, this writer had been independently introduced to the requirements of an old-fashioned tower (turret)[4] clock and to the medieval tradition of labor services after his family moved into an apartment whose landlord required the tenants to maintain a clock in the tower of an adjoining stable block, a local landmark. The clock, which probably dated from the early or mid-nineteenth century, had to be wound every couple of days. It had a striking train, as well as one for the hands on the face, and two very heavy weights that 14-year-old arms, when applied to the winding shafts, could raise only with difficulty. A hole in the tower floor allowed the weights to descend as far as the floor of the hayloft below, giving perhaps 4 meters of travel, although one was never supposed to allow them to fall so far. The anchor escapement and gears also had to be oiled at intervals. Access was limited by the very strong iron frame needed to support the axles, weights, bell, gearing, and pendulum, and only with difficulty could one squeeze around it to get at the other side. It was itself supported by the sturdy timberwork of the tower. So it is the existence of the frame, rather than the details of the mechanism, that sticks in the memory.

Medieval and early-modern clocks that have been removed from churches and other towers for display in museums or on the church floor have very substantial open box-like frames, in medieval examples normally of wrought iron joined with mortises, tusk-tenons, eyes, and iron wedges, a technique derived from carpentry. According to some writers the earlier type, a minority had two-post door-frame structures.[5] They are usually ornamented with projecting knobs or finials that would serve a practical purpose if the clock and its frame had to be removed and manhandled (Figure 6.1).[6] The church clock at East Hendred, Oxon (formerly Berks),

---

2 Lynn White, Jr., *Medieval Technology and Social Change* [hereafter *MTSC*] (Oxford: Oxford University Press, 1962), 120–29.

3 Carlo Cipolla, *Clocks and Culture* (London: Collins, 1967), 20.

4 Modern horologists classify these clocks as "turret clocks," since, from the early modern period, clocks of the same general type were found in turrets over the roofs of buildings. C.F.C. Beeson, *English Church Clocks 1280–1950* (London: Brant Wright, 1977), ch. 2.

5 M. Maltin and C. Dannemann, 'Dating the Salisbury Cathedral Clock', online at http://clocknet.org.uk/wiki/doku.php?id=dating_salisbury.

6 Beeson, *English Church Clocks*, 20, 23–24, 27–29, and 38–89.

Figure 6.1 Turret clock of *circa* 1600 to 1620 from Cassiobury (Hertfordshire, England), now in the British Museum

Source: Reproduced by permission of the trustees: © the Trustees of the British Museum.

England, for example, which is one of the earliest both still *in situ* and functioning, was made by Henry (or John) Seymour of Wantage in 1525, although much repaired and reconstructed since. It has a box frame of flat iron bars, joined with projecting eyes and pegs, and integrated into substantial supporting timberwork (Figure 6.2).[7]

It is therefore surprising that illustrations, ancient and modern, of medieval clocks often omit the holding frame entirely.[8] The mid-thirteenth-century miniature of a chamber clock reproduced by White is a partial exception. What may be

---

7 E.R. Manley, *A Descriptive Account of East Hendred* (East Hendred: self-published, 1969), 37; Beeson, *English Church Clocks*, 64–65 (giving John Seymour); 144, fig. 96, showing signature 'SEYMOUR WANTAGE 1525'; C.F.C. Beeson, *Clockmaking in Oxfordshire 1400–1850*, ed. A.V. Simcock (Oxford: Museum of the History of Science, 1989), 20, giving Henry Seymour. Nothing more seems to be known of this Seymour, but a John Seymour was making clocks in Wantage in 1712: F.J. Britten, *Old Clocks and Watches and Their Makers*, 15th ed. (London: E. & F.N. Spon, 1922), 775.

8 Beeson, *English Church Clocks*, is exceptional in illustrating frames and their analysis.

Figure 6.2 Left half of the frame of East Hendred church clock, after E.R. Manley

Note: The right half is obscured by timberwork.

a cutaway view of a tower shows, either in front of a turret or below and possibly supporting it, a two-tiered arch: in the upper tier, narrow (presumably timber) posts support a straight-sided arch, from the top of which hang five bells in a row, actuated by a large toothed wheel that sits below them on a dog-legged supporting arm. White notes that the wheel appears to be composed of fifteen cones and infers that their spacing indicates an hourly rotation of the wheel. In the lower tier, columns surmounted by imposts or capitals, set within the posts of the upper arch, support a semicircular arch from whose center a gargoyle-like spout descends; from its mouth water is pouring into a bowl on a four-legged stand. Apart from the dog-legged arm, however, the frame supporting the wheel and the rest of the mechanism is not shown.[9] Villard's drawing of *li masons don orologe* at folio 6v is of a clock tower or outer housing, not of the frame.[10] It shows a four-stage tower, each stage of which has an open arcaded gallery and above the arcades at each stage is a tiled or shingled roof. Above stages 1, 3, and 4 are gables with variously trefoil or cinquefoil cusping, and a spire rises above the top stage. The clock itself and any structure supporting it are concealed in the interior of the building.

---

   9   White, *MTSC*, pl. 10.
   10 Carl F. Barnes, Jr., ed., *The Portfolio of Villard de Honnecourt: A New Critical Edition and Color Facsimile* (Farnham and Burlington, VT: Ashgate, 2009), pl. 15.

The tradition of omitting the frame and showing the mechanism as if it were floating in suspension, or with only part of the frame structure, goes back at least as far as the drawings of the 1327 St. Albans clock by Richard of Wallingford. One drawing of the variable-velocity drive shows a rectangular outline that may be meant to represent part of the frame but does not show how the wheels, axles, and gears are attached to it; another, of the astronomical train, is said to show "two of the four compartments of the vast clock frame" but, in fact, displays only a geometrical rectangle round a detailed and highly specific plan of the axles, gears, and connecting mechanisms, identified with text and Arabic numerals but not clearly fastened to any frame.[11] Wallingford wrote within less than 60 years of the invention of weight-driven mechanical clocks. Drawings by Giovanni de Dondi later in the fourteenth century, and by Leonardo da Vinci in the fifteenth, likewise show only fragments of mechanism and no frame.[12] This tradition continues today.[13]

Hoisting machinery

Several authors have considered medieval hoisting machinery for raising heavy weights in the building trade, although detailed measured drawings and dating of surviving examples have been rare. Any relationship with clocks or their frames has seemed remote, partly because studies have concentrated on large cranes and treadmill hoists. Matthies's 1992 article, taking in a large number of manuscript illustrations of building works, archival evidence, and about 23 surviving examples from Belgium, England, France, Germany, and Sweden, still seems to be the most extensive study.[14] Hewett in 1985 illustrated some eight examples, including windlasses and treadmills, but his evidence is hard to use because his drawings are reconstruction drawings rather than record drawings.[15] He did draw attention to the distinction between compass arms with spokes and framed clasped arms for turning the hoist, pointing out that the latter were already known to Villard; Matthies notes that Villard's drawing is of a wheel

---

11   John North, *God's Clockmaker: Richard of Wallingford and the Invention of Time* (London: Hambledon and London, 2005), 175–76, figs. 30 and 31.

12   Ibid., 179, fig. 33 and 184, fig. 37.

13   For an example published during the writing of this article, *Church Times* [London], March 1, 2013, 15.

14   Andrea Matthies, "Medieval Treadwheels: Artists' Views of Building Construction," *Technology and Culture* 33, no. 3 (1992): 510–47.

15   Record drawings illustrate the structure or artefact as surveyed. Reconstruction drawings show what the artist thinks the artefact originally looked like: they omit features that are supposedly not original and include presumed original features that did not survive at the time of drawing.

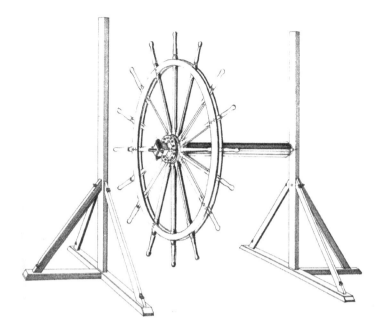

Figure 6.3 Windlass at Norwich cathedral

Source: Reproduced from C.A. Hewett, *English Cathedral and Monastic Carpentry* (Chichester: Phillimore, 1985), 195, fig. 194, by permission of the History Press.

only partly of clasped-arm technique.[16] Usually the remains of both are found dismounted, although occasionally mounted on a braced, freestanding trestle-like frame, like the compass-arm windlass at Norwich shown by Hewett (Figure 6.3), the windlass from Chesterfield church dendro-dated to between 1360 and 1400 and re-erected in Chesterfield Museum, or that at Auxerre cathedral with pairs of crossing sills and a clasped-arm wheel that still stands on the vault above the crossing (Figure 6.4). More typically, all that remains is the axle of a spoked compass-frame windlass, abandoned in the tower of a large church, as in the westworks of the colleges of St. Paul and Ste-Croix in Liège. It has therefore been supposed that the windlass or crane was repeatedly moved during building operations, ending up at the tower during the final stages of roof-construction.[17] The hoist that forms the subject of this chapter, by contrast, was fixed and built

---

16   Matthies, "Medieval Treadwheels," 526–27; C.A. Hewett, *English Cathedral and Monastic Carpentry* (Chichester: Phillimore, 1985), 188–99.

17   Matthies, "Medieval Treadwheels," 532–37.

Figure 6.4 Clasped-arm hoist above the crossing of nave and transepts at Auxerre cathedral

Source: Photo by the author, 2008.

into the original design of the roof where its remains still survive. It stands within a frame that is part of the roof and that has analogies to a clock frame and the way such frames support their mechanism. Those analogies are discussed after the hoist has been examined.

Because the hoist is part of the roof, it is necessary first to discuss in detail both the roof itself and its date, and regional investigations of the type of Romanesque common-tiebeam roof of which it forms an example:[18] other similar hoists may have survived in the thirteenth century in roofs since lost.

---

18   For the development of timber roofs in general in the region, Patrick Hoffsummer, et al., *Les Charpentes du xie au xixe siecle: Typologie et evolution en France du Nord et en Belgique*, Cahiers du Patrimoine 62 (Paris: Éditions du Patrimoine, 2002); Patrick Hoffsummer, ed., *Roof Frames from the 11th to the 19th century: Typology and Development in Northern France and Belgium – Analysis of CRMH Documentation*, Architectura medii aevi 3 (Turnhout: Brepols, 2009).

The roofs of the twelfth-century suburban collegiate church of St. Bartholomew (Barthélemy) at Liège have been the subject of repeated archaeological investigation. The Scheldt not only marks the historic boundary between the Holy Roman Empire and France, but that between two alternative approaches to medieval architectural history: the Franco-English to the west, which traditionally ignores everything above the vault or ceiling of the church, leaving the timberwork to be studied and drawn by separate specialists, and the German to the east, which regards the recording of roof carpentry as a normal part of the architectural historian's task. Canon Raymond Lemaire the elder (1878–1954), the pioneer investigator of the Romanesque in Brabant, certainly took that view, and his early work published in 1906 discusses roofs and includes a number of section drawings.[19]

The study of St. Bartholomew's, well east of Brabant, however, formed part of a more comprehensive general work of 1952 by the canon's nephew, Baron Raymond Lemaire, which referred to an original trussed-rafter roof in the nave.[20] It was followed by Janse and Devliegher, who published a cross section of the nave roof in 1962 and by a more detailed account with drawings and a photograph by Genicot in 1977.[21] They showed that the roof of the nave was of common-rafter, common-tiebeam type, with a collar and four vertical struts halved to the rafters at each couple. It was not, however, until proposals to restore the church in the 1990s gave rise to a detailed investigation of the fabric by a group of experts that a serious dendrochronological and typological study of the *charpentes* was undertaken by Professor Patrick Hoffsummer and colleagues.[22] This revealed that the Romanesque roofs fell into two phases: one dendro-dated to 1139 to 1151 on the transepts (with extensive fourteenth-century alteration in the north transept),

---

19 R. Lemaire, *Les origines du style gothique en Brabant: 1. L'architecture romane* (Brussels: Vromant, 1906). His nephew confusingly published a work with a similar title after World War II: Raymond M. Lemaire, *Les Origines du style gothique en Brabant. 2e partie, La Formation du style gothique brabançon* (Anvers: De Nederlandsche boekhandel, 1949).

20 R.M. Lemaire, *De Romaanse bouwkunst in de Nederlanden* (Brussels: Davidsfonds, 1952), 108–9.

21 H. Janse and L. Devliegher, "Middeleuwse Bekappingen in het vroegere Graafschap Vlaanderen," *Koninklije Commissee Voor Monumenten en Landschappen* new ser. 13 (1962): 308–21 at 318, afb. 20; L.F. Genicot, "Charpentes du xie au xixe siècle en Wallonie (2)," *Bulletin de la commission royale des monuments et des sites*, new ser. 6 (1977): 136–60 at 141–42.

22 P. Hoffsummer, David Houbrechts, and Jérôme Eckhout, "Analyses dendrochronologiques et étude typologique des charpentes," *Etudes préalables à la restauration de l'église Saint-Barthélémy à Liège*, Dossier de la Commission royale des monuments, sites et fouilles 8 (Liège: Commission royale des monuments sites et fouilles de la Région wallonne, 2001), 99–103; see also p. 75. Part of the dendrochronological results were given in Patrick Hoffsummer, *Les Charpentes de Toitures en Wallonie*, Etudes et documents monuments et sites 1, 2nd ed. (Namur: Ministère de la région, 1999), 79.

the crossing, and the extreme east of the nave, and the other, built with timber felled in the winter of 1187–1188, on the rest of the nave as far as the westwork. In the earlier, eastern part, fifteenth-century trusses had been intercalated between the early common-tiebeam trusses, but the western roof was largely unchanged.

The two Romanesque phases were distinguished not only in date but also in the jointing of the trusses: the earlier roof has plain or slightly barefaced-dovetail halvings, and the struts are halved to the tiebeams, and most of the halvings are on the west face. The later roof has well-cut notched-lap halvings with clear *ergots* on the east face of the trusses, and the struts mortised to the tiebeams.

Both parts of the roof have some form of longitudinal stabilization, unusual in surviving common-tiebeam roofs. In the eastern half one set of light purlins is pegged to the soffits of the common rafters; it is not clear if this is original or part of the later alterations. In the western half there are no purlins; instead, very long diagonal braces are pegged to the inner faces of the inner pair of struts (*poteaux*) on each truss. The braces are undoubtedly original work of *circa* 1188, as confirmed by dendrochronology. Oddly, they took a long time to be shown in drawings: Genicot's photograph clearly shows them, but he does not comment on them or draw them, while Hoffsummer's 2001 text draws attention to them, but his long section omits them. A sample length across four rafters is, however, shown in summary drawings of the roof in Hoffsummer's more recent general publication.[23] This kind of reinforcement, as Hoffsummer notes, is rare in surviving common-tiebeam roofs.[24] It can be paralleled in a few examples, where there may even be a more elaborate box with plates on the tiebeams supporting the verticals, as in the transepts at St. Georges-de-Boscherville, Normandy.[25]

It is a deliberate, original, variation in the form of longitudinal stabilization that confirms the antiquity of the hoist. Toward the middle of the nave, for three bays, across four trusses, the long braces are omitted by design – not cut off secondarily – and instead, a horizontal rail is attached to the inner faces of the *poteaux*, almost at their tops but below the abutment of long brace and rafter (Figure 6.5; H, D, and R in Figure 6.6). Although the braces barely butt up against the rafter (Figure 6.5), on the north side at any rate, a peg is driven through the horizontal rail (H in Figure 6.6), through the strut (S in Figure 6.6), and into the rafter (R in Figure 6.6), where it split the wood in a manner that is apparently more likely to be observed when the wood is green than when it has already hardened with age. In other words, the pegging and the rail, which forms the upper boundary of the box that holds the hoist, are original work of *circa* 1188.

---

23   Hoffsummer et al., *Les Charpentes: Typologie*, 166, fig. 1e; Hoffsummer, *Roof Frames*, 166, fig. 1e.

24   Hoffsummer et al., "Analyses dendrochronologiques," 99.

25   L.T. Courtenay, N.W. Alcock, and E.A. Impey, "An Early Common Tiebeam Roof: St Georges-de-Boscherville, Seine Maritime, France," *Medieval Archaeology* 42 (1998): 54–67.

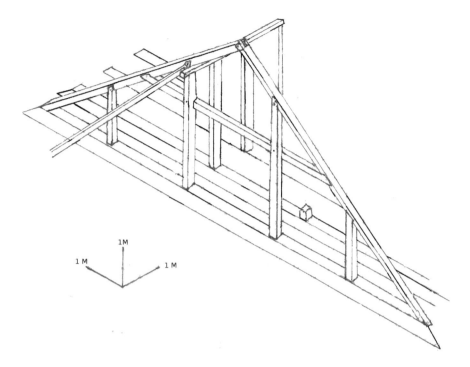

Figure 6.5 St. Barthélemy, Liège, nave roof

Source: Drawing by author.

Note: Isometric view of the relationship of the box to the trusses, showing the rail and the diagonal brace. Rafters behind the front pair are omitted for clarity.

In the middle bay of the three, the southern rail, at least, has a circular rebate for a wide pulley, with a deeper hole for a peg on which the pulley could rotate (Figure 6.7), though the matching pulley hole was not verified on the northern rail, whose face could not be seen during the visit. In the easternmost of the three bays, about a third of the way up the struts is fixed a windlass that was already noted by Genicot, who also provided a clear elevation of the windlass mounting, with a cross section of the axle. He observed that a former windlass (*treuil*) survives, reinforced by nailed supports, between the 23rd and 24th trusses of the nave.[26] Unfortunately, it is not clear where his numbering started. He does not note that the windlass mounting was fixed to the trusses, but this point was observed in 1999 by Hoffsummer, who reproduced Genicot's drawing and stated that it "is

---

26   Genicot, "Charpentes du xie au xixe siècle en Wallonie (2)," 141–42.

Figure 6.6 Pegging of the rail, strut, and rafter

Source: Photo by author, 2008.

Note: D – diagonal brace, H – horizontal rail, S – strut (*poteau*), R – rafter, X – the transfixing peg.

not impossible" that it was used in the construction of the roof dendro-dated to 1187–88.[27] Neither author commented on, or perhaps even noticed, the upper rail or its pulley hole or showed precisely how the supports for the windlass stand.

It is not altogether obvious from Genicot's drawing that at the south end of the axle there is a pair of brackets nailed to the inner east and west sides of the studs. On the brackets is lodged a short lower rail apparently lapped and pegged to the north face of the struts, between which it runs and is held in place by modern boarding (Figure 6.8). The end of the windlass is mounted on this lower rail at a point about one-third of the distance from the rail's east end. At the north end of the windlass, by contrast, the brackets are nailed to the *south* faces of the struts, and the rail is carried entirely on the south side of the struts, though it is again

---

27 Hoffsummer, *Les Charpentes de Toitures en Wallonie*, 73.

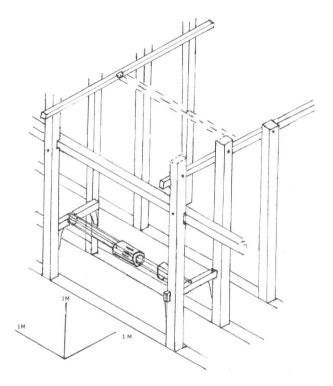

Figure 6.7 Isometric view showing the pulley rebate and the windlass axle in relation to the box

Source: Drawing by author.

Note: Former position of the pulley axle shown by a dashed line at top center. Rafters omitted.

pegged to them. The windlass axle itself is a single octagonal-sectioned piece of timber, with two bushes cut from the solid, each having mortices for spokes. The bushes are set quite closely together (about 35 cm apart), while the bush-free south end would have served as the drum or spool for the hoisting rope. The north end of the axle has shallow rebate about 1.5 to 2.0 centimeters wide for a lost metal band around the axle.

Oddly, the peg or dowel that projects from the north end of the axle into a slot in the rail is slightly eccentric to the center of the axle (Figure 6.8), which would prevent smooth winding – it effectively turns the axle into a cam. That may have been intended to prevent disastrous unwinding (although a bar inserted between the spokes would also have achieved that aim), or it may indicate a later modification or thoughtless repair. The asymmetry between the northern and southern bracket mountings for the axle is strange and may show that, in its present form,

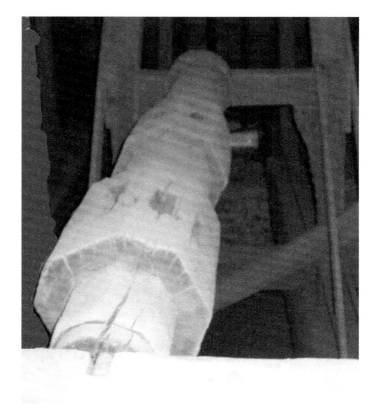

Figure 6.8 The windlass axle from the north
Source: Photo by author, 2008.

the windlass is not original. Nevertheless, the evidence of the upper rail and pulley rebate shows that a windlass of some sort was designed to stand there from the first. Possibly the original arrangement relied on halved and pegged lower rails at each end of the axle, and the nailed brackets were added after use had begun to show that the pegs and half-laps were not strong enough to carry any significant weight.

It is not entirely clear how the windlass would have been worked. The maximum possible length of the spokes is restricted by the position of the tiebeams below and the collars above, and since the lower rails are not even halfway up the struts, an adult could hardly have worked it as a treadmill. The axle is conveniently placed near waist height, however, for someone working the windlass by hand from a platform between the inner and outer struts at the north side.

The use of a fixed hoist designed as part of the roof frame, rather than the more usual kind that could be dismantled and moved to another part of the building, might be a result of rapid roofing over the western nave, as the uniform dates given by the dendrochronology also imply. This might have implications for the dating of the stonework of the supporting walls, but they cannot be explored here.

The hoist and clock frames

The design of this three-bayed box hoist, with its rectangular struts and rails, have some similarities to the box-like, two or three-compartment clock frames discussed earlier. We have noted that the jointing of metal clock frames mimics timber technology. The rails of the Liège hoist, as noted, are pegged to the inner faces of the struts. Similarly, the rails of a clock are attached to the inner faces of the standards (corner metal posts) and to the intermediate verticals. The axle supporting the drum of a clock, on which the rope holding the weight is coiled and the great wheel that drives the train, is carried about a third of the way up the compartment, like the windlass axle of the box hoist. The rest of the gearing is normally fixed on higher-up axles ("arbors" in horological terminology). The pulley at the top of the hoist is echoed at the same position on the frame by the fly arbor of the striking train of a clock, and sometimes by gearing connecting the going train to the escapement. These similarities might be explained if such box hoists were part of the mental background of the technologists designing early weight-driven clocks and their frames.

It is not being suggested here that Liège was the seat of invention of the weight-driven mechanical clock in the late thirteenth century. Still, various factors from the city would have made it a suitable site of innovation: it had a tradition as a center of metalworking; it was the center of often quite advanced roof carpentry, continuing in the thirteenth and fourteenth centuries, which also used metalwork at key points (as Professor Hoffsummer has shown); and its numerous colleges and churches would have supported a large number of potentially learned clergy that could have made the connection between the two mechanical ideas.

That said, box hoists of the St. Bartholomew's type may have been more common across a wide area than now appears. The common-tiebeam roof with four vertical struts is the commonest surviving type of late-Romanesque roof in northern France and Belgium, perhaps equaling or outnumbering all other common-tiebeam designs put together. It was also widely used in Germany, where examples continued to be built well into the thirteenth century. A minority of surviving examples had lengthwise bracing. At Konstanz Minster between 1223 and 1236, for example, the verticals rest on plates and there are both diagonal braces and horizontal rails attached to the inner faces of the inner struts (*poteaux*).[28] In south Germany, vernacular examples of this type of roof were still being built as late

---

28 Gunther Binding, *Das Dachwerk auf Kirchen im deutschen Sprachraum vom Mittelalter bis zum 18. Jahrhundert* (Munich: Deutsche Kunstverlag, 1991), 37, fig. 30.

as the 1330s.[29] Thus, in the later thirteenth century, before many examples had been replaced by Gothic designs, there would be far more such roofs standing than now, and a significant minority could have incorporated box hoists, which could thus have formed part of the mental furniture of whoever designed the first weight-driven mechanical clocks. Conversely, with the displacement of common-tiebeam, four-strut trusses for the design of new roofs by Gothic forms during the thirteenth century,[30] there was no longer structural support for box hoists framed into the roof. Thus, movable treadwheel hoists or windlasses fixed to stone towers necessarily supplanted them. (Matthies implies that treadwheel hoists were not widespread until *ca.* 1240.) The forms of hoisting machinery, which had itself been apparently reintroduced to Western Europe only in the 12th century,[31] and those of clock-frames, thus diverged sharply thereafter.

Another aspect of the design of the hoist at St. Barthélemy may be relevant to the origins of weight-driven clocks. Large treadmill cranes tend to be of the clasped-arm type, while surviving windlass axles may have their spoke slots set widely apart along the axle. The two closely spaced bushes at St. Barthélemy, however, bring to mind the strob escapement of the early fourteenth-century St. Albans clock design expounded by North. In that, two wheels set closely on a single axle (arbor) have fixed on their outer rims dowels or pins, at different positions on the two sides; a horizontal bar suspended above the two wheels supports the verge shaft between them; on the shaft a semicircular double pallet engages the staggered pins on the wheel rims in an oscillating motion.[32] Similar staggered pins, into which a rod or beam could be inserted as a brake, might have been used on windlasses. Hewett shows some examples of windlasses with projecting pins, but, with two exceptions, they project laterally, not in the plane of the wheels.[33] Two-bush windlasses with in-plane pins may, however, have helped to suggest the idea of the strob escapement.

Conclusion

The revival of hoisting machinery in the twelfth century led to the development of both fixed and movable types of hoist. The first included box hoists fixed in the roof, of which that at St. Barthélemy, Liège, dates in its original form from

---

29   Ibid., 39; G. Binding, U. Mainzer, and A. Wiedenau, *Kleine Kunstgeschichte des Deutschen Fachwerkbaus*, 3rd ed. (Darmstadt: Wissenschaftlicher Buchgesellschaft, 1984), 63.
30   See, in general, Hoffsummer, *Roof Frames*; Binding, *Das Dachwerk*.
31   Matthies, "Medieval Treadwheels," 512–14.
32   North, *God's Clockmaker*, 180–81, figs. 34 and 35.
33   Hewett, *English Monastic and Cathedral Carpentry*, figs. 186, 188, 194, and 198.

1188. Box hoists may have been common in those parts of Europe (now northern France, Belgium, and Germany) where the common-tiebeam roof with four struts predominated in the later twelfth century. In the thirteenth century, new roof types, spreading eastwards from France with Gothic construction, favored movable treadwheel hoists, or hoists fixed to stone towers, but enough box hoists may have survived to provide a construction template both the frame design and one form of early escapement of tower (turret) clocks by *circa* 1300.

Acknowledgments

I am especially grateful to Professor Patrick Hoffsummer for arranging a special visit for me to the lofts of several Liège churches, including St. Barthélemy, in October 2008, and for guiding me through the roof. I am also grateful to Dr. Dan Miles for advice on a technical point of pegging, and to Dr. Dominik Mączyński for photographs that, although not reproduced here, were crucial in understanding how to draw the hoist. Also, many thanks to the British Museum Image Service for permission to reproduce the photograph in Figure 6.1 and to Anette Fuhrmeister of the History Press for permission to use the drawing reproduced in Figure 6.3. The editor is thanked for helpful comments that I hope have improved the chapter.

Chapter 7

Industrial milling and the prolific growth of the Cistercian order in the twelfth and thirteenth centuries

Christie Peters

The recognition of medieval technology as a legitimate field of study owes much to the scholarship of Lynn White, Jr., who proclaimed in 1940 that,

> the chief glory of the later Middle Ages was not its cathedrals or its epics or its scholasticism: it was the building for the first time in history of a complex civilization which rested not on the backs of sweating slaves or coolies, but primarily on non-human power.[1]

Inspired by groundbreaking works in this field by scholars such as Marc Bloch and Lewis Mumford early in the twentieth century,[2] White wrote his seminal work *Medieval Technology and Social Change* (*MTSC*) in 1962 to make up for what he considered a lack of literature on the role of technological development in medieval human affairs. In the third chapter of *MTSC*, which is dedicated to the exploration of medieval mechanical power and devices, White credits Hellenistic society with the development of the cam and basic gearing mechanisms that are necessary for various types of milling but contends that the real development of power sources like the water mill and windmill took place in the High Middle Ages, and was due largely to the work of monastics.[3] According to White, these monks drew their inspiration

---

[1] Lynn White, Jr., "Technology and Invention in the Middle Ages," *Speculum* 15, no. 2 (1940): 141–59.

[2] Marc Bloch, "Les Inventions Médiévales," *Annales d'histoire économique et sociale* 7 (1935): 634–43; Lewis Mumford, *Technics and Civilization* (New York: Harcourt, Brace, and Co., 1934).

[3] Lynn White, Jr., *Medieval Technology and Social Change* (Oxford: Oxford University Press, 1962) [hereafter *MTSC*].

from St. Benedict of Nursia (d. 543), who changed the very nature of technological development in the West by exalting labor as a way to praise and serve God and by encouraging a tradition of learning among monastics. This combination of technology and attitudes toward labor and learning resulted in a social environment favorable to scientific and technological development.[4] While we now know that diverse milling technologies did, in fact, exist in later antiquity, the medieval attitude toward milling technology and technology in general still asks for clarification.

Lynn White, Jr. had strong opinions about the nature of technological development in the Middle Ages, but they were not as one dimensional as scholars have claimed over the years. Technological determinism in the strictest sense is the theory that technology drives history independently of all other contributing factors.[5] MacKenzie and Wajcman cite White's theories regarding the influence of the stirrup on the development of feudalism as an example of technological determinism in the introduction of their book on the social shaping of technology, but they fail to note his arguments concerning the influence of Christianity on the development of technology in the Middle Ages.[6] This is a curious omission given that White's arguments foreshadow their own. Similarly, Perdue argues that White used a 'single-factor' method of investigation when he singled out a number of individual technologies such as the heavy plough and stirrup as the primary drivers of historical change in Western Europe in the Middle Ages.[7] He acknowledges that White shifted towards cultural determinism in later writings, namely in *Medieval Religion and Technology* (1978),[8] but questions whether White's later reliance on Christianity as a driving force for technological development was compatible with his earlier views. What Perdue fails to note is that *MRT* is a compilation of essays that White wrote throughout his career. In 1940, well before the publication of *MTSC*, White argued that the theological assumption of infinite worth that is due to even the lowest among us drove the development of labor-saving power machines in the Occident in the later Middle Ages.[9]

The intention here is not to dismiss the deterministic slant of White's arguments, but to point out that the strongly deterministic nature of *MTSC* (or its reception in that way) has resulted over time in an obfuscation of the emphasis that White placed on the social construction of technology, particularly the role that Christianity played

---

4   Lynn White, Jr., "Dynamo and Virgin Reconsidered," *The American Scholar* 27 (1958): 188–89.

5   Merritt Roe Smith and Leo Marx, eds., *Does Technology Drive History? The Dilemma of Technological Determinism* (Cambridge, MA: The MIT Press, 1994).

6   Donald Mackenzie and Judy Wajcman, eds., *The Social Shaping of Technology* (Philadelphia: Open University Press, 1985).

7   Peter C. Perdue, "Technological Determinism in Agrarian Societies," in *Does Technology Drive History?* 174–78.

8   Lynn White, Jr., *Medieval Religion and Technology* (Berkeley: University of California Press, 1978) [hereafter MRT].

9   Lynn White, Jr., "Technology and Invention in the Middle Ages," in MRT, 156. For further thoughts on this topic, see Susan J. White, *Christian Worship and Technological Change* (Nashville: Abingdon Press, 1994).

in the development of technology in the Middle Ages. Perhaps nowhere is this demonstrated more clearly than in his work on the development of medieval power technology by monks. White argued in *Dynamo and Virgin Reconsidered* (1958) that the greatest glory of the Middle Ages was the concept of labor-saving power technology and that the White Benedictines (Cistercians) often led the way in the use of power.[10] White's contemporary, Bertrand Gille, agreed, stating that perhaps no group was more effective at developing sources of power than the Cistercian order beginning in the twelfth century.[11] In *Technological Progress in the Western Middle Ages* (1963), White further argued that Cistercians led in the application of water power to industrial processes.[12] These arguments and others like them voiced by historians of technology during the first half of the twentieth century provided the foundation for the idea that an industrial revolution took place in the Middle Ages, a revolution in which the Cistercian order played a significant role.

Archaeological evidence came to light in the later part of the twentieth century that demonstrated that the discontinuity of ancient and medieval industrial watermill technology has been greatly overstated, largely disproving the existence of a medieval industrial revolution.[13] Scholars now acknowledge that medieval monasteries made extensive use of existing technology without necessarily contributing significantly to its development, although Cistercians do appear to have been pioneers in certain industrial applications of water-mill technology, such as its application to the manufacture of iron.[14]

Unfortunately, the gradual abandonment of the idea of a medieval industrial revolution has resulted in an unwarranted trend to overlook the symbiotic relationship between Cistercians and waterpower. The argument that I present here is that the preexistence of advanced industrial milling technology in France at the time of the

---

10 Lynn White, Jr., "Dynamo and Virgin Reconsidered," in *MRT*, 190.

11 Bertrand Gille, "The Medieval Age of the West (Fifth Century to 1350)," in *A History of Technology and Invention: Progress through the Ages*, ed. Maurice Daumas (New York: Crown Publishers, 1969), 559; Anna Gotlind, *The Messengers of Medieval Technology? Cistercians and Technology in Medieval Scandinavia* (Alingsas: Viktoria Bokforlag, 1990).

12 Lynn White, Jr., "Technological Progress in Western Middle Ages," in *Scientific Change: Historical Studies in the Intellectual, Social, and Technical Conditions for Scientific Discovery and Technical Invention, from Antiquity to the Present*, Symposium on the History of Science, University of Oxford, July 9–15, 1961, ed. A.C. Crombie (New York: Basic Books Inc., 1963), 290.

13 Örjan Wikander, *Exploitation of Water-Power or Technological Stagnation? A Reappraisal of the Productive Forces of the Roman Empire* (Lund, Sweden: CWK Gleerup, 1984); Catherine Verna, *Les mines et les forges des Cisterciens en Champagne Méridionale et en Bourgogne du Nord Xiie–Xv^e Siècle* (Paris: A.E.D.E.H., 1995).

14 Adam Robert Lucas, "The Role of Monasteries in the Development of Medieval Milling," in *Wind and Water: Fluid Technologies from Antiquity to the Rennaissance*, ed. Steven A. Walton (Tempe, AZ: ACMRS, 2006), 106; Verna, *Les Mines et Les Forges des Cisterciens*.

Cistercian order's foundation in 1098, in conjunction with the order's focus on its unique mission to be self-sufficient, enabled the prolific expansion and economic growth of the Cistercian order in the twelfth and thirteenth centuries. While technology alone did not drive the expansion of the order, the Cistercian order would have been incapable of growing at the rate that it did without the presence and systematic implementation of this preexisting technology. This inverts the idea espoused by White and his peers that an already rapidly expanding and technologically adept Cistercian order initiated the revolutionary development and proliferation of water-mill technology in the Middle Ages. It is in keeping, however, with White's assertion that the heart of the Western Middle Ages lay between the Loire and the Rhine, which also happens to be the birthplace of the Cistercian order.[15] While the two arguments are essentially at odds with one another, they both tie Cistercians to water-mill technology and economic expansion in the Middle Ages.

The birth of the Cistercian order can be traced back to the foundation of Cîteaux in 1098 by a group of monks, led by Robert of Molesme, who were discontent with what they perceived to be increasing laxity in observation of the Benedictine Rule at the abbey of Molesme in Burgundy. Over the course of the following decade, under the subsequent leadership of Alberic and Stephen Harding, the Cistercian order began to take shape as liturgical and juridical regulations began to solidify.[16] The Benedictine Rule mandates that each monastery have "all of the necessities" to sustain itself inasmuch as possible, including "water, a mill, garden, fishpond, and [other] diverse arts."[17] The rule did not prohibit commerce, as long as the monks took care not to be greedy and to offer a fair price for their goods.[18] The earliest Cistercian legislative documents took these stipulations further by specifying that the order possess only for its own use streams, woodland, vineyards, meadows, and lands far removed from secular dwellings and animals,[19] and strictly prohibiting revenues from milling. While this later prohibition restricted the order's development

---

15 White, "Technological Progress in Western Middle Ages," 280.

16 Jean-Baptiste Van Damme, *The Three Founders of Cîteaux*, trans. Nicholas Groves and Christian Carr, Cistercian Studies 176 (Kalamazoo, MI: Cistercian Institute Publications, 1998).

17 *S.P. Benedicti Regula Cum Commentariis*, in *Sancti Benedicti monachorum occidentalium patris. Opera omnia*, Patrologiae cursus completus, series latina [PLL] 66 (Paris: Apud editorem, 1847), col. 900: Caput LXVI. *De ostiariis monasterii*. Monasterium autem, si potest fieri, ita debet constitui, ut omnia necessaria, id est, aqua, molendinum, hortus, pistrinum, vel artes diversae, intra monasterium exerceantur, ut non sit necessitas monachis vagandi foras, quia omnino non expedit animabus eorum.

18 Ibid., col. 801: Caput LVII. *De artificibus monasterii*. Si quid vero ex operibus artificum venundandum est, videant ipsi per quorum manus transigenda sunt: ne aliquam fraudem monasterio facere praesumant. . . . In ipsis autem pretiis non subripiat avaritiae malum: sed semper aliquantulum vilius detur quam ab aliis saecularibus datur, ut in omnibus glorificetur Deus.

19 Jean de la Croix Bouton and Jean-Baptiste Van Damme, eds., *Les plus anciens textes de Cîteaux: sources, textes et notes historiques*, Cîteaux studia et documenta 2 (Achel:

of surplus capacity in both agricultural and industrial milling, the Cistercian order began to realize a profit on its surplus almost immediately.

In 1115, St. Bernard founded Clairvaux, the last of the four principle daughter houses of Cîteaux. In 1135, under Bernard's leadership, the monks of Clairvaux began construction of a permanent abbey church at a site somewhat removed from its original location.[20] There are numerous instances of Cistercian abbeys relocating after their initial foundation for reasons that included uncomfortably close proximity to civilization, the inability of the abbey to expand to accommodate growth, and inadequate proximity to water.[21] Clairvaux was no exception. While not the first Cistercian abbey to be founded, Clairvaux was the first to construct its permanent abbey church. Monasterium Vetus, the original site of Clairvaux, is denoted Clairvaux I in the annotated version of Dom Milley's 1708 plan of the monastery (Figure 7.1).[22]

Geoffrey, prior of Clairvaux and future bishop of Langres, and a "wise and constant man," appealed to Bernard to allow the new monastic complex to be moved farther upstream in order for the monastery to make better use of the river for the utility of the community. He argued that they

> had settled in a narrow and inconvenient place which was not capable of so great a multitude [of tasks]; and with the daily increase in the number of arriving crowds, they could not be received within the structures of the factory and the *oratorium solis* barely [held] enough monks.

Instead, Geoffrey "considered a way appropriate to the plain below, and that lower place can make use of the river." That place would be

> spacious to all of the monastery needs: meadows, colonies, shrubs, and vines, and if it were seen that the forest enclosure were wanting [*videatur deesse*; to be seen to be wanting], walls of stone would be easy [to construct], for there was a vast [supply of stone] there for replacements.[23]

Abbaye Cistercienne, 1974), 123: Unde licet nobis possidere ad proprios usus aquas, silvas, vineas, prata, terras a saecularium hominum habitatione semotas et animalia.

20   Jean-Francois Leroux-Dhuys, *Cistercian Abbeys: History and Architecture* (Koln: Konemann, 1998), 37.

21   Marcel Aubert, *L'architecture Cistercienne en France* (Paris: Vanoest, 1947), 1: ###.

22   Watkin Williams, *Saint Bernard of Clairvaux* (Westminster, MD: The Newman Press, 1952), 396.

23   *De Reditu Bernardi ex Italia, et de Monasterii Clarae-Vallis in locum capaciorem translatione*, in *Opera Omnia*, ed. Bernardus, PLL 185 (1854; Paris: Migne, 1981), col. 284c–285a: Hic ergo atque alii plures viri provide, et de communi utilitate solliciti, Virum Dei, cujus conversatio in coelis erat, aliquando descendere compellebant, et indicabant ei quae domus necessitas exigebat. Insinuant itaque ei locum angustum et incommodum in quo consederant, nec capacem tantae multitudinis; et cum quotidie catervatim

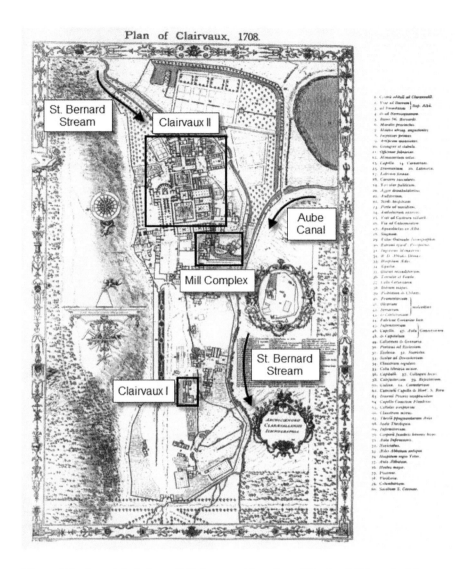

Figure 7.1 Annotated plan of Clairvaux abbey from Nicolas Milley, *Archicoenobii Claraevallensis ichnographia* (1708)

Source: Modified from Watkin Williams, *Saint Bernard of Clairvaux* (Westminster, MD: The Newman Press, 1952), p. 396, after the original in the Bibliotheque Nationale de France.

After some hesitation, St. Bernard agreed. The relocation of the new abbey church and accompanying monastic compound (Clairvaux II) to a position a few hundred meters up the St. Bernard stream allowed for the construction of a 3.5-kilometer millrace off the river Aube that provided adequate power for the compound's new milling facility. After its completion, St. Bernard went on to ensure that Clairvaux II become the standard of early Cistercian architecture that subsequent Cistercian houses were expected to emulate, a standard that included a hydraulic network conducive to both agricultural and industrial milling. This is evidenced by the fact that all sixty-nine of Clairvaux's daughter houses that were constructed prior to the death of St. Bernard in 1153 conformed to the programmatic principles of Clairvaux II.[24]

Arnold of Bonneval, correspondent and biographer of St. Bernard, recorded an enthusiastic description of Clairvaux II's hydraulic system during a visit in 1136:

> They spared no expenses, and hiring employees quickly, they set down all the work for the brothers. Some cut down trees, some squared up [*conquadrabant*] stones, some built walls, some dammed and channeled [*diffuses limitibus partiebantur fluvium*: divided up limits of the river], and helped the forest's water to the mill. But fullers, bakers, tanners, smiths, and various other artificers, appropriately adapted its activities [to] engines as it issued and came forth. Wherever appropriate the underground stream was escorted, rushing [*ebulliens*], in channels to every home.[25]

Arnold's account provides our earliest documented evidence of Cistercian industrial milling, and he mentions these industrial activities in a manner that seems to take them for granted. This leads to the logical conclusion that Arnold was familiar with industrial milling prior to that time. Another description from one of Arnold's contemporaries similarly celebrates the majesty of the milling complex of Clairvaux II:

> But the river does not give up here. It is the turn of the fullers working next to the mill to call upon it. Having concerned itself with preparing nourishment for the monks it now thinks of their clothing. It never refuses to do what is asked of it. It raises and lowers in turn the heavy pounders, hammers, or to put it another way,

---

adventantium numerus augeretur, non posse eos intra constructas recipi officinas, et vix oratorium solis sufficere monachis. Addunt etiam se considerasse inferius aptam planitiem, et opportunitatem fluminis quod infra illabitur, ibique locum -esse spatiosum ad omnes monasterii necessitates, ad prata, ad colonias, ad virgulta et vineas: et si silvae videatur deesse clausura, facile hoc parietibus lapideis, quorum ingens ibi copia est, posse suppleri.

24 Anselme Dimier, *Recueil de plans d'églises Cisterciennes* (Grignan, Drôme: Abbaye Notre-Dame D'Aiguebelle, 1949).

25 *De Reditu Bernardi ex Italia*, col. 285c–d: Abundantibus sumptibus, conductis festinanter operariis, ipsi fratres per omnia incumbebant operibus. Alii caedebant ligna, alii lapides conquadrabant, alii muros struebant, alii diffusis limitibus partiebantur fluvium, et extollebant saltus aquarum ad molas. Sed et fullones, et pistores, et coriarii, et fabri, alique artifices, congruas aptabant suis operibus machinas, ut scaturiret et prodiret, ubicunque opportunum esset, in omni domo subterraneis canalibus deductus rivus ultro ebulliens.

the wooden feet, thus sparing the brothers much heavy labor . . . Next it enters the tannery, where it prepares the leather needed for the brothers' footwear. It is both hard working and energetic.[26]

The planning and implementation of such an advanced hydraulic system so early in the order's history clearly indicate that the monks of Clairvaux recognized the importance of water power to their success and that they were comfortable integrating water power into their monastic complex prior to the order's prolific expansion.

Most medieval mills, including those owned and operated by Cistercians, were agricultural mills dedicated to grinding grain. All but two of the mills at Cîteaux and fourteen of fifteen at La Bussiere were grain mills.[27] The Rule of St. Benedict called for one weighed pound of bread per day to each monk, a significant demand for burgeoning monasteries.[28] For the order to remain self-sufficient, Cistercians had to supply the grain, mills, and manpower necessary to bake this bread. In 1148, a mere thirty-three years after its foundation, Clairvaux housed approximately 700 individuals, a number that included both novices and lay brothers.[29] That translates into a requirement of almost 20,000 pounds of bread per month for Clairvaux alone. As astounding as these numbers are, Bernard's contemporaries highlighted the industrial milling capacity of Clairvaux in their writings.

While far fewer in number than agricultural mills, industrial mills were essential for the Cistercian order to remain self-sufficient. Undershot, vertical water wheels were most commonly used in France to power industrial mills. The topography of France made it difficult to create a waterfall large enough to power overshot wheels,

---

26 *Descriptio positionis seu situationis monasterii Clarae-Vallensis*, in Bernardus, *Opera Omnia*, PLL 185, col. 570c–71b: Eum enim ad se fullones invitant, qui sunt molendino confines, rationis jure exigentes, ut sicut in molendino sollicitus est, quo fratres vescantur, ita apud eos paret, quo et vestiantur. Ille autem non contradicit, nec quidquam eorum negat quae petuntur: sed graves illos, sive pistillos, sive malleos dicere mavis, vel certe pedes ligneos (nam hoc nomen saltuoso fullonum negotio magis videtur congruere) alternatim elevans atque deponens, gravi labore fullones absolvit: et si joculare quidpiam licet interserere seriis, peccati eorum poenas absolvit. . . . Excipitur dehinc a domo coriaria, ubi conficiendis his quae ad fratrum calceamenta sunt necessaria, operosam exhibit sedulitatem. Translation from Leroux-Dhuys, *Cistercian Abbeys* (note 20, above), 48. This passage is more freely paraphrased in Jean Gimpel, *The Medieval Machine* (London: Victor Gollancz, 1977), 5–6 and James Burke, *The Axemaker's Gift* (New York: Doubleday, 1996), 108.

27 Karine Berthier and Josephine Rouillard, "Nouvelles Recherches sur L'hydraulique Cistercienne en Bourgogne, Champagne et Franche-Comte," *Archéologie Médiévale* 28 (1999): 142.

28 *S.P. Benedicti regula cum commentariis* (note 17, above), col. 613D–14D: Panis libra una propensa sufficiat in die, sive una sit refection, sive prandii et coenae. Quod si coenaturi sunt, de eadem libra tertia pars a cellerario reservetur reddenda coenaturis.

29 Aubert, *L'architecture Cistercienne en France*, 1: 15.

and the more powerful vertical wheels were better suited for industrial processes like fulling that required the reciprocating motion of hammers to pound cloth. These hammers were powered by cams placed on a drum fixed to the horizontal shaft of a vertical water wheel.[30] By mounting the cams directly, the horizontal axle of the wheel did not require gears that could reduce the amount of energy available or cause undue mechanical problems.[31] As the wheel turned, the cams tripped hammers that generated the power needed for a variety of industrial processes.

Industrial mills processed materials other than grain. Fulling mills, for example, automated the process of shrinking, felting, and cleansing newly made cloth, while tanning mills macerated oak bark to extract the tannins necessary to tan leather.[32] But as the order was strongly dedicated to remaining self-sufficient, they had to produce many necessary items like shoes, clothing, and tools using industrial watermill technology.[33] It is no surprise, therefore, that the Cistercian order has been associated with industrial milling to an extent that that its contemporaries who could outsource these needs have not. By the end of the twelfth century, Cistercians were acquiring industrial mills in numbers that resulted in a production capacity far exceeding the needs of their monastic community resulting in participation in commercial exchange in spite of the order's self-imposed restrictions. A 1218 reference to the activities of Brother Ancher, a monk responsible for selling the excess products of Clairvaux and acquiring those products that the abbey could not produce, demonstrates this point.[34] When one considers this commercial activity in conjunction with the order's targeted exploitation of granges by the middle of the thirteenth century, it becomes clear that Cistercians were purchasing mills specifically for their income-generating potential by this time.[35]

---

30 Bertrand Gille, "Le moulin à eau: une révolution technique médiévale," *Techniques et civilisation* 3, no. 1 (1954): 8–9; Wikander, *Exploitation of Water-Power* (note 13, above), 8; Adam Robert Lucas, *Wind, Water, Work: Ancient and Medieval Milling Technology*, Technology and Change in History 8 (Leiden: Brill, 2006), 244; E.M. Carus-Wilson, "An Industrial Revolution of the Thirteenth Century," *The Economic History Review* 11, no. 1 (1941): 43.

31 Paul Benoit and Josephine Rouillard, "Medieval Hydraulics in France," in *Working with Water in Medieval Europe: Technology and Resource Use*, ed. Paulo Squatriti, Technology and Change in History 3 (Leiden: Brill, 2000), 161–216 at 204.

32 Lucas, *Wind, Water, Work*, 243.

33 Adam Robert Lucas, "Industrial Milling in the Ancient and Medieval Worlds: A Survey of the Evidence for an Industrial Revolution in Medieval Europe," *Technology and Culture* 46, no. 1 (2005): 6.

34 M.H. d'Arbois, *Études sur l'état intérieur des abbayes Cistercienne, et principalement de Clairvaux, au xiie et au xiiie siècle* (Hildesheim: Strauss & Cramer, 1858), 240.

35 Paul Benoit, "L'industrie Cistercienne (xiie – premiere moitie du xivème siècle)," in *Monachisme et technologie dans la société médiévale du xe au xiiie siècle*, Actes du Colloque Scientifique International, Cluny, Septembre 4–6, 1991 (Cluny: Centre d'Enseignement et de Recherche de Cluny, 1991), 74; François Blary, "Les Établissements Agricoles et

Fulling mills that produced cloth and forge mills that produced iron are the first industrial mills for which we have documented evidence in France and the Cistercian applications for which we have the most documentary and archaeological evidence.[36] In a charter dated to 1080, the abbey of St. Wandrille in the diocese of Rouen was given the tithes of a fulling mill, and Anne-Marie Bautier documents a water-powered fulling mill located in Annegecq, Normandy, in 1086.[37] The earliest evidence of an industrial mill to appear in a Cistercian charter is the 1133 agreement between Pontigny and the Benedictine monastery of Saint-Germain d'Auxerre regarding the Espillard mill, a fulling mill in Revisy.[38] The two monasteries agreed to share the expenses and profits of this mill, while Pontigny retained the exclusive right to fish and fisheries within the defined boundaries, as well as the right to choose the miller. This charter clearly indicates that the miller of the Espillard mill was expected to be secular through its provision for his payment in corn, an interesting arrangement given the charter's early date. This provides clear evidence that Cistercian abbeys were struggling to balance their mandate of self-sufficiency with the reality of life in medieval France quite early in the order's history.

In *Wind, Water, Work: Ancient and Medieval Milling Technology* (2006), Adam Lucas argues that Benedictine and Cistercian application of water mills to industrial processes appears to have been overstated by historians of technology.[39] He supports this assertion with a compiled list of approximately 400 documented references to ancient and medieval industrial mills that date from 700 to 1600 CE. For documentation of French mills, Lucas relies heavily on Bautier's study, *Les Plus*

Industriels de l'abbaye Cistercienne de Chaalis (Oise)," in *Les Abbayes Cistercienne et Leurs Granges*, ed. G. Duby (Paris: Ligue Urbaine et Rurale, 1991), 42.

36 Bradford Blaine, "The Application of Water-Power to Industry During the Middle Ages." PhD dissertation, University of California at Los Angeles, 1966.

37 Anne-Marie Bautier, "Les plus anciennes mentions de moulins hydrauliques industriels et de moulins à vent," *Bulletin philologique et historique* (1960): 150.

38 Martine Garrigues, *Le premier Cartulaire de L'abbaye Cistercienne de Pontigny* (XIIe–XIIIe siècles), Collection de documents inedits sur l'histoire de France 14 (Paris: Bibliothèque Nationale, 1981), 171: Successorum memoriae presenti scripto commendare studuimus, inter nos scilicet aecclesiam Sancti Germani Autisiodorensis et Beatae Mariae Pontiniacensis, agentibus abbatibus Gervasio atque Hugone, de molendino quod est in alodio Revisiaci, nomine Espaillardo, taliter convenisse. Utrumque siquidem laudavit capitulum ut expensas molendini communiter mitterent et reditus omnes aequali portione inter se dividerent. Aecclesia tamen Pontiniacensis ad quam proprie molendini sedes et aqua pertinebat, omnes ejusdem aquae pisces atque piscationes infra terminus aquae suae sibi specialiter retinuit. Ad eamdem quoque pertinebit aecclesiam molendinarium eligere, mittere atque mutare subque jure suo quantum dumtaxat ad molendinum pertinent, specialiter habere. Ipse vero molendinarius utrique aecclesie de parte sua fidelitatem faciet atque de communibus molendini reditibus modium annonae pro mercede recipient cum certeris exacturis quae ad hujus modi mercennarios universali consuetudine pertinere noscuntur.

39 Lucas, *Wind, Water, Work* (note 30, above), 224.

Anciennes Mentions de Moulins Hydrauliques Industriels et de Moulins à Vent (1960). More than 50 years after its publication, this work remains the most comprehensive source of information regarding French industrial mills that existed from 1086 to 1200. Unfortunately, Bautier relied heavily on documentation found within Du Cange's *Glossarium*, an extensive Latin reference work first compiled in France in 1678.[40] While Du Cange is an immensely useful historical resource, it does not include most known Cistercian mills. For example, Louis Dubois has identified fifteen to twenty fulling mills associated with the abbey of Morimond, none of which appear on Bautier's list. This is an impressive number of fulling mills to be associated with a single abbey, given that just over seventy such mills have been identified in all of England and Wales, the first not being documented until 1185 and that owned and operated by the Templars.[41]

It is possible that Morimond required such a large number of fulling mills due to the monastery's unusual practice of establishing granges in areas where future daughter houses were envisioned.[42] The surplus cloth generated by the mills owned by Morimond and other Cistercian abbeys may have provided a source of income for needs not met by the various granges, as well as for the purchase of more land and funds to establish new abbeys. It is easy to see how the drive to establish daughter houses could have innocently resulted in the generation of income above and beyond what Cistercian abbeys needed to sustain themselves and contributed to the rapid proliferation of the order in the twelfth and thirteenth centuries. The fact that so many well-documented Cistercian mills are not listed in Lucas's work brings his argument that downplays the Cistercian application of industrial water-mill technology into question and highlights the need for an updated, comprehensive list of French industrial mills, as well as those of other regions.

Georges Duby proclaimed that the Cistercian order built its forges with as much majesty as its sanctuaries,[43] and evidence does indicate that Cistercians made a significant technological contribution to the industrial application of iron production. Centered largely in Champagne and Burgundy, Cistercian iron production was

---

40 Charles du Fresne Du Cange, et al., *Glossarium Mediae et Infirmae Latinitatis*, ed. Léopold Favre, 10 vols. (Niort: Favre, 1883–1887).

41 Louis Dubois, *Histoire de L'abbaye de Morimond: Quatrième fille de Cîteaux*, 3rd ed. (Dijon: Imprimerie Darantiere, 1879), 158; C. James Bond, "Cistercian Mills in England and Wales: A Preliminary Survey," in *L'espace Cistercien*, ed. Léon Pressouyre (Paris: Comité des travaux historique et scientifiques, 1994), 372; Carus-Wilson, "An Industrial Revolution of the Thirteenth Century" (note 30, above), 44.

42 Jean Salmon, "Morimond et ses Granges," in *Actes du 38e Congrès de L'association Bourguignonne des Sociétés Savantes* (Langres: Société historique et archéologique, 1969), 124.

43 Georges Duby, *Saint Bernard: L'art Cistercien* (Paris: Arts et Metiers Graphiques, 1976), 116.

often associated with granges dedicated to pasturage.[44] Iron production provided a source of income that helped to compensate for the less productive, heavily wooded granges where iron was often found but arable land was not. In Champagne, centers of iron production were located in the heart of the forests of Othe, Wassy, and La Chaume.[45] Cîteaux and Clairvaux, along with their daughter houses Vauluisant, Pontigny, La Crête, Longuay, Auberive, Fontenay, and LaBussière, were all active in the production of iron in this region.[46] An 1168 charter of Clairvaux documents an unusually detailed donation related to the production of iron by Walter, bishop of Langres.[47] This charter gave the abbey the exclusive right to extract iron from the land in the forest of La Chaume, to build a forge on that land, and to use wood from the forest as needed for the forge. The industry in Burgundy, located primarily in Gissey-on-Ouche, Montbard, and Cussey-les-Forge, developed somewhat later. The monasteries associated with these sites in Burgundy included Cîteaux, Fontenay, La Bussiere, and Auberive.[48] Cistercians appear to have produced iron for internal needs alone until the middle of the twelfth century, a time that corresponds with an increasing demand for iron products in the West.[49] With few competitors prior to the early thirteenth century and exemptions still in place that resulted in a greater than average market value for their goods, the order had much to gain by exploiting this market. By the thirteenth century, Cistercians were enthusiastically producing a surplus of iron to meet these external needs.

As with fulling, waterpower-driven iron production applies a cam system to the hammers, thus allowing for larger forge hammers and more constant production than was possible with ironworkers alone.[50] The abbey of Fontenay yields the most evidence for water usage in relation to the Cistercian iron industry. The milling complex of Fontenay is known to have been established in the twelfth century and nearby deposits of slag, a by-product of the metallurgy process, provide evidence that Fontenay had an early water-driven forge equipped with a hydraulic

---

44   Benoit, "L'industrie Cistercienne" (note 35, above), 82; Verna, *Les mines et les forges des Cisterciens* (note 13, above), 45.
45   Ibid., 15.
46   Ibid., 7.
47   Jean Waquet, ed., *Recueil des chartes de L'abbaye de Clairvaux, xiie siecle* (Troyes: Archives Départementales de l'Aube, 1950–1982), 2: 141: Ego Galterus, Dei gratia Lingonensis episcopus, notum esse volo presentibus et futuris me dedisse et concessisse in elemosinam domui Clarevallensi et fratribus ejusdem monasterii ut in finagio ville nostre de Chalma mineriam ferri extrahant et acceptam deferant libere sine contradiction, et si voluerint in eodem territorio de Chalma fabricam habeant et quod necessarium fuerit ad necessitate et utilitatem prefate domus habeant et exerceant mineriam prout utile sibi fratres idem judicaverint ad proprios usus Clarevallensis ecclesie cunctis diebus.
48   Verna, *Les mines et les forges des Cisterciens*, 30–31.
49   Ibid., 50.
50   Benoit and Rouillard, *Medieval Hydraulics in France* (note 31, above), 194.

hammer.[51] Similar evidence has been cited for the mill of Cérilly that belonged to the abbey of Vauluisant.[52] In Germany, Cistercian forge mills also powered bellows that enabled temperatures high enough to liquefy metal in blast furnaces.[53] While the Cistercian iron industry did not develop in earnest until the middle of the twelfth century, the description of Clairvaux II by Arnold of Bonneval clearly documents a water-driven hydraulic forge. Physical and documentary evidence indicates that Cistercians were active in the iron industry quite early in the order's history and that water power was used for this purpose when feasible.

Even with the significant omission of documented Cistercian mills from Lucas's list, 47% of the industrial mills listed in his compilation were located in France. His list also reveals a significant difference between the industrial mills in France and those in other countries. While fulling mills composed the majority of industrial mills in most countries, fewer than 50% of the industrial mills in France were of this type. Malt mills (which Lucas argues are industrial rather than agricultural mills), tanning mills, tool-sharpening mills, hemp mills, and sawmills are associated with France in numbers that far exceed these types of mills in other countries. In addition, 75% of the fulling mills and the only tanning mills that date to a time prior to the foundation of the Cistercian order were located in France.[54] All these observations reinforce the idea that France was a leader in the application of industrial water-mill technology well before and quite apart from the foundation of the Cistercian order.

According to Richard Holt, many of England's medieval mills were incorporated into the demesne sector by English lords who were concerned first and foremost with profit.[55] Because fulling mills in England were much less profitable than agricultural mills, a preference developed for corn mills in areas of England where there was an abundance of water. This resulted in a conservative policy toward watermill acquisition and development in that country.[56] Holt broadly con-

---

51 Benoit, "L'industrie Cistercienne" (note 35, above), 89.

52 Ibid.

53 Albrecht Hoffmann, "The Management of Water Power by the Medieval Monasteries in Central Europe," in *Actas Do Simpósio Internacional Hydráulica Monástica Medieval e Moderna, Convento da Arrábida, Novembro 15–17, 1993*, ed. José Manuel P.B. de Mascarenhas, Maria Helena Abecasis, and Virgolino Ferreira Jorge (Lisboa: Fundação Oriente, 1996), 146. For the later furnace revolution, see Brian G. Awty, "The Development and Dissemination of the Walloon Method of Ironworking," *Technology and Culture* 48, no. 4 (2007): 783–803.

54 These numbers were obtained through examination of the tables provided in the following publications: Bautier, "Les Plus Anciennes Mentions" (note 37, above) and Lucas, *Wind, Water, Work* (note 30, above).

55 Richard Holt, "The Medieval Mill: A Productivity Breakthrough," *History Today* 39, no. 7 (1989): 31.

56 Richard Holt, "Whose Were the Profits of Corn Milling? An Aspect of the Changing Relationship between the Abbots of Glastonbury and Their Tenants 1086–1350," *Past &*

cluded from this geographically isolated fact that "the medieval application of water-power to a limited range of industrial processes has been exaggerated by historians of technology because, excited by the novelty of it all, they have failed to see how little economic impact it had."[57] Between the tenth and the twelfth centuries, however, ownership of mills in northern France shifted from lay and Episcopal authorities to chapter houses and suburban abbeys.[58] The intentional break of Cistercians with feudal land management practices and their commitment to self-sufficiency led to a more liberal, open-minded approach to milling than that of their English neighbors, an approach surely encouraged by the preexistence of a robust industrial milling industry in France. This, in conjunction with the economic influence of tithe exemptions that Cistercians were granted in the twelfth century, resulted in a profitable industrial milling scenario for Cistercians in France and other parts of Europe from the twelfth century onward. Evidence from both France and Italy has shown that fulling mills in those areas earned as much, if not more, than grain mills in some parts of Europe.[59]

English scholarship on medieval watermills, as evidenced by the work of Holt and Lucas, has focused predominately on English watermills, but as can be seen from examining the lists of industrial mills provided by Bautier and Lucas, watermill development and usage in England differed significantly from that in the rest of Europe. Holt acknowledges that industrial mills may have had a more significant impact on the economy in other countries, but he claims that there is insufficient evidence to make such an assertion.[60] The importance of industrial milling to the economic success of the Cistercian order in twelfth-century France, as evidenced here, demonstrates that this is simply not true. It is clear from the evidence presented here that generalizations about the economic impact of industrial milling on the Cistercian order should not be based on English regional studies alone.

When one considers that Cistercian abbeys were mandated by the order itself, and from their inception, to produce the tremendous volume of clothing, leather, tools, and building materials that they required, and then not only survive but also

---

Present 116 (1987): 7–11, 13–22; John Langdon, "Was England a Technological Backwater in the Middle Ages?" in *Medieval Farming and Technology: The Impact of Agricultural Change in Northwest Europe*, ed. Grenville G. Astill and John Langdon, Technology and Change in History 2 (Leiden: Brill, 1997), 285.

57 Holt, "The Medieval Mill," 31.

58 Andre Guillerme, *The Age of Water: The Urban Environment in the North of France, A.D. 300 to 1800*, Environmental History Series 9 (College Station, TX: Texas A&M University Press, 1988), 94.

59 John Muendel, "The Distribution of Mills in the Florentine Countryside during the Late Middle Ages," in *Pathways to Medieval Peasants*, ed. J.A. Raftis (Toronto: Pontifical Institute of Medieval Studies, 1981), 89–95.

60 Richard Holt, "Medieval Technology and the Historians: The Evidence for the Mill," in *Technological Change: Methods and Themes in the History of Technology*, ed. Robert Fox (New York: Routledge, 1996), 111.

to thrive, it is reasonable to conclude that order could not have proliferated as it did in the twelfth and thirteenth centuries without an extensive preexisting network of industrial technology in France. Evidence has shown that contrary to popular belief, the majority of Cistercian mills were acquired by various means and not built by the monks themselves.[61] Only those mills in immediate proximity to the monastery were a regular exception, and they were built for the most part using existing technology without any significant innovative Cistercian contribution as far as can be determined.[62] If Thomas Hughes's concept of technological systems is applied very broadly to the scenario presented here, the technological system for which the Cistercian order is so well known was not developed by the order from the ground up. Rather, it was an open system in which the primary artifacts (industrial mills) were constructed by system builders who preceded the Cistercians.[63] The order's visible success as evidenced by its rapid proliferation in the twelfth and thirteenth centuries resulted in the long-standing, but mistaken, impression that Cistercians played an exaggerated role in technological development in the Middle Ages, as exemplified in Lynn White's work.

Unfortunately, when scholars dispelled the idea of an industrial revolution in the Middle Ages at the end of the twentieth century, a general sense of disillusionment with the technological prowess of the order and a subsequent tendency to overlook the complex, interwoven relationship that Cistercians had with water power pervaded the literature. The multifaceted interplay of theological devotion, monastic regulation, preexisting French milling technology, and a willingness to deviate from a rule of strict self-sufficiency as time progressed and circumstances changed allowed the Cistercian order to grow rapidly in the twelfth and thirteenth centuries. When Cistercian houses began to exploit the natural resources particular to their region, as those in Champagne and Burgundy exploited iron, the effect on the economy was profound. While the Cistercian order is no longer considered to be the instigator of an industrial revolution in the Middle Ages, as argued by Lynn White, Jr., the order's masterful use and development of preexisting watermill technology did contribute significantly to the prolific expansion of the order and the economic development of the rest of Europe in the twelfth and thirteenth centuries.

---

61 Paul Benoit and Karine Berthier, "L'innovation dans L'exploitation de L'énergie hydraulique d'après le cas des monastères Cisterciens de Bourgogne, Champagne et Franche-Comté," in *L'innovation Technique au Moyen Age*, Actes du vi[e] Congrès International d'Archéologie Medieval, ed. Patrice Beck (Paris: Éditions Errances, 1998), 59. Evidence indicates that only 3 of 11 mills at Pontigny, 3 of 17 at Boulancourt, 1 of 17 at Morimond, and 1 of 4 at Auberive were built by Cistercians.

62 Benoit, "L'industrie Cistercienne" (note 35, above), 76.

63 Thomas P. Hughes, "The Evolution of Large Technological Systems," in *The Social Construction of Technological Systems: New Directions in the Sociology and History of Technology*, ed. Wiebe E. Bijker, Thomas P. Hughes, and Trevor Pinch (Cambridge, MA: MIT Press, 1987), 45–76.

Chapter 8

Cistercian nuns and forest management in northern France

Constance H. Berman

This article centers on the evidence for the two houses of Cistercian nuns founded by Queen Blanche of Castile in northern France, at Maubuisson near Pontoise and le Lys near Melun.[1] It looks briefly as well at documents for several other such early thirteenth-century foundations for Cistercian nuns in northern France, including those at Lieu-Notre-Dame de Romorantin and les Clairets (both west of Paris) and Saint-Antoine-des-Champs just outside the medieval walls of the city of Paris itself. This explicit evidence surviving for those houses of nuns provides a picture of Cistercian prudence and rationality in the thirteenth-century management of forest; there is likely similar evidence for houses of Cistercian monks in this region at this time, but that is beyond the purview of the research on which this chapter draws.[2] In treating Cistercians and forest management, I am using the term *forest* for any medieval woodland resources, not limiting it to areas officially considered "forest" in a legal sense. It is probably no longer necessary to assert either that these abbeys of Cistercian nuns were as much a part of the order and of its economic practices as were the order's houses of monks or that such communities of religious women were as likely to practice the most up-to-date forest management as others would.[3]

---

1 Parts of this chapter were presented at the International Conference for Medieval Studies, Kalamazoo, Michigan, in May 2012; the Society for French Historical Studies annual meeting, Cambridge, Massachusetts, in April 2013; and at a conference on monasticism at University of Stirling, Scotland, in July 2013.
 2 This chapter draws on research from a larger study of Cistercian nuns: Constance H. Berman, *The White Nuns: Cistercian Abbeys for Women in Medieval Europe* (Philadelphia: University of Pennsylvania Press, 2018).
 3 See Constance H. Berman, "Were There Twelfth-Century Cistercian Nuns?" *Church History* 68 (1999): 824–64, and Janet Burton, *The Yorkshire Nunneries in the Twelfth and Thirteenth Centuries*, Borthwick Paper 56 (York, UK: University of York, Borthwick Institute of Historical Research, 1979). In our discussion of communities of

The issue of Cistercians and forests is associated with a long-term debate about Cistercians as pioneers, in which I have argued that Cistercians most often settled in places that were already cleared and cultivated, where they instituted grange agriculture by a considerable investment in reassembling fragmented landholdings. Often but not always their sites had become available to them as a result of a secular movement of village formation, although their foundations might also be used by powerful lords to occupy spaces that might otherwise become those of rival castles.[4] The granges that we associate with the Cistercians were created by investing savings from their austere lifestyles in rationalizing and consolidated fragmented land. Whatever reclamation work they may have done was usually secondary, in that land was either cleared or drained or occupied in some fashion before they acquired it.[5]

Such approaches are in contradiction to a traditional picture based on Cistercian rhetoric that identified them as founding their houses and living "far from cities, castles and human habitations" and "by the labor of their own hands" found in early documents produced by the order.[6] Cistercian authors continued to repeat this rhetorical theme of Cistercian plantations amid savagery as found, for instance, in Walter Daniel's mid-twelfth-century biography of Aelred of Rievaulx.[7] The assertions by monastic authors of the order's "pioneering" origins led an earlier generation of medievalists to conclude that Cistercian foundations everywhere were encountering

---

religious women in the later Middle Ages, we must abandon old assumptions about female frailty and incompetence. Cistercian abbesses were just as likely as Cistercian abbots to be good property managers and to invest in the amelioration of their holdings houses of Cistercian nuns that I have investigated in northern France were neither poor nor ill managed; there is no indication that they were in debt, but they were often maligned by monastic officials. See Constance H. Berman, "The Labors of Hercules, the Cartulary, Church and Abbey for Nuns of La Cour-Notre-Dame-de-Michery," *Journal of Medieval History* 26 (2000): 33–70.

4 On this see Constance H. Berman, plenary, "Amelioration and Investment by Cistercian Monks and Nuns," from the "Plantations Amidst Savagery?" conference in July 2013 on monasticism at Stirling University, organized by Richard Oram.

5 Constance H. Berman, *Medieval Agriculture, the Southern-French Countryside, and the Early Cistercians. A Study of Forty-Three Monasteries*, Transactions of the American Philosophical Society 76, pt. 5 (Philadelphia: APS, 1986).

6 Long quoted from the so-called Prima collectio, the dating of those documents is discussed in Constance H. Berman, *The Cistercian Evolution. The Invention of a Religious Order in Twelfth-Century Europe* (Philadelphia: University of Pennsylvania Press, 2000; rpt. 2nd ed. 2010).

7 Walter Daniel, *The Life of Alred of Rievaulx*, trans. F.M. Powicke (Kalamazoo, MI: Cistercian Institute Publications, 1994), 124–25: "The father (Aelred) went down to Galloway to visit and comfort a daughter-house of Rievaulx. . . . It is a wild country where the inhabitants are like beasts and is altogether barbarous. . . . Rievaulx made a foundation in this savagery which now, by the help of God, who gives the increase to a new plantation, bears much fruit." Querying these remarks was the theme for the 2013 conference on monasticism at Stirling.

land never before cultivated and that the Cistercian economic successes were inadvertent, but could be explained by the "bumper crops" of soils never before brought under the plow. But this rhetoric of solitudinous sites was a traditional monastic rhetoric long espoused by monks and nuns describing themselves as seeking out deserts and settling in wild and forested places. As a recent study by Ellen F. Arnold has made very clear, it long anticipated the late eleventh-century arrival of the Cistercians.[8] Interestingly enough, while the texts assert settlement in wilderness and forest, they rarely mention actual forest clearance by the Cistercians and only occasionally even evoke forest themes, historians have frequently pointed to manuscript illuminations to make that argument.[9] Several bits of such iconographic evidence have been used to argue for Cistercian pioneering activities but most often only cite early manuscript paintings from the early Cîteaux manuscript of the *Moralia in Job*, which depict monks laboring at various agricultural, household, and industrial tasks. What an art historian has recently told us about this picture is that "[w]hat is being shown here on the literal level is the act of land clearance.... [T]he extreme removal of the Cistercians in the early days to undeveloped regions typically necessitated extensive land clearance."[10]

This illustration of a Cistercian monk appearing to cut down a tree while a layman is in its top branches, using traditional tools to lop off branches probably to provide animal food and small poles for use as animal food and bedding, shows, in fact, two aspects of forest management. The top of the picture illustrates a kind of pollarding (and, by extension, coppicing), while the bottom reflects cutting down a tree for lumber. The art historian Conrad Rudolph, who described this painting as depicting "the act of land clearance," was misled by traditional interpretations. It, too, like other paintings in the *Moralia in Job* is a depiction of the struggle between good and evil, with the evil monk (tonsured) cutting down the tree while the "good" layman above him is having the tree cut down under him.[11]

A second frequently reproduced and similarly cited as evidence of Cistercians being involved in land clearance is an image from an early thirteenth-century manuscript commentary on the Apocalypse in the Cambridge University Library. This is apparently the first attempt to trace earlier history from the time of the Revelation of Saint John to the present and contains a series of such triptychs depicting important events such as the Life of Benedict and the spread of

---

8 Ellen F. Arnold, *Negotiating the Landscape: Environment and Monastic Identity in the Medieval Ardennes* (Philadelphia: University of Pennsylvania Press, 2013).

9 One rare use of forest imagery is found in the opening of the chronicle of Silvanès, see Beverly Kienzle, "Pons of Leras: A Twelfth-Century Cistercian," *Cîteaux: commentarii cistercienses* 40 (1989): 215–26.

10 Conrad Rudolph, *Violence and Daily Life: Reading, Art, and Polemics in the Cîteaux Moralia in Job* (Princeton: Princeton University Press, 1997), 67.

11 The tool used by the layman in the tree is one still used for cutting fodder in northern Europe. My thanks to Dr. Oystein Ekroll for this information.

the Cistercians. Once again, the image most likely depicts Cistercian forest management rather than clearance, particularly given that trees were cut back at just above the heads of the monks and laborers depicted there. Such harvesting of branches at head height above the reach of gracing animals allowed new growth to sprout out at that level.[12] Indeed, this may be a standard view more suggestive of pollarding than of any sort of clearance of never-before cleared forest.

That these two images reflect forest management and maintenance by the Cistercians, rather than any extensive clearance or other reclamation activities, is what is suggested by the materials from thirteenth-century foundations of houses of Cistercian nuns that I discuss in the following. This conforms with recent interpretations that new monks and nuns, like those of the Cistercian Order, participated not in the first stages of medieval reclamation activities but in a second stage of land management and amelioration. Such amelioration, for instance, in the expensive construction of dikes and large-scale drainage ditches, was the work often undertaken by monastic groups after the land had already been cleared, drained, and brought under cultivation by anonymous peasants.[13] As Robert Fossier long ago opined, "Cistercians were so late in the reclamation movement that they almost missed the train as it was leaving the station."[14]

The abbey of Notre-Dame-du-Lys near Melun was one of two foundations for Cistercian nuns made by Queen Blanche of Castile. It was begun in 1244 and completed by 1248 just before Louis IX left on his first Crusade. Its location southeast of Paris near the forest of Othe was in a region where forest reclamation and village formation were still relatively recent in the mid-thirteenth century.[15] Forest rights and management along this political frontier between France and Champagne have been intensively studied and provide a context for our understanding of le Lys's forest acquisitions. There kings of France and counts of Champagne alike, as well as the archbishops of Sens, established new towns or villages (*villeneuves*) to which they attempted to attract settlers.[16] There some attempts at village

---

12 See Oliver Rackham, *Trees and Woodland in the British Landscape* (London: Dent, 1990).

13 This is especially apparent where great monastic corporations provide dikes to protect previously drained land from the sea; see William H. TeBrake, *Medieval Frontier: Culture and Ecology in Rijnland* (College Station, TX: Texas A&M University Press, 1985), and Erin L. Jordan, *Women, Power, and Religious Patronage in the Middle Ages* (New York: Palgrave Macmillan, 2006).

14 Robert Fossier, "L'économie cistercienne dans les plaines du nord-ouest de l'Europe," *L'économie cistercienne. Géographie, mutations* (Centre culturel de l'abbaye de Flaran: Troisièmes journées internationales d'histoire, Septembre 16–18, 1981), *Bulletin Monumentale* 142, no. 2 (1983): 53–74.

15 Charles Higounet, *Défrichements et villeneuves du Bassin parisien, XIe–XIVe siècles* (Paris: CNRS, 1990).

16 See Richard Keyser, "The Transformation of Traditional Woodland Management: Commercial Sylviculture in Medieval Champagne," *French Historical Studies* 32, no. 3

foundation were short-lived and were soon replaced by the foundation of granges by le Lys and earlier monastic foundations. Elsewhere, new monastic sites and granges were located in the interstices between those *villeneuves*. For le Lys this is seen particularly clearly for the Cistercian nuns' grange at Mâlay, located in lands associated with the villages of Mâlay-le-Roi and Mâlay-le-Comte. The surviving documents for le Lys's acquisitions for this grange are much more extensive than those found for properties elsewhere.[17] There le Lys's nuns profited in its establishment of a grange from the relatively recent foundation of new settlements whose owners (some of them ecclesiastical ones) and tenants seemed quite willing to sell land to the nuns.

Many of the nuns' acquisitions at Mâlay were undertaken by le Lys's first abbess, Alice of Mâcon (1248–1259), one of Blanche of Castile's cousins who had inherited the county of Mâcon and sold the entire county to Louis IX in about 1237, shortly before her husband's death. The cash payment along with a lifetime annuity for Alice provided an annual income (possibly received even after she became abbess), which she used to fund purchases for le Lys.[18] Indeed, from her installation in 1248, Abbess Alice began acquiring rights south of Melun in a variety of lordships. Thus, she purchased 260 *arpents* of woodland along with 65 *arpents* of agricultural land at Tillières in the parish of Villiers-en-Brie from Hugh de la Grange for 600 livres of cash.[19] Her acquisition of forest rights along the Seine at Fontaine le Port or Fontaine le Farcy led to a dispute already in 1252 over cutting brush along the river.[20] In that year too, she acquired property upriver (*i.e.*, south) on the Seine in the city of Sens where she acquired a house, a wine cellar, and dependencies in the parish of Saint-Hilaire for 194 *livres tournois* from Felix of Pontarlier and his wife Isabelle.[21]

Abbess Alice also began to acquire rights in "Mâlay-le-Roi" and "Mâlay-le-Comte" just north of Sens along the Vanne River a tributary flowing east from the Seine. Thus, in 1253 she paid 100 *livres tournois* to the convent of Clairlieu for

---

(2009): 353–84; cf. William Duba, "The Cartulary of Vauluisant: A Critical Edition." MA thesis, University of Iowa, 1994.

17   For this grange, unlike others, medieval charters survive in all their detail because they were deposited in Sens rather than Melun at the time of the Revolution; see publication of summaries by L'Huillier, "Inventaire des titres concernant la seigneurie que les religieuses de l'abbaye royale de Notre-Dame du Lys Possèdaient à Mâlay-le-Roi," *Bulletin de la Société Historique de Sens* 10 (1882): 34–50.

18   See further discussion in Constance H. Berman, "Two Medieval Women's Control of Property and Religious Benefactions: Eleanor of Vermandois and Blanche of Castile," *Viator* 41, no. 2 (2010): 151–82.

19   Melun A.D. Seine-et-Marne H566, no. 25. An *arpent* is an area of square land measurement, approximately 0.85 acres (or about 3 *arpents* in a hectare), depending on which local foot measure was being used.

20   Ibid., no. 31.

21   L'Huillier, "Inventaire," 347–52.

half a vineyard at la Garenne in Mâlay-le-Roi; this included rights over a winepress, wine sheds, and a fourth share of a willow grove located on the pond of Mâlay at la Saulsaie. She also paid 665 *livres tournois* to Peter of Chateauvieux of Sens and his wife Felicia for a house, a barn, a barnyard, vineyards, and other rights in the *censive* (a seigneurial tract of land) and lordship of the lord king at Mâlay-le-Roi. Included in the sale were 14 *quarrelles*, possibly of vineyards, on the bank of the river Vanne, a meadow, and 20 pieces of land containing 24½ *arpents* at l'Espinette de Pasqui, rights at Île-Peche-Veron, and so on. These properties had been held by the late Guy Le Gaigneur, who also had held rights in the king's forest at Mâlay for which he had paid the king an annual rent of 40 livres. We can only speculate as to what his rights there were; they could have been to cut wood, to coppice, or simply for a pig pasture. Two years later, in June 1255, Louis IX, back from his first Crusade, transferred the rights in the forest of Mâlay to le Lys.[22] There and nearly everywhere in the vicinity where the nuns of le Lys made acquisitions we see them acquiring land holdings by extensive purchases, in part to acquire or establish vineyards or have them planted by nearby villagers.

By the time of her death in 1259, Abbess Alice herself would have expended nearly 1,400 *livres* acquiring rights at Malay (Table 8.1). These included 45 *arpents* of land at Mâlay, along with 5 *arpents* of willow groves, 10 of vineyards, a large amount of pasture, and a house and barn that Louis IX confirmed to le Lys in December 1260. By 1263 references to warrens, willow groves, and "the woods of le Lys" evidence the nuns' growing assets in the forested area, where, if nothing more, they were getting sufficient material to make barrels to ship wine down the Vanne, the Yonne, and the Seine for sale in Paris. Such acquisitions by the nuns continued right up to their purchase in 1296 of a house at Mâlay-le-Roi with its court and dependencies from Isabelle, widow of Geoffrey.[23]

Rights at Mâlay had included those in what had once been royal forest along the border with Champagne, but there were other concessions of royal forest to le Lys as well, recorded in a fourteenth-century cartulary devoted to rights granted by Louis IX and Blanche of Castile to that abbey.[24] About to depart on his 1248 Crusade, Louis IX granted le Lys 200 *arpents* in the forest of Bièvre. One hundred of these were described as including rights to collect wood for heating; for construction and repair of the abbey, its mills, or its dependent farms; and for up to 300 pigs to feed there at the proper season. The other 100 *arpents* were simply described as those at

---

22   Ibid., and Melun A.D. Seine-et-Marne H566, no. 35 (1253) lists a "foullerie."
23   L'Huillier, "Inventaire," 347–52.
24   See "Cartulaire du Lys," Paris, BnF, Latin MS 13,892. Armande Prieur's thesis on this manuscript is calendared in *Ecole nationale des Chartes. Positions des thèses de 1945* (Paris: Daupeley-Gouverneur, 1945), 119–24, which provides a summary of Prieure, "Histoire de l'abbaye Notre-Dame du Lys-la-Royale au diocèse de Sens." I have consulted this text in Melun, A.D. Seine-et-Marne, 100J149I, and in Inventaire H566, as well as the original cartulary in Paris.

Table 8.1 Sixty-three contracts for Mâlay from L'Huillier, 1252–55

Year	Gifts Received	Purchases Made	Average Purchase Price (livres tournois)	Total expended (livres tournois)
1252	1	1	194	194
1253	0	2	382½	765
1254	1	6	70	419¼
1255	1	2	20¼	20¼
TOTALS	3	11		1,398½

the Quai or Port of le Lys on the Seine. Le Lys thus received usage rights in royal forests that included pasture in season for pigs, a certain number of carts of firewood each week, and of larger materials, possibly even obtained by cutting trees, for building churches and abbey complexes, granges, and mills. Le Lys soon acquired additional rights to woodland and vineyards, often located along the Seine near the abbey itself in areas often described as in the censive, or lordship of the king. These included rights at Farcy, Fontanne-le-Port, les Boissettes, and Boissises-le-Roi, the last clearly an area in which the king had lordship but in which rights were pieced together in small conveyances. Thus, in March 1250 Lauran Guignard granted five *quartiers* of vineyards at Boissises-le-Roi that had owed twelve pennies of rent. Jean of Boissises-le-Roi granted six shillings in rent, a house, an *arpent* of vineyard, and two pieces of land in the same place, all held earlier from the king. In April 1260 Aveline la Bouchière sold the nuns a piece of vineyard at Boissises-le-Roi located in the censive of the king on which three pennies were owed. In June 1262 Gerard of Boissises gave one piece of land at Boissises-le-Roi in the king's censive owing 20 shillings. In March 1269 Louis IX amortized to the nuns (granted them the right to hold in mainmort) all the nuns' acquisition of these rents at Boissises and elsewhere nearby, for instance, at Bretagnes and Rubella.[25] In the end, the nuns had acquired considerable properties at royal forests' edges. Indeed, the analysis of Armande Prieur in 1945 listed the abbey's holdings by the seventeenth century as 1,750 *arpents* of property, describing the nuns as practicing a regular forest-cutting rotation over ten years, with woodland products in ten-year rotation cycles for use as building materials, for making wine barrels, and for firewood and animal fodder.[26]

Whereas the abbey of Cistercian nuns at le Lys was founded in an area adjoining the borderlands between Capetians and counts of Champagne, those at Notre-Dame-la-Royale or Maubuisson, also founded by Queen Blanche of Castile, were on a different political frontier, on the edge of newly acquired royal territories in Normandy. Maubuisson's location approximately forty miles west of Paris in the parish of Saint-Ouen-d'Aulnay, today part of Pontoise, was near the confluence of the Oise and Seine. Queen Blanche founded it between 1236 and 1242 on dower lands granted by her

---

25   Melun A.D. Seine-et-Marne H566, nos. 20, 29, and 30.
26   Prieure, *Histoire*, 139–66.

son (probably in anticipation of a settlement formalized in 1240), and for its construction, she had access to materials in the nearby royal forest of Cergy. Although in 1240 Blanche was limited by her son, the king, from permanently alienating more than a tiny portion of her dower properties, she had access to income and materials from her dower lands, as well as to her cash in the treasury in Paris, with which to begin this project.[27]

Maubuisson's charters provide evidence for substantial forest acquisitions by its nuns in nearby wooded lands as well as further afield. In 1245 Louis IX granted Maubuisson rights to feed 300 pigs in the woods of Guise and in those of Retz in the Vermandois north of Paris.[28] It was probably also in 1245 that Louis IX gave Maubuisson rights northward and upriver on the Oise to collect each week seven three-horse cartloads of firewood in the forest called "Alathe," described as near the woods of Bonfosse, which, in turn, was described as between Verneuil and Pont-Saint-Maxent.[29] While visiting Maubuisson in October 1245, Louis IX gave additional forest rights in "le bois Ageux" and 100 *arpents* of woodland at Bonfosse. The latter adjoined woods belonging to Royaumont, on one side, and those of Peter Cook, knight, on the other.[30] In October 1250 this Peter Cook made a gift of another 20 *arpents* of woodland to Maubuisson and then in November 1250 sold those nuns another 150 *arpents* of woods there for 600 livres.[31] In 1255 Cook also sold them woods that adjoined those belonging to other lords including those of the lord king for 160 livres.[32]

---

27 For resettlement by Louis IX, see *Layettes*, vol. 2, no. 2885 (1240) and vol. 5, no. 514 (June 1248). After 1240, the queen began to consolidate rights at the abbey site by repurchasing claims from other holders. Thus, in 1241, Robert of Maubuisson; his wife, Odeline; and their son, Nicholas, sold to the queen their claims in the estate of Maubuisson, which they held from the abbot of Joyenval, a house of Premonstratensians (who confirmed the sale), "for the work of the new abbey." The conveyance included two houses near the abbey and all their holdings at Maubuisson, described as 15 *arpents* of land, vineyards, and meadows and their woodland of la Nova or la Novella. They were paid 402 livres, of which 40 were reserved for their son, Enjorrand, when he came of age. *Cartulaire de Maubuisson*, nos. 91–92 (1241–43) and Pontoise, A.D. Val d'Oise "Achatz," fol. 38ᵛ (1242) and fols. 40ᵛ–41ʳ. Although Armelle Bonis, *Abbaye cistercienne de Maubuisson. La Formation du Temporel (1236 à 1356)* (Saint-Ouen-l'Aumône: Conseil Général du Val-d'Oise, 1990), 29, suggests that there once existed a conveyance of the site in the villa of Aulnay from the abbey of Saint-Martin of Pontoise, more likely Saint-Martin of Pontoise had claims to tithes there. Grantors to the nuns occasionally mention holding their lands in fief from the lord king or lady queen; see the following discussion. Founded before 1227, the Premonstratensian house of Joyenval was located south of Poissy near Chambourcy in the diocese of Chartres (later Versailles) See A. Dutilleux, *Notice sur l'abbaye de Joyenval* (Versailles: Cerf et fils, 1891).
28 *Cartulaire de Maubuisson*, no. 8 (May 1245).
29 Ibid., no. 38 (1272).
30 Ibid., no. 244 (October 1245).
31 Ibid., nos. 245–48 (1250).
32 Ibid., nos. 171–74, 189–91, 198, and 204 (1247–71).

In 1246, just before his departure on his first Crusade, Louis IX made a huge grant of income to Maubuisson: 400 livres per annum from new assarts in the forest of Breteuil near Evreux. To have purchased such rights would have cost 4,000 livres.[33] Such a concession made by the king shortly before his departure not only garnered prayers for the success of his expedition but also may have protected from usurpation such recently assarted lands in what was still a fragile border region with the Angevins.[34] In 1248 Queen Blanche herself also purchased additional rights for Maubuisson near Evreux in the forest at Bretagnolles for 1,500 livres.[35] Some income from the forests in Normandy is included in the account book discussed later (see Appendix A.1).

The abbey and church must have been nearly complete when Blanche of Castile announced in this foundation charter that she had used her own funds to build it. The church would be consecrated in 1244.[36] The foundation charter for Maubuisson is dated 1241/42. In it, Blanche asserted that she had built the abbey with her own funds. She went on to say that this abbey's foundation would be as pleasing in the heavenly realm as was the conversion of pagans to Christianity:

> The doctors of the most holy mother Church assert that the blessed angels are filled with joy at the baptism of the reborn [newly converted] Christian, but to do this is difficult in our present times.... Therefore to increase the affection of those heavenly friends and for the honor of the omnipotent Deity and especially his most glorious, ever-virgin Mother, and everyone in that heavenly city.... We [Blanche] with the approval of our dear son, Louis [IX], King of the Franks, and with our own funds, have founded and built a house of nuns of the Cistercian Order [at Maubuisson].... We do this for the health of our soul, and those of the late Alphonse, illustrious and well-renowned King of Castile, our father, and Queen Eleanor, his wife, our mother, and for our dearest Lord and beloved husband of great renown, Louis VIII, the late King of the Franks, and for our dear son Louis IX and all our children.... We have founded this abbey of nuns of the Cistercian Order ... on the estate of Aulnay next to Pontoise. And we shall call it Notre- Dame-la-Royale, because it is to be founded in honor of the Celestial Queen. We concede to it in perpetuity ... the place itself and the land on which it is sited, the monastery [and its church], the dormitory, the refectory, the cellar, and all the necessary buildings contained within its walls, those buildings and walls and whatever is within them, from their length and breadth, right and left. All this was acquired with our own personal funds.[37]

The early account book, called on its cover *Achatz d'héritage de Maubuisson* (Purchases of Endowment of Maubuisson) bears out Blanche's assertion that she had built it with her own funds. This parchment volume of about 90 folios, containing

---

33 Ibid., no. 329 (1246) is a concession of 400 *livres* per year, not 40.
34 Part of these forest rights were later sold with the King's consent; *Cartulaire de Maubuisson*, nos. 94 (1253), 285 (1256), and 287 (1253).
35 Ibid., nos. 252 (1246), 256, and 257 (1248).
36 Ibid., no. 5 (1244).
37 Ibid., no. 1 (1241–1242), variants in Pontoise: A.D. Val'd'Oise 72H115.

records from 1236 to 1260, records a total of 24,430 livres in cash expended on behalf of Blanche in the years between 1236 and 1242.[38] The volume describes its own genesis on folio 5[r]:

> In the year of the lord 1236 a new abbey was founded near Pontoise by the illustrious Blanche by grace of God Queen of the Franks. And these are the receipts that Master Richard of Tornay had for the construction of that abbey that was founded in the first week after Pentecost.[39]

Pentecost in 1236 would have been May 25 and from a week later until 1242, Queen Blanche was presented with such accounts three times a year and participated directly in the acquisition of endowment. She must have begun with the cash sum left to her by Louis VIII in his will.[40]

Receipts for Maubuisson included frequent deliveries of cash from Blanche's treasury at the Temple in Paris, but there is included there as well what appears to be local income or produce from Pontoise in the reckoning of fall 1239: nearly 18 livres paid from tolls at Lyencourt and smaller sums coming from sale of local produce: pigs, red brisia (*brasilia*, a dyestuff?), leeks, iron, lime for the king's houses at Pontoise, and wooden planks (*merrenus*) for work at the *Domus Dei* (or Poor House) at Asnières. Some of these are obviously forest products, others from gardens, and in mid-Lent 1239/40, six livres from the Bois de Cergy.[41]

The book contains much more than its thrice-yearly sums of expenditures include details about the price of nails, glass, or cut stone at the time and lists of expenditures for wages and for acquiring property for endowment. In 1242 the queen handed the reins over to Maubuisson's first abbess, Guillelma, who had been sent to Maubuisson with nuns from the abbey of Cistercian women at Saint-Antoine-des-Champs in Paris. Abbess Guillelma appears occasionally from about 1240 and continued to make and appear in entries in the accounts after the queen disappeared from them.

There were also purchases of forest recorded in the account book. Thus, on folio 40[r] the volume records that the Lady Abbess paid 140 *livres parisis* to the

---

38 Pontoise, A.D. Val d'Oise "Achatz," fol. 13[r].

39 Pontoise, A.D. Val d'Oise 72H12, fol. 5[r]: "Anno Domini millesimo ducentesimo tricesimo sexto (1236) fundata fuit nova abbacia iuxta Ponthisarium ab illustria Blancha Dei gratia Regina Francorum. Et hec est recepta Magistri Richardi de Torni pro operibus dicte abbacie que fundata fuit prima ebdomada post Penthecosten." Parts of its contents were published in 1850. I am preparing an edition.

40 *Layettes*, vol. 2, no. 1710 (1225) gave her 30,000 livres; in a 1240 resettlement a larger sum of 45,000 livres is mentioned, but whether that was in addition to the original 30,000 is not clear.

41 Pontoise, A.D. Val d'Oise "Achatz," 1239 quire 1, fol. 3[r] repeated on quire 2, fol. 2[r], col. a.

knight Lord Thibaut of Fic to purchase forest "behind Mahaut" and then 16 livres, 13 shilling, and 4 pennies to Heloise of Atro and her relatives for confirming the purchase.[42] In 1241, the knight Lord Peter of Pleissy received 10 livres and then another 20 livres for the lordship of the vacarrie and that of the woods that Robert of Malodun and Mathias of Wautel, mayor of Petralata, sold to the lady queen. That was seven *arpents* of woodland (*bosci*) called Boscum of Novella next to Bessancourt that they held from Lord Peter of Pleissy, for *calcaria* and *decimata* or five sous of relief for each *arpent*, totaling 27 livres.[43] On the vigil of the Birth of Christ in 1241, those sellers had 130 *arpents* of land in the Garenne next to the woods of Bertencourt of Roseriis. They also had 67 *arpents* of what is probably brushland (*bruetie*) and 2½ *arpents* of vineyard at Bessencourt, for which they paid 200 livres. All the preceding was in the fief of the lady queen.[44] Then in 1259, Jacqueline and Alice, daughters of the late knight Adam of Méry, sold seven-and-a-half *arpents*, less 15 perches of woods (*nemoris*: grove, glade, pasture, woods) located in the *capite* of the woods of Rosieres toward Mery, to the lady abbess of the Blessed Mary la Royale next to Pontoise (Maubuisson), for 19 livres and 16 shillings *parisis*.[45] And in the same year, Nicholas of Atro of Bessancour sold to the monastery of Maubuisson 15 *arpents* and a half one *quarellum* less, located behind the house of Cistercian monks at Val-Notre-Dame at Meriel for 70 *livres parisis*.[46]

---

42   Ibid., fol. 40ʳ (1240): ¶ Item per manu Domine Abbatisse Domino Theobaldo de Fic, militi, pro nemore empta ab ipso sita retro Mahut VIIXX £. Par. ¶ Item Heluysi de Atro et famulie ipsius pro laudem predicti nemoris XVI £. XIII s. IIIId.

43   Ibid., fol. 36ʳ⁻ᵛ (1241): ¶ Item Dominus Petrus de Plesseio, miles, habuit super venditionem quam fecit de domino Vacarrie et dominio nemoris quod vendiderunt Robertus de Malo Dumo et Maior de Petra Lata in festo Beati Andree X £. Item die Jovis post octavo nativitatem Domini XX £. ¶ Robertus de Malodumo et Mathias de Wautel maior de Petra Lata vendiderunt Domine Regine septem arpenta et dimidium bosci quod vulgiter appellatur Boscum de Novella iuxta Bertencuriam quod tenebant de Domino Petro de Plessiaco, milite, pro calcaria et decimata vel quinque s. de relevagio quemlibet arpentum LXX s. de quibus habuerunt XXVII £.

44   Ibid., fols. 36ᵛ–37ʳ: ¶ Anno XL⁰ primo (1241) in vigilia Nativitatem Domini habuit VIXX X [130] arpenta terre in Garenna prope nemus Bertencuriam de Roseriis. ¶ Item LXVII arpenta Bruetie et duo arpenta et dimidium vinee apud Bertencuriam. Et est precium venditionis IIcc £. [200] De quibus sunt pagati. Omnia autem supradicta tenebant in feodum de Domine Regine.

45   Ibid., fol. 47ʳ (1259) [in a new hand]: ¶ Eodem anno (1259) vendiderunt Jaqueline et Aelidis filie quondam defunct Ade de Meriaco, militis, septem arpenta et dimidium quinze perticis minus nemoris sita in capite nemoris de Roseriis versus Meriacum Domine Abbatisse Beate Marie Regalis iuxta Pontisaram pro viginti novem (29) £. Par. et sexdecim s. De quibus sunt pagate.

46   Ibid., fol. 47ʳ: ¶ Eodem anno (1259) Nicholaus de Atio de Bertencuria vendidit monasterio Beate Marie regalis quinze arpenta nemoris et dimidium, unum quartellum minus, sita retro domum Beate Marie de Valle que dicitur Meriel pro sexaginta decem (70) £. Par. De quibus est pagatus.

The dates of these accounts suggest that even before the documented settlement in 1240 of Blanche of Castile's dower/dowry rights by Louis IX, he had granted Blanche the site and other rights in Pontoise, for by 1239, if not earlier, materials for construction were coming from the forest of Cergy. Evidence about forest management, by or for the nuns in the account book, includes three pages concerning work in the bois de Cergy for 1239. They reveal sums paid to woodsmen for getting materials out of the forest over the course of more than a year. There are three different types of accounting for sums and materials in three lists. Overall, these three pages document that materials from Cergy were being used in 1239 (and probably earlier) for the construction of Maubuisson.

First are payments for expenses in managing the forest of Cergy, starting with Peter of Marinus and Master Michael of Villerii. These woodsmen received 100 sous (*i.e.*, five livres) from Master Richard, Blanche's chief agent at Maubuisson, for what appears to be surveying in the woods of Cergy (*agromensuras*): "*quando boscus mensuratus fuit*" (in the next line, *diffinirendum* may mean to define or lay out boundaries).[47] For 1239, we can see what expenses were incurred in providing materials for construction in the forest of Cergy (see Appendix A.2).

Then there are receipts for casual sales of charcoal, *brisia*, bark, and the occasional sale of lumber. Since there are no indications of quantities tabulating the amounts would prove nothing, but most mentioned item is bark (*cortex/cortices*). This list includes the day-to-day operations of cutting, sawing, making planks, and transporting building materials by horses or mules and by boat, and guarding the river bank or port, from which these items would be moved to the abbey. Receipts for casual sales totaled 80 livres, 55 shillings, and 2 pennies. In the second list – *de expletis bosci cirgie* – exploitation means customary usage and rights (see Appendix A.3). In a third list there were another 987 livres for the associated expenses of exploiting those woods and converting wood to charcoal, trees to planks and so on, but particularly for transport (*vectura*). Thus, we find entries for laths (and *escanda*, which may be lath as well), general wood, boards, and beams, as well as Merrengi wood (*matieramum*) for construction and entries for debarking trees and guarding the port (see Appendix A.4).

So how is it that for 1239 the account book has three page sides (folios 20ʳ–21ᵛ) concerning the bois de Cergy? There is first of payments for work done in the woods of Cergy. Clearly given that more was paid than taken out and paid for, this is a record of getting wood for construction. These may sometimes coincide with other entries in the account book and are definitely related to lists of cash paid into the hands of Richard, the Templar master of works, for Blanche's construction, and from the forest of Cergy came materials from Blanche's dower lands, but while this may have reduced costs of materials as they owned them whether

---

47 The Saints' Days as references for dates are interesting in that they follow the calendar, suggesting a running list copied into the volume.

standing as timber or hewn into lumber, costs of labor and transport still had to be paid.

Several other items in the account book are of interest. An intrusion in the account book from mid-century reveals something about the income coming from cutting or coppicing in those woods at Bonfosse from 1248 to 1250 and then from 1257 to 1259. Payment from Bonfosse came on All Saints' and Assumption Days in 1248/49 and again in 1249/50. These totaled 53 livres over the first year in the academic sense and 54 in the second. Presumably, it was a result of the gifts and purchases in the 1250s just described that payments increased to an average of nearly 72 livres per annum by 1257 through 1259.

A different intrusion in the volume concerning forest rights from about 1260 is a list of *coupages*, a "cutting list" for the woods of Rosières near the abbey and possibly part of the royal forest of Cergy.[48] It begins "Ce sont les coupes des bois de Rosieres et des autres bois autour de Bertencuria ens arpentz du Roy." In my view, and given the evidence from the earlier intrusion as well as from le Lys, what follows is a list of annual cuttings for nine years in this forest, a list that would presumably be restarted in the tenth year. Such annual cuttings amounted to (as they are recorded) 30, 46, 60½, 59½, 55½, 65 plus 11, 67½, 65½, and 60 *arpents* for a total of 520½ *arpents* and thus averaging about 58 *arpents* cut per year.[49] On the other hand, this could be only a list of areas available for cutting on a more irregular basis.

The transfer from Louis IX to Blanche of rights in the royal forest of Cergy would have been for her life. Moreover, there is no evidence from her lifetime that the forest of Cergy was ever granted to Maubuisson, as opposed to remaining part of Blanche's dower rights. Consequently, forest access would have become a problem for the nuns after Blanche's death in November 1252. This might explain why in the summer of 1253 Louis IX, on Crusade in the East and, possibly upon hearing of his mother's death, wrote from Sidon (now in Lebanon) to Master Garnier of Cergy, who was asked to concede to Maubuisson the rights at Cergy that he (Garnier) held from the king, who, in turn, promised Garnier rights elsewhere.[50] The request from Sidon may have been the first actual grant to Maubuisson of rights at Cergy, although

---

48 Pontoise, A.D. Val d'Oise "Achatz," fol. 43[r] it immediately follows items from the late 1250s, so might be dated to c.1260 with a later insertion from 1314.

49 If so, in the next decade, the second cut at Coupillet was done in 1274 and measured 69½ Montmorency *arpents* as opposed to the 46 royal ones, a ratio of just under 1½ royal to each Montmorency arpent. They indicate what is considered proper exploitation of such dower or what is considered proper forest cutting or coppicing as implied by the intrusions about Rosieres and Bonfosse.

50 *Cartulaire de Maubuisson*, no. 94 (August 1253). This is probably the same Master Garnier (of Sognolles) who had sold rents at Aulnay for four *livres* minus eight shillings in 1244; "Achatz d'héritages," fol. 38[v] (1244). He also appears, with regard to Evreux tithes, in 1256 conflict. Sources cited by Keyser on royal accounts in 1202 do not mention Pontoise or Cergy. My thanks to Wendy Pfeffer, who looked in Paris.

other conveyances of smaller areas of woodland, like those of Rosières, may have been of tenurial rights in that forest from feudal holders from the king.

The nuns of Les Clairets (near Nogent-le-Rotrou, in the Perche, west of Chartres), an abbey of Cistercian nuns founded in 1204 by Matilda, countess of la Perche, a granddaughter of Henry II of England and Eleanor of Aquitaine, would have not only very extensive rights in milling facilities but also forest usage granted by the counts of le Perche and others. One of Les Clairets's documents suggests the ways in which *forestaria* might be held by hereditary tenants and the types of rights associated with their guardianship of woodlands (Appendix B). The agreement with forester Matthew in 1252 confirmed that the post of forester was to be passed from father to son and confirmed to the next generation by the abbey and community whom that new forester swore to serve faithfully. It also stated that if forest sales were made, said Matthew and his heirs ought to receive payment of two-and-a-half shillings from the sale price from the abbess and community of nuns. He had, moreover, pannage for his pigs and pasture for his animals. Moreover, Matthew and his heirs had to agree to any sale, gift, or transfer of their claims to the debris (dead wood, boards, and lopped-off leaves) when any trees were given or cut down for usage rights. The document appears as well to limit who got which rights if noble owners and nuns both decided to cut down trees simultaneously. The point here is that pasture and mast were available to the forester, so was some claim on the debris in the vicinity of that cutting: dead wood, the tree branches, and whatever was lopped off. Terminology suggests managed practice, although the details are somewhat obscure.[51]

Documents for Notre-Dame de Lieu-lez-Romorantin provide a slightly different picture. The abbey of Cistercian nuns at Lieu-Notre-Dame was located in the southern part of the diocese of Chartres with holdings that stretched into that of Orleans and toward Amboise into the Loire River valley. There in marshy areas in the Loire valley in which reclamation was still underway in the thirteenth century, clearance of forest may have involved some cutting and drainage of waste or scrublands as well. From as early as their first gifts in 1222, Lieu's founder, Isabelle, countess of Chartres, who had inherited the position from a nephew, and her husband, John of Oisy, were granting holdings in land adjoining the abbey site, including 36 *arpents* of uncultivated land.[52] That the founders intended that the nuns oversee reclamation of such uncultivated land in the vicinity of the abbey is confirmed in a 1232 concession by Isabelle's sole daughter, Matilda of Amboise, and her husband, Richard of Beaumont. They gave to the nuns of Lieu rights additional to those granted by Isabelle of up to one 100 *arpents* of uncultivated land free of rents and rights to land beyond those 100 *arpents* if the nuns paid rent to

---

51 *Abbaye Royale de Notre-Dame des Clairets: Histoire et Cartulaire*, ed. H. de Souance (Vannes: Lafolye, 1894), no. 52 (1251/1252). See Appendix B.

52 *Cartulaire de l'abbaye royale du Lieu-Notre-Dame-lèz-Romorantin*, ed. Ernest Prat (Romorantin: A. Standachar et cie, 1892) no. 33 (1222).

the donors at the usual rate.[53] That woodland was what was at issue in grants by that family is confirmed in Isabelle's last testament of 1247 in which she gave even more such properties with permission for the nuns "to reduce it to cultivation."[54]

These nuns were not pioneers in cutting down great forests any more than were most other Cistercians, although their tenants may have been. The lists of rents found in the 1270s' cartulary suggest that Lieu-Notre-Dame had numerous tenants who may have been undertaking such assarting. That their tenants were undertaking such clearance and reclamation is suggested as well by the terminology for paying rents there called *terrages* (*terragia*), a new form of rents on land that are usually described as shares in the harvest on newly cultivated land. This is documented in several lists of rents to be paid to the nuns of Lieu found in the abbey's cartulary, such as one "Hec sunt terragia de Morays," which goes on to name 14 individuals, some appearing more than once, who owed payments in kind for one or more pieces of land "uprooted" or "adjoining the marsh" at Morays. Another list, "Hec sunt terragia de la Sotaere," is described as stretching to "the marshes of Pinart, Loumemort (Eaumort?), and Platereau." In this list, more than 70 persons appear with payments owed for about 100 pieces of land. A third list is for Laubertière (l'Aubertière) with 16 individuals listed as paying rent for 20 holdings. Finally, in a list for la Bodanière, fifty individuals pay rents on a slightly greater number of pieces of land. There is some obvious overlap, but combined with lists of either head taxes or plough duties, these four lists confirm that by the 1260s, if not earlier, there were between 100 and 150 families who owed rents to the nuns for tenancies on lands that probably had been brought under cultivation by those peasants and now owned by those nuns.

Recent reduction to cultivation in their lands is also indicated by Lieu's nuns' involvement in disputes over the tithes on *noval* and ancient lands at Mur and Salbeut, parts of which had only recently been brought into cultivation. In 1244 Isabelle of Chartres redeemed for the nuns half the original tithes of the parish of Mur from the mortgage of 120 livres over them that had been made by the knight Roger le Bugle to the church of Saint-Sauveur in Blois in 1234. Then in 1247 Roger sold the other half of those tithes to Isabelle for 180 livres.[55] In 1249 Isabelle's grant of those tithes to the nuns of Lieu was confirmed after her death by her daughter and heir, Matilda of Amboise, who mentioned that Roger was her liegeman.[56] By August 1249, however, a dispute had arisen between the parish priest of Mur and the nuns of Lieu over the *noval* tithes there; arbitrars declared that the nuns should have both *noval* and ancient tithes but should pay Peter, the parish priest, annual payments in lieu of the tithes: six *sestiers* of rye on the *noval* tithes and seven *sestiers* of rye for the ancient ones.[57] At this time, a considerable amount of land

---

53 *Cartulaire de Lieu*, no. 24 (1232).
54 Ibid., no. 1 (1247).
55 Ibid., no. 66 (1234) and see nos. 67 (1244), 68 (1234), and 69 (1249).
56 Ibid., no. 71 (1247).
57 Ibid., no. 70 (1249) and see nos. no. 76 (1252), 77 (1252), and no. 79 (1263).

subject to *noval* tithes had been brought under cultivation in the recent past. The Cistercians, including the order's nuns, remained exempt even after 1215, but the near parity of the rate paid to Peter suggests they were near in value.[58]

Thus, references to such *noval* tithes suggest that the nuns' tenants had been actively creating new land for cultivation at Mur. This appears to have been the same situation in the parish of Soetaerio. Countess Matilda of Amboise oversaw the sale of tithes there to Lieu for 145 livres in 1251 by the squire William of Cornamain.[59] That the nuns had been encouraged in this activity by their founders is confirmed by the document from 1249 following her mother's death in which Matilda confirmed anniversaries for her father and mother. In it, she confirmed that in woods near the abbey and its great pond, the nuns could have ditches to limit access and warrens in which to raise rabbits and have exclusive hunting of small animals.[60] Matilda also gave woodland rights in all her woods in the castellany of Romorentin between the road from Millencay to the new mill and that from Cornil to Romorentin near the grange of Hagueville. In that area the nuns could "custodire, vendere, dare, extirpare et ad agriculturam reducere."[61] The nuns of Lieu also acquired usage rights in forest and waste in areas that were *not* to be developed. For example, in 1247 Isabelle gave Lieu rights for up to 100 pigs to be kept in her woodlands, along with rights to hunt or trap small game such as rabbits and to build a mill at a designated site.[62]

The Cistercian nuns of the great abbey of Saint-Antoine-des-Champs just outside Paris would appear from the properties considered in their cartularies as having taken little interest in forest acquisition. There were a few concessions like those at Aulnay, or Cressonessart, that may have included woodland along with other rights, but these rights to woodland were the limited ones that any tenant within a village would have had. Charters show that most of Saint-Antoine's thirteenth-century acquisition efforts were focused on those rural properties making up its granges at Aulnay, Champagnes, and Montreuil, where it had cereal cultivation and viticultural rights and on other rights like meadows and fishing weirs.[63] Those nuns also had extensive acquisitions of properties and rents over them in the city of Paris itself.[64]

---

58 That the abbey of Cistercian nuns at Lieu founded in 1222 and thus, after the Fourth Lateran Council of 1215, was involved in controversies over tithes was precisely because at issue were the tithes on newly cleared (*noval*) land for which new Cistercian lands continued to be exempt. On this aspect of Cistercian tithes, see James S. Donnelly, *The Decline of the Medieval Cistercian Laybrotherhood* (New York: Fordham University Press, 1949).

59 *Cartulaire de Lieu*, no. 82 (1251), etc.
60 Ibid., no. 37 (1249).
61 Ibid., no. 36 (1249).
62 Ibid., no. 1 (1247).
63 Paris, A.N., S*4386, fol. 8ʳ.
64 Paris, A.N., LL1595, *passim*.

Yet, if one actually adds up the amounts expended by Saint-Antoine's nuns in the middle of the thirteenth century, it appears that its largest purchases were the exceptional two purchases in 1243/44 for 200 *arpents* of property in the woodlands of Bois de Sariel between Tournans and Ozoir la Ferriere in Brie east of the city of Paris. One hundred thirty *arpents* cost them four livres each, and the other seventy *arpents* cost them five livres each, making a total of 870 *livres tournois* expended in that year for those woodlands. This was the largest documented sum the abbey spent at any point in the thirteenth century on what was essentially a single tract of property, so its significance is considerable.[65] The first conveyance by the knight John of Parossey and his wife Alice tells us that she had inherited those rights to property owing *cens* (rent) in the lordship of the late knight William of Gleseria and that they, the sellers, guaranteed to Amicia abbess of Saint-Antoine and her community that woodland with the land on which it was located (*nemus et fundo*) in full mainmorte to that abbess and community and the children of the late William of Gleseria did so as well along with all other overlords.[66] The second sale by the squire Peter of Champs and his wife Juliana, although with a higher price was similarly worded, confirmed, and guaranteed.[67] Several other confirmations followed, but they do not add any information on what use the nuns intended for those woods at Sariel. Later in 1261 Abbess Jeanne of Saint-Antoine contracted to rent an additional 25 or so *arpents* adjoining their own property at Sariel from the abbot and a community of Premonstratensians at Hermières. After only a little more than ten years, in 1272, however, the nuns were claiming that they were paying excessive rent in terms of "just price"; by 1278 a lower payment had been instituted.[68] While nothing is said about how it was to be used, the value of such forest, whether acquired in the outright purchase or in rental agreements, far outweighed any other of Saint-Antoine's acquisitions at *that* time. Probably what was at issue were usage rights similar to those explicitly outlined for les Clairets, although the possibility of a cell of nuns there, perhaps replacing a house of Premonstratensian sisters, cannot be wholly ruled out.

Such references as these add understanding of how houses of Cistercian nuns, as well as the order's monks, handled their acquisitions of forest and other wasteland rights at least by the thirteenth century. Thus, the documents for the nuns elucidate aspects of Cistercian forest management that at least in northern France were probably practiced more generally among Cistercians in the thirteenth century. These surviving documents add complexity to what was once an excessively

---

65 Other large amounts paid in a single year for adjoining properties included 400 *livres tournois* paid in 1259; see Berman, *The White Nuns* (note 2).
66 Paris, A.N., S*4386, fols. 11^v–12^v (January 1243, ns. 1244).
67 Ibid., fols. 12^v–13^v (January 1243, ns. 1244).
68 Ibid., fols. 11^r–16^r (1243–1278).

simple association of Cistercians and forest, enlarging or converting that understanding to one of forest management.

Appendix A: accounts from Pontoise

1. After 1255.[69]

¶ Tales sunt redditus abbacie Beate Marie Regalis et ad tales terminos:..
¶ Item in festo Beati Michaelis...
¶ Item de nemoribus Rosseriarum C £....
¶ Item de redditibus Normannie IIIIc £. Tur. valent III^{CC} XX £. Par.
¶ Item de nemore de Bonfosse L £.
¶ Item de nemore Airouelli (Eragnes?) XX £. [these last two replaced with "XXXVII £."]
¶ Item de nemora qui vocatur defensus prope Plesilliacum circa XL £. XXVII £....
¶ Item apud Coingnoles super domum Bernardi Forestarii decem s. censuales....
¶ Item tres sestarios castaneorum que valent circa XII s.

2. 1238–39.[70]

¶ Hec receperunt Petrus de Marinus et Magister Michaelus de Villerii a Magistro Richardo pro operibus bosci Cirgie quando boscus mensuratus fuit in expensis aciarium C s. [surveying?]
¶ Item tradidit magister Ricardus Petri de Marinus X £. ad diffinirendum in Cergie. [laying out boundaries]
¶ Item quando magister fuit in Cergie die Jovis ante festum Beatorum Gervasii et Protasii [June 19] XX £.
¶ Item in vigilia octavo Petri et Pauli [June 29] pro Petrum de Marino XXX £.
¶ Item in festo Sancti Arnulphi [of Soissons, Aug. 14] XVII £.
¶ Item die Jovis ante fest Beati Petri ad Vincula [Aug. 1] pro Michaelis XI £.
¶ Item in die Assumptionis Beate Marie [Aug. 15] pro Michaelis XX s.
¶ Item die Veneris post fest Beati Bartholomei [Aug.24] pro Michaelis de Villerii XXV £.
¶ Item in die Nativitatem Beate Marie [Sept. 8] pro Petrum de Marinus XX £.
¶ Item in festo Beati Mathei Evangeliste [Sept. 21] pro Petrum XXXII £.
¶ Item in festo Beati Dyonisii [Oct. 9] pro Petrum XX £.

---

69 Pontoise, A.D. Val d'Oise "Achatz," fols. 41^v–42^r. The account is undated, but the previous folio is dated 1255.
70 Ibid., fol. 20^{r-v}.

¶ Item in festo Beati Melloni [Oct. 21] pro Michaelis de Vilerii XX £.
¶ Item Cineri de Compendus [Oct. 22?] pro vectura VIII £. (transport)
¶ Item die Sabbati post festum Omnium Sanctorum [Nov. 1] XL £.
¶ Item in Crastino Beate Katherine [25 Nov.] pro Michaelis XVIII £.

Summa III^{CC} £.

¶ Item Dominica proxima post festum Beati Nicholai Hyemalis [Dec. 6] pro Petrum XX £.
¶ Item Dominica ante Nativitatem Domini [Dec. 25] pro Michaeli X £.
¶ Item die Martis ante Epiphanyam [Jan. 6, 1239] pro Petrum de Marinus XXX £.
¶ Item die Dominica proxima post Candelosem [Feb. 2] pro Petrum XL £.
¶ Item die Lune ante mediam Quadragesima [mid-Lent] ad opera Martini Roberti de Gonesse XXX £.
¶ Item die Veneris ante Paschalis florida [Palm Sunday, which was Mar. 20 in 1239?] habuit Petrus de Martinus XXX £.
¶ Item die Jovis post Paschalis [Mar. 27?] XXX £.
¶ Item die Jovis ante festum Apostolorum Philippi et Jacobi [May 1, also Beltane] XL £.
¶ Item in die Trinitatis [first Sunday after Pentecost; Pentecost was May 22 in 1239] XX £.
¶ Item die Martis ante festum Nativitatem Beati Johannis Baptiste [Jun. 24] XL £.
¶ Item die Lune ante festum Beate Marie Magdalenis [Jul. 22] XL £.
¶ Item in Crastine Sanctorum Egidii et Lupi [Sep. 1] apud Pontisariam XL £.
¶ Item Jacobo de Suessionis pro vectura merregni XII £. X s.
¶ Item die Martis proxima ante festum Apostolorum Symonis et Jude [Oct. 28] pro Magistrum? Michaelis? et pro clericum XLIII £. XII s.
¶ Item Jacobo de Suessionis pro duabis naves XIII £. XIIII s.
¶ Item Jacobo Similiter pro vectura XLIX s.
¶ Item Petro de Marinus pro gagiis XII £. X s. X d. [then two blank spaces]

Summa VIII^{CC} III £. XV s. X d. 803/15/10.usque ad festum Omnium Sanctorum [Nov. 1] anno Domini M° CC° XXX° nono [1239]

3. 1239.[71]

¶ Recepit de Petri de Marine de expletis [usage] Bosci Cirgie.
¶ Item de carbone [charcoal] vendito LX £. or sol?

---

71 Ibid., fol. 21^r.

¶ Item de brisia (brazilwood dye) vendita XXXIII s.
¶ Item de ligno ad summam [best quality wood] XXVI £.
¶ Item de cortice [bark] VIII £. X s.
¶ Item recepti de ligno [ordinary wood] LX s.
¶ Et de cortice V s.
¶ Item de cortice XXVII s.
¶ Item de cortice XLV s.
¶ Item de minuto ligno [light-weight wood/poles?] vendito XL s.
¶ Item de Johanne de Moriers pro ligno vendito IIII £.
¶ Item de Firmio de Ausay et de Bartholomeo de Oneis pro cortice VI £. XIIII s.
¶ Item pro cortice XL s. IIII d.
¶ Item pro ligno XIIII £. XV s.
¶ Item pro cortice pellis [peeled bark?] LXX s.
¶ Item de brisia LXXVI s. II den
¶ Item de carbone vendito XXXVI £. V s.
¶ Item de carbone VI £. XV s. IIII d. minus

Summa LXXX £. LV s. II d. [80/55/2]

4. 1239.[72]

¶ Pro factura carbonis [making charcoal] X £. V s.
¶ Pro vectura ligni ad summam [carrying best quality wood] de bosco usque ad portum XI £. II s. VI d.
¶ Item pro facturas late, ligni, planches, asserum [laths, wood, boards, beams] XVI £. III s.
¶ Item pro peler escorche [peeling bark] LXXI s. VI d.
¶ Pro expensis Petri de Marinus IIII £. II s. VIII d.
¶ Item Droconi pro custodia portus; IIII £. II s.
¶ Item Matheo pro custodia portus XXXIIII s.
¶ Item Rogero Aurige IIII £. XVII s. VIII d.
¶ Item scio [saw] Rogeri XXVII s.
¶ Item pro expensis equorum [horse expenses] XXXI £. VI d.
¶ Pro vectura nave [boat transport] IIII^{XX} X £. III s.
¶ Item operariis nemoris [woodmen's work?] IX^{XX} £. III s.
¶ Item pro vectura merregni de bosco ad portum CXI £. X s.
¶ Item Petro de Marinus XL £. XIII s. minus.
¶ Item Jacobo de Suessionis pro vectura VII £.
¶ Item Gerardo de Choisiaco pro vectura merregni VIII £. X s.

---

72 Ibid., fol. 22^r.

CISTERCIAN NUNS AND FOREST MANAGEMENT 185

¶ Item Michaelis de Chauni pro duabus naves XI £. VII s. VI d.
¶ Item Guiniero pro tribus naves XI £. V s.
¶ Item Roberto Bacive pro unam navem IIII £.
¶ Item Jacobo de Suessionis pro XV naves LXI £.
¶ Item pro vectura merregni a bosco usque ad portum LV £. [or solidi?]
¶ Item pro eodem VIII £. IIII s.
¶ Item per vectura similiter X £.
¶ Item pro vectura merregni LX s.
¶ Item Reginaldo de Sancto Oenio Alneto pro lignis XVIII £. X s.
¶ Item Rogero et custodi portus XVI £. XVI s.
¶ Item pro expensis equorum LXII £.
¶ Item pro factura escande et vectura eiusdem VI £.
¶ Item pro vectura merregni D [500] £. IIII. s.
¶ Item pro factura late en forcie XV s.
¶ Item pro scinta asserum et plancheii VIII £. X s.
¶ Pro scinta plancii VI £. III s.
¶ Item socio scio Rogeri VI £. IX s.
¶ Item Petro de Marine pro sagiis [mules?] XII £. X s. X d.
¶ Item carpentariis&operariis nemoris pro Petrum & Michaelis XLIII £. XIIs.
¶ Item Jacobo pro vectura nave XLIX s
¶ Item eidem Jacobo pro duabus naves XIII £. XIIII s.
¶ Item operariis nemoris LXXVIII £. V s. VII d.
¶ Item Jacobo pro vectura unius nave XLIX s.

Summa usque ad festum Omnium Sanctorum, A.D. M° CC° XXX° nono [1239]: IX^{CC} IIII^{XX} VII £. XI s. [987/11]

¶ Item operariis nemoris X £. X s.
¶ Item operariis nemoris Cirgie X £. quas tradidit Johannes Morier.

Appendix B: document on *forestaria* **for the Cistercian abbey of Les Clairets**

Universis praesentes litteras inspecturis, magister Lucas, decanus ecclesiae Sancti Johannis de Nogento-Rotrodi, et Guillelmus Decanus ecclesiae Omnium Sanctorum de Mauritania, salutem in Domino. Noverint universi quod, cum Matheus Marescalli peteret a religiosis mulieribus, abbatissa et conventu de Claretis Cisterciensis ordinis, forestariam in nemoribus de Pertico quae habuerunt a nobilibus viris comite Britanniae et Jacobo Castrigonterii et Nogenti domino, videlicet de omnibus arboribus captis ab usuariis, datis seu venditis, ramos et cospellos, castaguum suum quantum ad nemus mortuum, pasturam ad animalia, pasnagium ad porcos, custodiam nemoris, ramum et fracturam arboris, arboremque cadentem et de forestis nemorum emendam, quae omnia dicebat, idem Matheus ad se et suos haeredes forestarios esse. Et super hoc tam dicti abbatissa et conventus quam idem Matheus in nos tamquam in arbitros electos compromissent, promittentes sub pena quadraginta librarum turonensium, prout in litteris eorum vidimus contineri, quod arbitrium nostrum tenerent. Nos, die lunae proxima post festum beati Silvestri assignata partibus ad nostrum arbitrium proferendum, praesentibus partibus de bonorum virorum consilio et etiam de ipsorum partium consensu, arbitrium nostrum protulimus in hunc modum: Videlicet quod dicta nemora quiete et libere remanent in perpetuum dictis monialibus ad faciendam omnino voluntatem suam, prout dicti nobiles in suis nemoribus fecerunt et tanquam domini facere poterunt. Ita tamen quod Matheus et haeredes sui successive erunt forestarii in dictis nemoribus praedictorum abbatissae et conventus; et eidem in dicta abbatia facient juramentum de haerede in haeredem quod praedicta nemora servabunt fideliter, et forestam dictarum nemorum eisdem significabunt. Et si forte de forestis emenda debita fuerit, praedicti Matheuws et heredes sui de dicta emenda duos solidos et dimidios et nihil amplius per manum abbatissae et conventus recipient et habebunt. Panagium vero ad porcos suos, pasturam ad animalia sua, usuagium suum ad nemus mortuum, ramos et cospellos de omnibus arboribus datis et captis ab usuariis, habebunt similiter idem Matheus et haeredes sui et de ipsis suam poterunt facere voluntatem, contradictione praedictarum abbatisse et conventus non obstante; adjunctum est etiam, quod si in dictis nemoribus praedictorum nobilium et abbatissae et conventus simul caducum fuit, solam arborem vel ramum solum, sive fracturam solam de illo caduco habebunt praedicti Matheus et haeredes sui. Erit tamen in optione dictorum Mathei et haeredum suorum arborem seu ramum vel fracturiam quae cecidit in caduco saepedicte Matheus et haeredes sui caperint, ea vice in arbore, ramo vel fractura, sive in arboribus, ramis vel fracturis quae in nemore dictarum monialium ceciderint, nihil poterunt idem Matheus et haeredes sui petere seu etiam reclamare. Praeterea sciendum est quod, si in nemore dictarum monialium, solum arbores, rami, vel fracturae ceciderint seu per caducum commune in nemoribus dictarum monialium et dictorum nobilium et dicti Matheus et haeredes sui in nemoribus dictarum monialium arborem vel ramum, seu fracturam capere voluerint, dictae moniales unum de praedictis eligent et capient quod maluerint; post electionem vero dictarum monialium supradicti Matheus et haeredes sui aliud, quod maluerint, eligent, et habebunt, et de ipso suam poterunt facere voluntatem, contradictione dictarum monialium non obstante. Quod ut ratum et stabile perpetuo perseveret, praesentes litteras sigillorum nostrorum minimine duximus roborandas. Actum anno graciae millesimo ducentesimo quinquagesimo primo, mense januarii.[73]

---

73 *Abbaye Royale de Notre-Dame des Clairets*, no. 53 (1251/52).

Chapter 9

Cold, rain, and famine
Three subsistence crises in the Burgundian Low Countries during the fifteenth century

Chantal Camenisch

In the course of the fourteenth and fifteenth centuries the territories of present-day Belgium, the Netherlands, Luxembourg, and parts of northern France fell under the rule of the dukes of Burgundy before they were controlled by their Habsburg heirs in the sixteenth century.[1] The so-called Low Countries were one of the most progressive regions in medieval Europe: densely populated and intensively agricultural.[2] The population density was particularly high in the coastal areas of Flanders and South Holland, where dozens of big cities and their seaports were situated. Fewer people lived in Brabant, Liège, North Holland, and Hainault. The most sparsely populated areas were Artois, the Picardy, and Frisia.[3]

The Burgundian Low Countries were additionally characterized by a remarkably high degree of urbanization. Around 1470 about 44% of Holland's inhabitants lived in towns, 33% in Flanders, and 29% in Brabant, while most regions of Europe did not have more than 20% to 25% at the end of the Middle Ages.[4]

---

1   Andrew Brown and Graeme Small, *Court and Civic Society in the Burgundian Low Countries c.1420–1530* (Manchester: Manchester University Press, 2007), 3–6.

2   Willem Pieter Blockmans and Walter Prevenier, *The Promised Lands: The Low Countries Under Burgundian Rule, 1369–1530*, trans. Elizabeth Fackelmann (Philadelphia: University of Pennsylvania Press, 1999), 5; Bas van Bavel, *Manors and Markets. Economy and Society in the Low Countries, 500–1600* (Oxford: Oxford University Press, 2010), 1–3; Jan de Vries, *European Urbanization 1500–1800* (London: Methuen, 1984), 29.

3   Walter Prevenier and Willem Pieter Blockmans, *Die burgundischen Niederlande* (Weinheim: Acta humaniora, 1986), 29–30.

4   Blockmans and Prevenier, *Promised Lands*, 152. Ulf Dirlmeier, Gerhard Fouquet, and Bernd Fuhrmann, *Europa im Spätmittelalter 1215–1378*, Oldenburg Grundrisse der Geschichte 8 (München: Oldenburg, 2003), 23.

A high degree of urbanization meant enhanced productivity, because comparatively few people working in the agricultural sector were able to feed the many others who worked in other occupations. In comparison with other regions the Burgundian Low Countries benefited from intensive agriculture and high yield ratios in terms of grain production. Accordingly, domestic trade was of great importance and some areas of the Burgundian Low Countries by the fifteenth century were already part of an integrated market. But as this was still not sufficient to supply the population, the region was linked by trade routes to many places, such as the British Isles, the Roman Empire, France, and even Spain and Italy. Plenty of grain reached the markets of the Low Countries from the Baltic, the Roman Empire, and other places.[5]

Despite this, a number of food price increases are documented for this area during the fifteenth century. Three of them were particularly significant. The first crisis occurred during the 1430s, the second at the beginning of the 1480s, and the third started at the end of the latter decade and extended into the first years of the 1490s. How could repeated subsistence crises occur in an area that was characterized by such a well-developed economy and society? An examination of these three crises shows substantial similarities in their preconditions, trigger events, structure, and impacts. Analysis of these similarities may help to explain why the Burgundian Low Countries were affected so markedly by the crises.

All three crises occurred during times of war and riots in the Burgundian Low Countries and their neighboring areas. The crises also coincided with periods of high taxes and turbulent trading conditions. In addition, for the seasons before and during the crises very unfavorable weather events are documented. Apparently these weather events were among the causes of the subsistence crises, a trigger in an already tense situation: "it is generally accepted that short-term (intra-annual, annual and inter-annual) variations in climate and weather, having an immediate effect on harvests and other economic activities, are relevant to short-term economic fluctuations."[6] Therefore, it is appropriate to make use of a model that shows what kind of impact climate and weather had on the economy and society. In 1985 Robert W. Kates developed different climate–society interaction models that were not linked to a certain region or period. Christian Pfister and Daniel

---

5   Karl Gunnar Persson, *An Economic History of Europe: Knowledge, Institutions and Growth, 600 to Present* (Cambridge: Cambridge University Press, 2010), 64–65. Blockmans and Prevenier, *Promised Lands*, 5–6, 155–56. Herman van der Wee, *The Growth of the Antwerp Market and the European Economy (Fourteenth–Sixteenth Centuries)* (The Hague: Martinus Nijhoff, 1963), 1: 23.

6   Martin J. Ingram, Graham Farmer, and Tom M.L. Wigley, "Past Climates and Their Impact on Man: A Review," in *Climate and History: Studies in Past Climates and Their Impact on Man*, ed. Tom M.L. Wigley, Martin J. Ingram, and Graham Farmer (Cambridge: Cambridge University Press, 1981), 18.

Krämer adapted the core of these models and transformed them into a simpler and more general model: simplified climate–society interaction.[7]

This model shows on a first level the so-called *First-Order Impact*: the biophysical effects of extreme weather events on primary production such as food and feed. In the model, the effects of sufficient or insufficient primary production on economic growth and human and animal health are described as *Second-Order Impacts*. The prices of biomass and transportation, as well as epidemics and epizootics (outbreaks of diseases in people and animals, respectively), belong to this type of impact.[8] This second-order impact interacts closely with the *Third-Order Impact*: demographic and social implications such as malnutrition, demographic growth, and social conflicts. Cultural responses and coping strategies form the *Fourth-Order Impact*. According to this model, the weather impacts decrease with every additional level of impact order. The higher the order of impact, the more they are influenced by other factors, although this simplified climate–society interaction model does not attempt to include all the factors that have an effect on the economy, society, and cultural activity of humans during a subsistence crisis. For this reason, other factors need to be discussed prior to the reconstruction of the crises on the basis of the model. Thereafter, it is necessary to reconstruct the weather conditions before and during the different subsistence crises because the entire model is based on extreme weather events. Among these extreme weather events, extensive rainy periods during spring, summer and fall and low temperatures in late spring and summer are particularly expected to cause crop failure.[9] Further-

---

7 Robert W. Kates, "The Interaction of Climate and Society," in *Climate Impact Assessment: Studies of the Interaction of Climate and Society*, ed. Robert W. Kates, Jesse H. Ausubel, and Mimi Berberian (Chichester, UK: John Wiley and Sons, 1985), 3–36; Christian Pfister, "Climatic Extremes, Recurrent Crises and Witch Hunts: Strategies of European Societies in Coping with Exogenous Shocks in the Late Sixteenth and Early Seventeenth Centuries," *The Medieval History Journal* 10 (2007): 37–43; Daniel Krämer, "Regional differences in social vulnerability after the harvest failure of 1816 in Switzerland" (paper presented at the conference "Historical Climatology – Past and Future" organized by the German Historical Institute, Paris, the Kulturwissenschaftliches Institut, Essen and the Université de Versailles Saint-Quentin-en-Yvelines Paris, Paris, France, September 5–6, 2011); Daniel Krämer, *'Menschen grasten nun mit dem Vieh'. Die letzte grosse Hungerkrise der Schweiz 1816/17*, Wirtschafts-, Sozial- und Umweltgeschichte 4 (Basel: Schwabe, 2015), 133–138

8 On the consequences of cattle plague and other epizootic diseases, cf. Philip Slavin, "The Great Bovine Pestilence and Its Economic and Environmental Consequences in England and Wales, 1318–50," *The Economic History Review* 65 (2012): 1239–66.

9 Bernard Hendrik Slicher van Bath, "Le climat et les récoltes au Haut Moyen Âge," in *Agricoltora e mondo rurale in occidente nell'alto medioevo*, Settimane del centro italiano di studi sull'alto medioevo 13 (Spoleto: Presso la sede del Centro, 1966), 399–402; Christian Pfister, *Klimageschichte der Schweiz von 1525–1860 und seine Bedeutung in der Geschichte von Bevölkerung und Landwirtschaft, Vol. 2: Bevölkerung, Klima und

more, extreme meteorological events during other seasons also need to be taken into consideration. Subsequent to the climate reconstruction, the different impacts need to be discussed.

The sequence of such subsistence crises has already been described by Ernest Labrousse and Wilhelm Abel.[10] These crises in the era before capitalism was established at the beginning of the nineteenth century are known as *crises type ancien*.[11] They began with a crop failure caused by unfavorable weather conditions that, in turn, caused an increase in grain prices. In consequence, people had to spend much more of their money on grain and grain products. Soon they were limited to the cheapest available food and could not afford craft products or other items not essential to their survival. Producers and traders of more expensive foods and crafts therefore lost their market and their income while they also had to pay more for their food. Obviously not all people were affected in the same way. Wealthy people who did not have to worry about their income certainly did not suffer from hunger. Landlords who could sell their grain for higher prices might even have earned a lot of money, as well as retained enough for themselves and immediate family and dependents.[12] Usually food crises had disastrous consequences for small leaseholders because their own production was not sufficient to feed them after they had paid the requisite duties and taxes. Wage earners were also threatened because they could buy less and less with their money even if they did not lose their jobs altogether.

Different kinds of historical sources can be taken into consideration in this type of research and the most useful here are narrative sources, because they contain weather-sensitive, as well as economy- and culture-related, information. This kind of evidence includes annals, chronicles, journals, and, beginning at the end of the fifteenth century, memoirs. Narrative sources have a descriptive and explanatory character. The most sensitive ones for this period and subject are chronicles. They are written in Latin, French, or Flemish. Many of them are edited. Nevertheless, some caution is advisable when one is dealing with this source type. The manner in which such narrative sources were generated and copied during the Middle Ages could cause errors in dating or inaccuracy in the description. Therefore, a critical source assessment and sufficient density of information are essential preconditions.[13]

Agrarmodernisierung 1525–1860, Academica Helvetica 6 (Bern, Stuttgart: Haupt, 1985), 35–37.

10 Ernest Labrousse, *La crise de l'économie française à la fin de l'Ancien Régime et au début de la Révolution* (Paris: Presses Universitaires de France, 1990), 173–81; Wilhelm Abel, *Massenarmut und Hungerkrisen im vorindustriellen Deutschland* (Göttingen: Vandenhoeck and Ruprecht, 1972), 58; Krämer, *'Menschen grasten mit dem Vieh'*, 117–180.

11 Werner Plumpe, *Wirtschaftskrisen. Geschichte und Gegenwart* (München: C.H. Beck, 2010), 9.

12 Alain Derville, *L'agriculture du Nord au Moyen Âge. Artois, Cambrésis, Flandre Wallonne* (Paris: Presses Universitaires du Septentrion, 1999), 215.

13 Christian Rohr, Chantal Camenisch, and Kathleen Pribyl, "European Middle Ages," in *Palgrave Handbook of Climate History*, ed. Sam White, Christian Pfister, and Franz Mauelshagen (London: Palgrave Macmillan, 2018), 247–263; Chantal Camenisch,

The crisis of the 1430s

The price increase in the 1430s is the best-known subsistence crisis in the fifteenth century and the worst crisis of this type since the beginning of the fourteenth century.[14] This supra-regional crisis in the second part of the 1430s occurred after a series of less extensive price increases of a more regional character during the first half of the same decade.[15]

In the spring of 1436, the first accounts of rising grain prices in the Burgundian Low Countries and the surrounding areas are given in different chronicles. It seems that during these months, regions in northwestern Europe like Flanders and Northern France were affected. In the following year, the number of descriptions of rising grain prices, food scarcity, and famine rose significantly. An increase of mortality is documented as well, especially in Flanders and Holland where an epidemic was raging. In 1438 the food supply situation worsened dramatically. Chroniclers describe famine, epidemics, and numerous deaths. A sixteenth-century chronicle records 24,000 deaths in Bruges alone between June and November 1438. In 1439 high food prices are still mentioned, although they decreased by the following year.[16] Several factors need to be taken into consideration to explain

---

Endlose Kälte Witterungsverlauf und Getreidepreise in den Burgundischen Niederlanden im 15. Jahrhundert, Wirtschafts-, Sozial- und Umweltgeschichte 5 (Basel: Schwabe, 2015), 40–58; Pierre Alexandre, *Le climat en Europe au Moyen Âge: Contribution à l'histoire des variations climatiques de 1000 à 1425, d'après les sources narratives de l'Europe occidentale* (Paris: Éditions de l'École des Hautes Études en Sciences Sociales, 1987), 19–23, 37–42.

14 Christian Jörg, *Teure, Hunger, Grosses Sterben. Hungersnöte und Versorgungskrisen in den Städten des Reiches während des 15. Jahrhunderts*, Monographien zur Geschichte des Mittelalters 55 (Stuttgart: Anton Hiersmann, 2008), 3–4; Walter Bauernfeind, *Materielle Grundstrukturen im Spätmittelalter und der Frühen Neuzeit. Preisentwicklung und Agrarkonjunktur am Nürnberger Getreidemarkt von 1399 bis 1670*, Nürnberger Werkstücke zur Stadt- und Landesgeschichte 50 (Nürnberg: Stadtarchiv, 1993), 357; Bruce M.S. Campbell, "Four Famines and a Pestilence: Harvest, Price, and Wage Variations in England, 13th–19th Centuries," in *Agrarhistoria på många sätt; 28 studier om manniskan och jorden. Festskrift till Janken Myrdal på hans 60-årsdag (Agrarian History Many Ways: 28 studies on humans and the land, Festschrift to Janke Myrdal 2009)*, ed. Britt Liljewall, et al. (Stockholm: Kungliga Skogs- och Lantbruksakademien, 2009), 28; Chantal Camenisch et al., "The 1430s: a cold period of extraordinary internal climate variability during the early Spörer Minimum with social and economic impacts in north-western and central Europe," *Climate of the Past* 12 (2016): 2107–2126. In about the same time, when this article was submitted, another study with a similar topic was published by a Dutch scholar: Remi van Schaïk, "Drie vijftiende-eeuwse crises in de Nederlanden: oorzaken, kenmerken en gevolgen," *Leidschrift. Historisch Tijdschrift* 28, no. 2 (2013): 67–84.

15 Jörg, *Teure, Hunger, Grosses Sterben*, 118.

16 Chantal Camenisch, "Kälte, Krieg und Hunger: Krisen im 15. Jahrhundert in den burgundischen Niederlanden unter besonderer Berücksichtigung der Witterung," in *Krisen. Ursachen, Deutungen und Folgen – Crises. Causes, interprétations et consequences*, ed.

such a dramatic rise in the mortality rate since no single reason provides a sufficient explanation for this demographic catastrophe.

In 1436, immediately before the crisis, a new phase of the Hundred Years' War began. In this year, the western part of Flanders was raided by English armies.[17] Additionally the trade between England and the Burgundian Low Countries was seriously affected by the policy of alliance adopted by the sovereigns of both countries. After the Treaty of Arras in 1435, the Burgundians became allies of the French.[18] In addition, the Hanseatic League left Bruges in the summer of 1436 after bruising conflicts with the local merchants; trade with Flanders was stopped and the blockade was not lifted before 1438.[19]

The weather conditions before and during the crisis merit particular attention. In the summer of 1436, it was rather wet and cold in the Burgundian Low Countries. The following winter was notable for its extremely low temperatures. Chroniclers write that the winter crops, vineyards, and orchards were ruined and cattle froze to death. Low temperatures during the following spring also caused significant damage to grain crops. In the neighborhood of the Burgundian Low Countries, two different periods of killing frost are reported in spring. At the end of March frost destroyed almost all the plants in Paris. On May 19, a second frost damaged grain and vineyards in Metz and Cologne. This suggests a poor (grain) harvest in summer 1437. The following fall was very rainy, which may have delayed the sowing of the winter crop. The winter of 1437/38 was also very cold but not as cold as the previous. In December and January, drifting ice was observed on the rivers of the Low Countries and the surrounding areas. In January, the River Meuse was covered by ice, which impeded shipping traffic on this important transportation route. The summer of 1438 stood out because of its biting cold and well-above-average precipitation. A chronicler writes that the temperatures in Paris on July 24 were as low as in February or March. Because of the continuous rain several rivers burst their banks in the area of the Burgundian Low Countries.[20]

Several chroniclers emphasize the relation between unfavorable weather and crop failure, the *First-Order Impact* in the simplified climate–society interaction model. In particular, these very or extremely cold periods in winter and spring and the long periods of extensive rainfalls in the summer and fall had, according to the chronicles,

---

Thomas David, et al., Schweizerisches Jahrbuch für Wirtschafts- und Sozialgeschichte 27 (Zürich: Chronos, 2012), 70; Camenisch, *Endlose Kälte*, 400–406.

17 Willem Pieter Blockmans, "Vlaanderen 1384–1482," in *Algemene Geschiedenis der Nederlanden 4, Middeleuwen* (Bussum: Unieboek bv, 1980), 213–15.

18 John A. Wagner, *Encyclopedia of the Hundred Years War* (Westport, CT: Greenwood Press, 2006), 29–30.

19 Blockmans, "Vlaanderen 1384–1482," 213–16.

20 Camenisch, "Kälte, Krieg und Hunger," 67–70; Camenisch, *Endlose Kälte*, 407–408; Camenisch et al., " The 1430s: a cold period," 2110–2112.

a strong impact on harvest yield. This relation has of course already been verified by prior research in which additional unfavorable weather patterns are listed.[21]

Following the climate–society interaction model, *Second-* and *Third-Order Impacts* need to be taken into consideration. Since they are linked very strongly, they should be discussed together. Crucial impacts caused by the crop failure were the price increases caused by insufficient supply that could not meet the constant demand for grain on the markets.[22] The contemporary chroniclers often mention this connection between crop failure and high prices. The high prices of staple food caused malnutrition (*Third-Order Impact*) that was closely associated with epidemics.[23] As a matter of fact, the chronicles usually attribute the immense losses of human life to famine and disease, as in 1437 and 1438.

From 1436 to 1438, the usual grain imports from the Baltic and other places to the Burgundian Low Countries were interrupted. The reasons for the blockade seem to be that the export regions were also hit by crop failure. In addition, their local governments wanted to prevent too much grain being sold in other regions for higher prices.[24]

The crisis of the 1480s

Another supraregional subsistence crisis occurred just over a generation later, at the beginning of the 1480s. In 1480, several chroniclers describe rising food prices and scarce grain supplies in the Burgundian Low Countries and the neighboring regions. In the following two years, poverty and scarcity are documented in the Low Countries, France, and Lorraine. In 1481 and 1482 an epidemic disease is described that caused high fever and terrible headaches. During these years, a rise in mortality is reported as a consequence of famine and disease.[25]

The endemic military activity in Europe in this period continued apace, but during the crisis of the 1480s, the reasons for military actions in the area were different.

---

21 Slicher van Bath, "Climat et récoltes," 400–2; Pfister, *Klimageschichte*, 35–37.

22 On the connection between crop failure and prices, cf. Emmanuel Le Roy Ladurie, *Histoire humaine et comparée du climat, Vol. 1: Canicules et glaciers (XIIIe–XVIIIe siècle)* (Paris: Libraire Arthème Fayard, 2004), 21–23; Jan de Vries, "Measuring the Impact of Climate on History: The Search for Appropriate Methodologies," *The Journal of Interdisciplinary History* 10 (1980): 599–630 at 619.

23 Cormac Ó. Gráda, *Famine: A Short History* (Princeton: Princeton University Press, 2010), 109.

24 Marie-Jeanne Tits-Dieuaide, *La formation des prix céréaliers en Brabant et en Flandre au XVe siècle* (Brussels: Editions de l'Université de Brussels, 1975), 224–28.

25 Camenisch, "Kälte, Krieg und Hunger," 71–73; Camenisch, *Endlose Kälte*, 410–413. For a general overview on Europe see also Chantal Camenisch, "Two Decades of Crisis: Famine and Dearth during the 1480s and 1490s in Western and Central Europe" in *Famines During the 'Little Ice Age' (1300–1800). Socionatural Entanglements in Premodern Societies*, ed. Dominik Collet, and Maximilian Schuh (Cham, Springer: 2018), 73–80.

On January 5, 1477, Charles the Bold, Duke of Burgundy, was killed in the Battle of Nancy while fighting the Duke of Lorraine and the Swiss Confederacy. He died without a male heir and was thus succeeded by his daughter Mary of Burgundy. The king of France would not recognize Mary's claims and for this reason, as well as the opportunity afforded by the defeat of the Burgundians by the Swiss, invaded parts of her territory. By mid-August, Mary had married Maximilian of Austria, the son of the Holy Roman Emperor and later Emperor Maximillian I (r. 1508–1519). With Maximilian's support, Mary fought against the French troops. During this war, the Burgundian territories close to the French border were systematically devastated. The grain-growing region of Artois, the "breadbasket" of the area, was badly affected by this incursion. In many regions of the Burgundian heritage, but particularly in Flanders, troops were levied. For this reason, the tax burden rose significantly after 1479 across the entire area. Duchess Mary died in 1482 after a riding accident, leaving her lands to her son Philippe (1478–1506, ruled as Philip IV of Burgundy and later Philip I of Castile), although the area was, at the time, ruled by Maximilian because Philippe was still a child. Riots resulted in the Burgundian Low Countries against Maximilian's regency, and this, too, affected the grain production in the region.[26]

Very unfavorable weather conditions before and during this subsistence crisis cannot go unmentioned. After a very dry and hot summer in 1479 that caused damage to the grain growth in Soest, 1480 experienced devastating meteorological conditions. The spring was so cold that there were no leaves on the vines of Lorraine by May 1. Frost and cold in May are mentioned by two different chroniclers. The temperatures during the summer were also very low. In addition, it rained continuously in July and August, and grain and other crops were destroyed in the fields. The precipitation caused floods. These wet conditions did not change until the end of the fall. The following winter of 1480/81 was extremely cold. In the Burgundian Low Countries, France, and the Holy Roman Empire, wide rivers and parts of the North Sea close to the coast were covered by ice. Many chroniclers mention a terrible frost that caused considerable damage to cattle, grain and orchards. In Lorraine, the wine that was stocked in the caves was frozen in the barrels. Spring was also very cold. The chronicles contain consistent descriptions of cold temperatures and frost in the months of March, April, and May. The growth of crops was severely disturbed by these very unfavorable conditions. At the end of May, no blossoms were visible in the orchards for a second straight year. The weather in the following summer was very cold and wet again. Chroniclers describe fruit damage and delayed development of the vegetation (*e.g.*, the Liège grain harvest was delayed until September 8) caused by the low temperatures and the continuous rain during June, July, and August.[27]

---

26 Steven Gunn, David Grummitt, and Hans Cools, *War, State and Society in England and the Netherlands 1477–1559* (Oxford: Oxford University Press, 2007), 12–13; Blockmans and Prevenier, *Promised Lands*, 193–201.

27 Camenisch, "Kälte, Krieg und Hunger," 71–73; Camenisch, *Endlose Kälte*, 413–416.

Also, during the crisis, the relation between unfavorable weather events and crop failure as a *First-Order Impact* was mentioned along with the grain price increases. In 1481 and 1482, the chroniclers describe malnutrition and the spread of human diseases and cattle were affected by epizootics. The situation worsened because from 1480 to 1483, no grain supplies reached the Burgundian Low Countries from the Baltic.[28] The reasons for the interrupted grain trade were probably the same as those during the crisis of the 1430s.

The crisis of the 1490s

Yet another devastating subsistence crisis occurred during the late 1480s and, especially, the early 1490s. First accounts of rising grain prices in Bruges appear in 1488. In the following year, increasing prices and an epidemic disease are described across the Burgundian Low Countries: chroniclers mention 20,000 deaths in Leuven, 25,000 in Brussels, and 40,000 in Ghent caused by famine and an unknown disease. The years from 1490 to 1493 are described as a time of high prices and scarcity, when common people in the towns and the countryside suffered from misery and hunger. Several chroniclers give an account of another price increase in 1491. In Bruges and Liège, people suffered from hunger so badly that numerous families left the region in order to find a better place to live. People sold their household effects and clothes and begged in the streets in order to feed their families and themselves. At night people stole premature grain on the fields in order to dry it in the stove. Not only humans suffered from the famine; their cattle also starved or died because of epizootic diseases. In Dortmund, 1,000 cows died, and the prices of dairy products rose there significantly. In 1492 children and poor people were still starving. Finally, in 1493 food prices decreased.[29]

These years were also marked by political and military turbulence. The aforementioned revolts against Maximilian of Austria that started at the beginning of the 1480s flared up repeatedly until 1492. During the 1480s and 1490s, Flanders was hit worst by war and occupation among the regions of the Burgundian Low Countries, but Holland and Brabant also suffered as a result of military actions. Maximilian and his opponents both raised high taxes in order to pay for their wars, and Flanders, especially the cities of Ghent and Bruges, led the rebellion. The conflict escalated in 1488 when Maximilian was captured in Bruges and his troops besieged the rebellious city of Ghent. Many Flemings took refuge in Brabant; the entire area was in a state of upheaval.[30]

---

28 Tits-Dieuaide, *Formation des prix*, 229–34.
29 Camenisch, "Kälte, Krieg und Hunger," 73–76; Camenisch, *Endlose Kälte*, 417–420; Camenisch, "Two Decades of Crisis", 80–86.
30 Van der Wee, *Growth of the Antwerp Market*, 2: 97–98.

In the same years a sequence of extreme weather events once again hit the Burgundian Low Countries. The beginning of spring 1488 saw good weather conditions during the sowing time, but in the middle of March temperatures dropped rapidly and brought the growth of the vegetation to a halt. In May, several chroniclers mention frost and repeated periods of rain. For this reason, at the beginning of June cherries, strawberries, and green beans were not yet ripe. The weather conditions did not change during the summer and fall of 1488. It stayed cold and wet, so the wine grapes did not ripen either. Around Metz, the wine harvest was not even completed before 1 November so late were the fruits in ripening on the vine. During November, the temperatures were so low that drifting ice was observed on the Meuse and in the harbor of Rotterdam. The weather conditions in the spring of 1489 were once again less than ideal. In April, frost damages to wine grapes are mentioned. The weather was rather cold and very wet during the following summer, and chroniclers mention floods in the summer and fall.

In contrast to the two subsistence crises earlier in the fifteenth century, the crisis of the 1490s is unusual for a second period of very harsh weather conditions. This second period had an even more severe impact on the food prices in the Burgundian Low Countries than the first period at the end of the 1480s. The temperatures in winter 1490/91 were so low in wide parts of Europe that water bodies in several parts of the continent were uncharacteristically frozen and passable. There are descriptions of frost damages to crops on the fields, trees and vineyards; even frozen people are mentioned in many chronicles. This frosty period lasted until spring, and a number of frosty days in May devastated different crops. Vines and trees lost their leaves in spring and the grain did not sprout. In summer, too, the weather conditions were disastrous. Continuous rain caused floods that submerged fields and meadows in wide parts of the Burgundian Low Countries. Because of the rain and the humidity, the grain did not ripen, and the premature grain brought into the barns rotted there. The continuous rain also caused problems during the fall as it was not possible to sow the winter crop. In the following February and March low temperatures delayed the ploughing and sowing of summer crops.[31]

Much like the other two subsistence crises, crop failure, increasing food prices, and malnutrition are mentioned from 1488 to 1493. Additionally, a terrible disease raged in the Burgundian Low Countries from 1490 to 1493. In 1491, the chronicles also refer to epizootics and a lack of feed. During this crisis, demographic changes were caused not only by increased mortality but also by migration as can be proved by reference to the sources. The chronicles mention that many people left the Burgundian Low Countries. This demographic development clearly influenced the grain prices as well, though the tradeoff between fewer mouths to feed but also fewer agricultural workers still meant instability. And to add insult to injury, from 1491 to 1492 the grain trade with the Baltic was interrupted yet again.[32]

---

31 Camenisch, "Kälte, Krieg und Hunger," 73–76; Camenisch, *Endlose Kälte*, 420–422.

32 Tits-Dieuaide, *Formation des prix*, 234–38.

Conclusion

The three major subsistence crises of the fifteenth century occurred during periods of political disturbance and war. In addition, before and during the crises very unfavorable weather conditions have been evidenced. Very cold periods during the spring season and late frost in May, as well as very wet or extremely wet summers and falls, are mentioned in the chronicles repeatedly. A number of the coldest winters during the fifteenth century occurred before and during the subsistence crises.

These extreme weather events led to crop failure according to the simplified climate–society interaction model. Furthermore, *Second-* and *Third-Order Impacts* such as food price increases, interrupted trade flows, malnutrition, epidemics, and mortality were caused by crop failure. The interaction of the different impact levels worsened the subsistence crises. It is very probable that subsistence crises of such dimensions occurred because the political and military unrest coincided with extreme weather events and the consecutive impacts. The sequence of the crises follows Labrousse's model of the *crise type ancien* as far as can be verified.

Index

Note: page numbers in **bold** indicate figures.

abbeys: Cîteaux 15, 153, 161; Clairvaux 154, **155**, 156–7; Fontenay 161–2; Les Clairets (W of Chartres, France) 178, 181, 185; Lieu-Notre-Dame (south of Chartres, France) 178–80; Maubisson (Notre-Dame-la-Royale, Pontoise, France) 171–2, 173, 174–7; Morimond 160; Notre-Dame-du-Lys, Melun 168–9; Saint-Antoine-des-Champes 180–1
Abel, Wilhelm 190
Aberth, John 85
Adams, Henry 109
agriculture 45, 48, 188, 189; agricultural revolution of the Middle Ages 6, 15, 80
Alberic 153
Alered of Rievaulx 166
Alice of Mâcon 169, 170
Ammianos, Marcus Aurelius 123
animal husbandry 45
Annales School 10, 37
Antikythera Mechanism 118–19, 121, 132, 133
archaeology 47
architectural history 14; regional traditions 141
architecture Romanesque 140–5, 148–9
Aristophanes 132
Arnold, Ellen F. 85, 167
Arnold of Bonneval 156, 162
assarting 166–8, 180
astronomical instruments 50
Ausonius *see* "Mosella" (4th C. poem)
automaton 132
axles 145, 146, **146**

Bachrach, Bernard S. 5, 63
Bacon, Francis 63–4
ball bearings 114
Barbegal (Arles, France) 50
Battle of Tours (732) 44

Bauer, Catherine 34
Bautier, Anne-Marie 159
Beattie, James 89
Bedford Hours (15th C. MS) 116, **120**
bells 137
Benedictines 45, 85; Rule 153, 157; work ethic 109
Berman, Constance H. 86
Bernard of Chartres 13, 30
Bible, *Genesis* 83
bibliographies 101
bibliometrics 51, 92, 97–104
Biringuccio, Vannoccio 129
Blanche, Queen of Castile 165, 168, 171–2, 173–4, 176, 177
blast furnaces 162
Bloch, Marc 10, 37, 64, 150
Boreas 129, 132
Bouman, Mark J. 59
Bridbury, A. R. 96
Bruges (Belgium) 191, 192
Buddhist technology 92
Burckhardt, Jacob 3
Burgundian Low Countries 16, 187–97
Burke, James 50

Campanella, Tommaso 54, 60
cams 145, 158, 161; camshafts 113
capital 50
capstans 127; *see also* windlass
carpentry 135
Carson, Rachel 72, 74
Cassiobury (Herefordshire, UK) **136**
catapults 63
cathedrals: Auxerre 139; Norwich 139; Salisbury 127
Catholic Church 39; *see also* Christianity
Charlemagne 46, 61
Charles Martel 63
Charles the Bold, Duke of Burgundy 193

charters 120, 172
Christianity 76, 79, 86, 115, 151; Latin 108; medieval 71; orthodox 72
chronicle sources 191–6
churches: Konstanz Minster 147; St. Batholomew (Barthélemey), Liege 141–4, **143**, **144**, 148; St. Georges-de-Boscherville, Normandy 142; St. Paul and Ste-Croix colleges, Liège 139
Cipolla, Carlo 55, 62–3, 92, 135
Cistercians 15, 49–50, 152–64, 165–85
citation analysis *see* bibliometrics
cities *see* urban environment/urbanism
Claggett, Marshall 96, 106
climate–society interaction model 189–90, 193
Clio (muse) 91
clocks 14, 40–2, 48, 50, 108, 134–8, 147–8; astronomical 138; frames 135–8; St. Albans 138, 148; turret (tower) 149, 135–8; water (*clepsydra*) 134; weight-driven 135–8, 147–8
Columbian encounter 87
compass, magnetic 108
condemnation of 1277 49
connecting rods 46, 123, 125; *see also* cranks
construction, building 48
consumers 87
Cowan, Ruth Schwartz 12
cranes 138, 148
cranks 7, 8, 14, 46, 55, 105, 107, 110, **119**, **120**, 122, 123, 127–9; August (Augusta Raurica, Switzerland) 126, 133; handle 128, 131; metal 129; possible **130**
crankshaft 113
Cranston, Alan 72
crop failures 189, 190–6
crop rotation ("three-field system") 46, 57; *see also* agriculture, agricultural revolution of the Middle Ages

Daedalus 123
Daniel, Walter 166
Darwin, Charles/Darwinism 11, 42
da Vigevano, Guido 128
da Vinci, Leonardo 138
deductive research 93
Deep Ecology 73
Deetz, James A. 11n33
de Honnecourt, Villard 137, 138
Delville, Louis 38

demographic change 189, 196; crisis "*type ancien*" (Labrousse) 190
Derr, Thomas Sieger 75, 84
determinism 85; Christian 78; cultural 151; technological (*see* technological determinism)
DeVries, Kelly 13
Diamond, Jared 92
di Dondi, Giovanni 50, 138
digital scholarship 93
dikes/ditches 168, 180
Domesday Book (1086) 121
dominion theology 89
Dortmund (Germany) 195
Dubois, Louis 160
Duby, Georges 160
Du Cange, Charle du Fresne 160
Dura Europos (Syria) 112
dynamo, electric 109

East Hendred (Oxon, UK) 135, **137**
ecocriticism 70
ecological imperialism 89
economics 53, 61, 90, 188, 190; history 79
ecotheology 14, 70, 73
Eleanor of Aquitaine 178
electrons 105, 108, 117
Ellul, Jacques 34
Elvin, Mark 81
environment/environmentalism 15, 48, 70, 74, 77, 79; ethics 70
environmental history 80, 84–5, 89; global 80, 82, 87; medieval 76, 82, 84–5
eotechnic 39; *see also* Mumford, Lewis
Ephesos (Selçuk, İzmir Province, Turkey) 8, 125–6
epidemics/epizootics 189, 193, 195, 196
escapements 135, 148; anchor 135; strob 148
Euripides 132

famines *see* crop failures
Farrell, Robert T. xii
Febrve, Lucien 37
feudalism 44, 63, 105, 151
Finley, M. I. 90
food prices 188
forest clearance *see* assarting
foresters 178
forest management 165–82

forests: Bievre 170; Bondosse 177; Breteuil 173; Cergy 176–7; Othe 168; Rosières 177–8
forges 162
fortifications 63, 131n42
Fortuna/Fortune's wheel 115, **117**
Fossier, Robert 168
frame, clock 135, 136
frost 196
fulling mills *see* mills, fulling

galaxies 105, 108, 117
gears/gearing 118, 123, 123
Geddes, Patrick 40n38
Geoffrey (prior of Clairvaux and Bishop of Langres) 154
Gerassa (Jerash, Jordan) 8, 123, 125, 126
Giedion, Siegfried 68
Gies, Frances and Joseph 92
Gille, Bertrand 38n30, 152
Gimpel, Jean 8, 13, 36–8, 48–50, 51, 53, 55–7, 61–2, 64, 66, 92, 121
Glacken, Clarence J. 87–8
Glastonbury (England) 50
Goldstone, Jack A. 79
granges 158, 160, 166, 180; Mâlay 169–70, 171
grindstones 54–5, 116, **118**, 129; *see also* cranks
grindstones, rotary 115, **116**
Guillelma, abbess of Maubisson 174
gunpowder 108

Hacker, Barton C. 55, 62, 63
Hall, A. Rupert 34
Hall, Bert S. xii, 9, 53, 63, 134
Hall, Phyllis A. 54, 60
Hanseatic League 192
Hardin, Garrett 74
Harding, Stephen 153
Haskins, Charles Homer 37
Headrick, Daniel 57
Henry II, king of England 178
Herlihy, David 84, 94
Hero of Alexandria 112, 132
Herrad von Landsberg *see Hortus Deliciarum* (12th C. MS)
Hierapolis (Phrygia, Anatolia, Greece) 8, 122, **122**, **124**, 125, 126, 129, 133
Hilton, R. H. 96
historical models 133

History of Science Society (HSS) 101, 103
history of technology 30–1, 38, 67; *see also* Society for the History of Technology (SHOT)
hodometer 119
Hoffman, Richard C. 85
Hoffsummer, Patrick 141–2
hoists 14, **120**, 127, 128, 138–49; box 139, 142–8; clasped-arm 138–9, 141, 148; windlass 139–40, 145–6, 147
Holmes, Sherlock 7n22
Holt, Richard 86, 120, 162
horses 49; harness 46
Hortus Deliciarum (12th C. MS) 116, **117**
Hughes, J. Donald 82, 84
Hughes, Thomas M. 164
Hundred Years' War (1337–1453) 192
hurdy-gurdy 116, **119**, 129
Hyams, Paul xii
hydraulic technology *see* mills

imperialism 57
impetus theory 135
industrial archaeology 49
industrial machinery 121, 126
industrial milling 152, 156, 158
industrial mills *see* mills, industrial
industrial revolution of the Middle Ages 15, 62, 152, 164
intellectual property 57
interdisciplinarity 84
International Medieval Bibliography (IMB) 101–4
invention, act of 38
iron production 152, 160–1
Isabel, countess of Chartres 178–9

Jamison, Andrew 55
Jeanne, abbess of Saint-Antoine 180
Jenkins, Willis 77, 84
John of Salisbury 30

Kates, Robert W. 188
Kelly, Kevin 8
keys cranked **130**, 131
Krämer, Daniel 188–9
Kroeber, Alfred 10, 37
Kuhn, Thomas S. 11, 12

INDEX

labor-saving devices 50, 152
Labrousse, Ernest 190
Lake Nemi ships 113, 123
Landels, J. G. 127
land management 165–81
land reclamation 166
landscape 87
Langdon, John 61
Lemaire, Raymond, Sr. and Jr. 141
Leopold, Aldo 74
Levine, David 80
Lewis, M. J. T. 54, 59, 60
Liège (Belgium) 195
Lienhard, John 11
light/lighting 59
Lone Ranger, The 93
Long, Pamela O. 57, 105
Louis IX, king of France 168–77 *passim*
Louis VIII, king of France 174
Lucas, Adam 86, 159
Luttrell Psalter (14th C. MS) 116, **118**, **119**
Lycurgus Cup *(krater)* 129–33

machinery 48
malnutrition *see* crop failures
Malthusianism 80
Mangartz, F. 125
Martel, Charles 44
Mary of Burgundy 193–4
materials 58
Matilda, countess of la Perche 178
Maximillian I, Holy Roman Emperor 194
McNeill, J. R. 87, 81, 83
McNeill, William 81
mechanical power 150
mechanical revolution of the Middle Ages 6, 14, 107
medieval science 99–101, **100**, 102
medieval technology 99, **100**
medieval workers 109
metaphorical reasoning 42
Metz (France) 196
military technology 56
millers 159
milling 61; facilities 178; millstones 111
mills 86, 108, 119, 120, 151; agricultural 157; Cérilly, France 162; forge 159; fulling 158–60, 162; horizontal 121; industrial 8, 159–60, 162, 163; malting 162; saw 113; saw, stonecutting 112, 122, **122**, 123–5, **124**, 126 (*see also*

Ephesos (Selçuk, İzmir Province, Turkey); Gerassa (Jerash, Jordan); Hierapolis (Phrygia, Anatolia, Greece)); tanning 158, 162; Vitruvian Mill 125; water 38n33, 49, 162–3; waterwheels 157; wind 108; wind, post 50
mining 48
Mitterauer, Michael 80
monasteries 42, 57, 85; Saint-Germaine d'Auxerre 159; *see also* abbeys; Benedictines; Cistercians
monastic orders 109
monastic rhetoric 167
Moralia in Job (*c.*1111 MS) 167
"Mosella" (4th C. poem) 112, 123, 126, 133
mountains: Ardennes 86
mounted shock combat *see* stirrup
Muir, John 74
Mumford, Lewis 8–9, 12, 13, 32, 33–5, 42–3, 51, 58, 62, 64, 66, 67, 150

Nash, James A. 83
natural theology 72
nature–culture divide 81
nebulae 91; *see also* galaxies
Needham, Joseph 95
neutron stars 91
n-grams 97–101
Noble, David F. 31n4
nuns 165–83

Oelschlager, Max 82
Open Syllabus Project 12, 69
Oribasius 112
Oriethyia 129

Paris region 15
parva (small things) 60, 174; *see also* Deetz, James A.
peasants 45, 109
pedagogy 64–5, 69
pegs 142, 144, **144**
perpetual motion 46
Pfister, Christian 188–9
Philip IV/I, king of Burgundy and Castile 194
pioneers *see* assarting
pipe organs 115
Pirenne, Henri 45
plough 45–6, 53, 61, 151
Plutarch 8

pollarding 167
Pontigny (France) 159
Pontoise (France) 182–5
Pope John Paul II 72
power, mechanical 134; sources 46–7; water 57, 62, 152
Premonstratensians 181
printing/printing press 39n34, 108
progress 49
pulleys 143–4, **145**, 147
pumps, bilge 113, 123

querns 111, 114, 123, 129

Radkau, Joachim 74, 87
Ranke, Leopold von 3
reason/rationality 49
religious women *see* nuns
Revelation of Saint John 167
Richard of Wallingford 50, 138
Richards, John F. 83
rivers: Aube (Marne, France) 156–7; Serchio (Tuscany, Italy) 46
Robert of Moselme 153
Robert the Englishman 135
Roberts, Michael 55, 62–3
Roland, Alex 5, 9, 10, 13, 56–7, 58
roofs: carpentry 140–7, 148; common-tiebeam 140, 141–3, 148–9; Romanesque 141–4
Rostow, Walt 90
Rotterdam 196
Rudolph, Conrad 167

Sagan, Carl 91
Saints: Benedict 151, 167; Bernard 154–5; Boniface 45; Francis 72
Sarton, Georges 37
sawmill *see* mills, saw
saws: frame 123; stone 8; *see also* mills, saw, stonecutting
Sawyer, P. H. 96
Scharper, Stephen Bede 77
Schiøler, T. 125, 126
Schumaker, E. R. 74
Schwarzschild, Steven 75
Second Crusade (1147–49) 60
Seymour, Henry (or John) 136
Sibley, Mulford Q. 63
siege warfare 63
Sierra Club 72

Simmons, I. G. 82
Simms, D. L. 113
Singer, Charles Joseph 95
slaves/slave labor 121
Smith, Cyril Stanley 34
Society for the History of Technology (SHOT) 2, 4, 10, 12, 34, 35–6, 38, 101, 103
Socrates 132
Sörlin, Sverker 83
stage equipment 132
Staudenmaier, John 43
Stavelot-Malmedy (Liège, Belgium) 86
steam engines 41, 48
Stenhouse, John 89
stewardship 79
stirrup 44, 53, 63, 65, 105, 151
Strayer, Joseph 37

technological determinism 4–5, 41, 53, 96, 105, 134, 151; dynamism 108–11; hubris 68; systems 164
technology 99, 104; studies of 103
Templars 160
temple key 129, **130**, 131
textiles 48
textual analysis 46
Thorndike, Lynn 96
time 41; *see also* clocks
tithes 180
tomb of the Haterii (Roman, 1st century) 127
trade 188
treadwheels 127, 138–9, 145, 148
Treaty of Arras (1435) 192
tripped hammers 158; *see also* cams
Tuan, Yi-fu 81

Unger, Richard 86
urban environment/urbanism 57, 59, 67
urbanization 187–8
Usher, Abott Payson 34
Utrecht Psalter 115, **116**, 127, 129

Van Crevald, Martin 58
van Dam, Petra J. E. M. 86
vase painting **130**
villeneuves 168
vineyards 170–1, 175, 196
Virgin Mary 109
Vitruvius 109, 110, 119, 120, 127, 132; "Vitruvian Mill" 120

Walter (Bishop of Langres) 161
Walton, Steven A. 86
Warde, Paul 83
Warner, Sam Bass, Jr. 66
watermills *see* mills, water
weather events 188–96 *passim*
Weiner, Douglas 81
Western exceptionalism 78
Western theology 109; *see also* Christianity
wheelbarrow 54, 59, 60
White, Lynn, Jr. 35–6, 43–8, 51, 52, 55, 56, 57, 59, 61–6, 68–9; career 1, 2; criticism 2, 75; legacy 70; medieval scholarship 75; military thesis 5

White, Lynn, Jr. works 16–29; "Historical Roots . . ." 14, 70–89; influence 98–9, **98**; *Medieval Technology and Social Change*: early reception 134; reputation 14; response to 53n74; reviews 94–7
Williams, Michael 88
windlass 112, 127, 128, 138–9, **139**, 143, **145**, 146, **146**, 147, 148
windmills *see* mills, wind
Winner, Langston 12
woodlands 15; products 176, 178
Worthen, Shana 9, 11–12

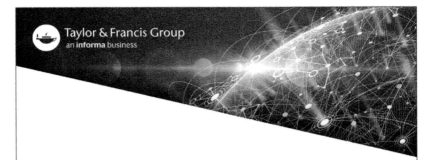